Joint Insolvency Examinations Board

Personal Insolvency

Study Manual

For the November 2010 examination

JIEB Personal Insolvency Study Manual

ISBN: 9780 7517 8266 0 (previous edition 9780 7517 6570 0)

Third edition November 2009
First edition 2008

All rights reserved. No part of this publication may be reproduced or transmitted in any form or by any means or stored in any retrieval system, or transmitted in, any form or by any means, electronic, mechanical, photocopying, recording or otherwise without the prior written permission of BPP Learning Media.

British Library Cataloguing-in-Publication Data
A catalogue record for this book has been applied for from the British Library

We are grateful to the Joint Insolvency Examinations Board for permission to reproduce the syllabus and past examination questions and answers.

Printed in the United Kingdom

Your learning materials, published by BPP Learning Media, are printed on paper sourced from sustainable, managed forests.

A note about copyright

Dear Customer

What does the little © mean and why does it matter?

Your market-leading BPP books, course materials and e-learning materials do not write and update themselves. People write them: on their own behalf or as employees of an organisation that invests in this activity. Copyright law protects their livelihoods. It does so by creating rights over the use of the content.

Breach of copyright is a form of theft – as well as being a criminal offence in some jurisdictions, it is potentially a serious breach of professional ethics.

With current technology, things might seem a bit hazy but, basically, without the express permission of BPP Learning Media:

- Photocopying our materials is a breach of copyright
- Scanning, ripcasting or conversion of our digital materials into different file formats, uploading them to facebook or emailing them to your friends is a breach of copyright

You can, of course, sell your books, in the form in which you have bought them – once you have finished with them. (Is this fair to your fellow students? We update for a reason.) But the e-products are sold on a single user license basis: we do not supply 'unlock' codes to people who have bought them second hand.

And what about outside the UK? BPP Learning Media strives to make our materials available at prices students can afford by local printing arrangements, pricing policies and partnerships which are clearly listed on our website. A tiny minority ignore this and indulge in criminal activity by illegally photocopying our material or supporting organisations that do. If they act illegally and unethically in one area, can you really trust them?

© BPP Learning Media 2009

Contents

		Page
▶	Introduction	v
▶	JIEB syllabus	vi
▶	The JIEB exam	xi
▶	How to use this study manual	xii
▶	Chapter summary	xiii
1	Insolvency Code of Ethics	1
2	Statements of Insolvency Practice	13
3	Options for debtor and creditors	25
4	Introduction to voluntary arrangements	39
5	Voluntary arrangement procedures	69
6	Post approval matters	91
7	Introduction to bankruptcy	107
8	Post bankruptcy order procedure	127
9	The trustee	153
10	Bankruptcy estate	175
11	Proofs of debt	209
12	Closure of bankruptcy	227
13	Partnership law	245
14	Administration of the estate of insolvent deceased individuals	267
15	Numbers questions	277
▶	Index	289

Personal Insolvency

Introduction

This is the third edition of BPP Learning Media's ground-breaking study manual for the Personal Insolvency paper of the Joint Insolvency Examinations Board. It has been published specifically for the November 2010 JIEB exam.

Features include:

- Full syllabus coverage.
- Fully up-to-date at 31 July 2009.
- A user friendly style for easy navigation.
- Chapter introductions to put the topic into context and explain its significance in the exam.
- Section overviews and chapter summaries.
- Self test questions and answers.
- Suggested practice on past exam questions.

Other JIEB papers and products

BPP Learning Media publishes a range of learning materials for the three JIEB examinations, including Question Banks, Passcards, Audio CDs and Home Study programmes.

For further information, or to order, call 0845 0751 100 (within the UK) or +44 (0)20 8740 2211 (from overseas) or order online at www.bpp.com/learningmedia

Feedback

We at BPP Learning Media always appreciate feedback about our products. If you have any comments about this book or any other products in the BPP Learning Media JIEB range, please contact Pippa Riley, Publishing Projects Director by e-mail at pippariley@bpp.com.

JIEB Personal Insolvency syllabus

The syllabus

Candidates must be able to demonstrate a thorough working knowledge of Insolvency Practice, including relevant law and guidance as described in this syllabus, sufficient to enable them to carry out the functions of an authorised insolvency practitioner. Insolvency Practice includes both non-formal and formal practice. Non-formal practice is defined as the provision of analysis and advice to stakeholders concerning an entity in financial difficulties. Formal practice is defined as acting as office holder, from appointment through all the stages of the relevant insolvency procedures to release from the office. The jurisdictions for the purposes of this syllabus are England and Wales; and Scotland. The offices and procedures described in this syllabus relate to both jurisdictions except to the extent that legislation applies differently between them. The relevant offices for the purposes of this syllabus are as follows: those described in the Insolvency Act 1986 and the Bankruptcy (Scotland) Act 1985; receiverships under the Law of Property Act 1925, the Agricultural Credits Act 1928 the Agricultural Credits (Scotland) Act 1929: court appointments; and offices held by virtue of EU Insolvency Regulation 1346/2000.

Relevant law and guidance comprises the legislation referred to above, the Company Directors' Disqualification Act 1986, the Insolvency Rules 1986, the Insolvency (Scotland) Rules 1986, all as from time to time amended, and any other primary legislation, secondary legislation, case law or other guidance that is directly relevant to the performance of an office holder's duties. Examination questions will be based on the relevant law and guidance in force on 30th April for the year of the examination. Questions will not require more recent case law, but demonstrating knowledge of any that is relevant may attract additional marks.

Candidates will also need to demonstrate knowledge of cross-border insolvency issues (including foreign entities located in the respective jurisdictions) but not of the insolvency legislation in foreign regimes. Candidates will need to be aware of industry licensing, environmental and other regulatory requirements, agency and other issues, and the civil and criminal risks arising from them, but will not need in-depth knowledge of industry-specific legislation.

Candidates will be assessed by means of three separate papers, all of which may include questions relating both to non-formal practice and to formal practice although the emphasis will be on the latter. The three papers are distinguished by the different types of entity and the different formal insolvency procedures to which they relate.

The Personal Insolvency paper may include questions relating to any of the following types of entity: individuals, partnerships (except Limited Liability Partnerships) and the estates of deceased individuals. Questions on formal practice will focus on the following procedures: Bankruptcy and Individual Voluntary Arrangements; Voluntary Trust Deeds and Sequestrations. However, questions may also test knowledge of Administrations, Liquidations and Receiverships as they relate to individuals (e.g., individuals in partnerships or individuals subject to Receivership).

The Liquidations paper may include questions relating to any of the following types of entity: all forms of registered and unregistered companies (whether or not in a group structure), including Limited Liability Partnerships (but excluding other partnerships). Questions on formal practice will be limited to the following procedures: Members' Voluntary Liquidations (including Section 110 schemes); Creditors' Voluntary Liquidations; Compulsory Liquidations; and the appointment of Provisional Liquidators or Special Managers. Candidates will be expected to recognise that the following types of entity require special treatment, but they will not be required to deal with these entities in detail: Industrial Societies, Provident Societies, Friendly Societies, Commonhold Associations and Community Interest Companies.

The Administrations, Company Voluntary Arrangements and Receiverships paper may include questions on any of the same types of entity as for the Liquidations paper. Questions on formal practice will be limited to the following procedures: Company Voluntary Arrangements; Partnership Voluntary Arrangements;

Administrations, Administrative Receiverships, Receiverships (Scotland), Court Appointed Receiverships and Receiverships under the Law of Property Act 1925.

Non-formal Insolvency Practice

This section of the syllabus refers to engagements for the provision of analysis and advice about matters relating to entities that might already be, or that are at risk of becoming, insolvent. The potential clients for this advice include the entities, their representatives, their creditors, and any other stakeholders.

Engagement

The following learning outcomes refer to the process of engagement for non-formal Insolvency Practice. They do not refer to the process of appointment to an office in a formal insolvency procedure, which is addressed later in the syllabus.

1. Candidates should be able to identify legal, regulatory and ethical considerations affecting the engagement, and also practical considerations (eg staffing levels, relevant experience, and qualifications) to determine whether the engagement can be accepted.

2. Candidates should be able to set out and confirm the adviser's and the client's duties, responsibilities and obligations in connection with the engagement.

Analysis and Advice

The following learning outcomes refer to analyses of the entity's financial affairs and to the provision of advice with regard to those affairs.

The analyses will be necessary to provide the basis for the advice, which is why the learning outcomes dealing with analyses are in this part of the syllabus. Similar analyses will be required for formal Insolvency Practice, which is addressed in the next section of the syllabus.

3. Candidates should be able to assess an entity's overall financial state and solvency by:
   - ascertaining the value of assets and the amount of liabilities, including contingent and prospective liabilities
   - considering the achievability of profit and loss, and cash flow forecasts.

4. Candidates should be able to establish whether an entity that appears to be insolvent should be made subject to a formal insolvency procedure or whether a non-formal insolvency procedure such as a turnaround or a debt management scheme might be appropriate. However, candidates are not required to be able to advise on the detailed techniques that may be used in any such non-formal insolvency procedures.

5. Candidates should be able to identify the most appropriate formal insolvency procedure and estimate the financial outcome of an entity's insolvency by:
   - ascertaining the values of assets and the amounts of liabilities that would arise in the formal insolvency
   - comparing and contrasting the estimated outcomes from the available procedures, and from alternative strategies within the available procedures.

6. Candidates should be able to provide advice to the entity or its representatives with regard to:
   - their duties, responsibilities and potential liabilities
   - any need to seek additional legal or other guidance
   - how best to proceed.

7. Candidates should be able to provide advice to others who are affected by the financial state of the entity with regard to protecting their interests.

8. Candidates should be able to adapt their advice to take account of new information and changing circumstances.

Formal Insolvency Practice

This section of the syllabus refers to appointments as office holder.

The different subsections refer in turn to case management, case strategy and the operational requirements to make realisations, to deal with any misconduct and to agree and pay claims.

Questions on formal Insolvency Practice may also include requirements to carry out the same sorts of analyses as are described above in the previous section of the syllabus on non-formal Insolvency Practice.

Case Management

The following learning outcomes refer to any appointment as an office holder under relevant legislation.

9 Candidates should be able to identify legal, regulatory and ethical considerations affecting the appointment as office holder and also practical considerations (eg staffing levels, relevant experience, and qualifications) to determine whether the appointment can be accepted.

10 Candidates should be able to manage the statutory, regulatory and contractual procedures required to institute, progress and close the relevant insolvency procedure, including:

- establishing and maintaining files, including Insolvency Practitioner Records.
- appointment to the office.
- obtaining bonding and insurance.
- calling and holding statutory meetings of relevant participants as required, including initial, general and final meetings.
- banking, managing and disbursing funds.
- obtaining sanction for specific actions, as required from creditors (or the relevant committee/s), the court, or the Official Receiver.
- ceasing to act and release from office.

11 Candidates should be able to prepare and file the relevant notices, reports and returns required by the office, including to:

- the insolvent entity.
- creditors.
- members.
- HM Revenue and Customs.
- the Secretary of State for the Department of Business Enterprise and Regulatory Reform.
- Companies House.
- the London Gazette.
- the relevant court.
- the Serious Organised Crime Agency.
- the office holder's authorising body.
- the Pension Protection Fund, the Pensions Regulator, and the trustees or managers of the pension scheme.

Case Strategy

The following learning outcomes refer to the overall strategies, which will guide the office holder's actions to optimise the result.

12 Candidates should be able to identify whether the optimum result is more likely to be achieved by:

- a formal procedure that involves disposals of assets; and/or
- a formal procedure not involving disposals but which may include, for example, voluntary contributions, debt rescheduling and/or debt restructuring.

13 Where appropriate, candidates should be able to identify the overall strategy that is likely to optimise realisations by means of disposals, which strategy may include:

- continued trading; and/or
- the sale of assets (either as a whole or piecemeal).

14 When determining the most appropriate strategy, candidates should be able to take into account:

- the taxation implications of the different possible strategies
- the possible effects of interactions between concurrent and/or consecutive procedures.

15 Candidates should be able to identify steps that might properly be taken to mitigate liabilities (including any liabilities arising from the strategy itself).

16 Candidates should be able to adapt their strategies to take account of new information and changing circumstances.

Realisations

The following learning outcomes provide a general list of the activities which candidates should be able to carry out to achieve realisations by disposals of the entity's assets and by other means as appropriate.

17 Candidates should be able to identify, seek out, establish ownership, take control of and protect the entity's assets and records, including by means of:

- investigation
- physical and practical controls
- legal proceedings
- insurance
- banking arrangements and investment of funds.

18 Candidates should be able to manage the continuation and/or cessation of an entity's business having proper regard to the rights of all affected parties, including dealing with:

- finances, using cash flow forecasts and trading budgets.
- employees, taking account of their rights (including Transfer of Undertakings and pension rights) and of the office holder's duties.
- management of operations.
- tax including VAT compliance.
- compliance with industry licensing, environmental and other regulatory requirements, including for personnel and premises.
- business assets, including:
    - freehold and leasehold premises
    - fixtures and fittings
    - plant and equipment
    - motor vehicles
    - stock and work in progress
    - contracts
    - intellectual property, including goodwill.

19 Candidates should be able to realise value from the entity by executing:

- sales of the business as a going concern, either as a whole or in part/s, making use of hive-down companies if appropriate; and/or
- sales of assets, either as a whole or piecemeal, including, where relevant and appropriate, dealing with assets that are subject to
    - security
    - execution, attachment or distress
    - lien
    - reservation of title

- special legal requirements
- onerous provisions.

20 Candidates should also be able to achieve realisations from sources other than asset disposals, including from:

- actions that may only be available to the office holder, including those in respect of misconduct, or voidable transactions.
- amounts that may be recoverable by the entity in its own name.
- contributions from net income.
- contributions from third parties.

21 Candidates should be able to identify circumstances that give rise to potential recovery actions, the creditors who might benefit from pursuing them, how such actions might be funded, and whether they should be pursued.

Dealing with Misconduct

The following learning outcomes refer to the duties of the office holder to assess and report on conduct.

22 Candidates should be able to identify and, where appropriate, investigate misconduct relating to the insolvency, including such matters as are identified in the Insolvency Act 1986 and in the Company Directors' Disqualification Act 1986.

23 Candidates should be able to prepare and submit reports as required in cases of misconduct, including to the:

- Official Receiver.
- Secretary of State for Business Enterprise and Regulatory Reform.
- Serious Organised Crime Agency.

Agreeing and Paying Claims

The following learning outcomes provide a general list of the activities by which candidates should be able to agree and pay claims in an insolvency procedure. Not all of them will apply in every case.

24 Candidates should be able to determine the validity of charges and the charge holders' rights and to compute the amounts payable.

25 Candidates should be able to determine the validity and quantum of preferential claims and compute the amounts payable.

26 Candidates should be able to evaluate and resolve claims in special categories, including:

- retention of title
- lien
- hire purchase and leasing
- execution and distress.

27 Candidates should be able to determine the validity and quantum of unsecured claims and compute the amounts payable.

28 Candidates should be able to rank all of the valid claims and duly pay them in the statutory order having taken into account, as appropriate, interest, set off, the Prescribed Part, subrogation and marshalling.

29 Where there is a surplus after the payment of relevant creditors, candidates should be able to determine the amounts and entitlements to the surplus and the procedures for passing it across.

The JIEB exam

The exam paper

(a) The JIEB exam consists of three papers each of three hours, with an additional 30 minutes reading time per session. (In 2010 the examination will be held on 1, 2, and 3 November).

(b) Exam questions are set on the basis of European and UK legislation on insolvency and statements of insolvency practice in force on the 30th day of April for the year of examination. Knowledge of case law after 30 April will not be specifically examined, however demonstration of knowledge of recent case law may attract additional marks.

(c) The subject of the three papers is:

    (i) Liquidations
    (ii) Administrations, Company Voluntary Arrangements and Receiverships
    (iii) Personal Insolvency.

(d) Each paper consists of four compulsory questions, with two questions attracting 20% of the marks and two questions attracting 30% of the marks.

(e) The examination is essentially practical and relevant experience, whilst not essential, is an advantage. The examination aims to assess whether candidates have sufficient knowledge of insolvency law and practice to enable them to carry out the functions of an authorised insolvency practitioner. Candidates are expected to have a basic knowledge of taxation, accountancy and business law, directly relevant to the performance of an office holder's duties in the practice of insolvency.

(f) Marks are awarded in the exam for the ability to communicate effectively.

(g) The exam is open book and candidates are provided, in the exam hall, with the latest edition of the Butterworths Insolvency Law Handbook.

How to use this study manual

This is the third edition of the BPP Learning Media study manual for the Personal Insolvency paper of the Joint Insolvency Examinations Board. It has been written to cover the JIEB syllabus.

To pass the examination you need a thorough understanding in all areas covered by the syllabus.

Recommended approach

(a) To pass you need to be able to answer questions on **everything** specified by the syllabus. Read the text very carefully and do not skip any of it.

(b) Learning is an **active** process. Do **all** the activities as you work through the manual so you can be sure you really understand what you have read.

(c) After you have covered the material in the Study Manual, work through the questions suggested in the Exam Practice section.

(d) Before you take the exam, check that you still remember the material using the following quick revision plan.

    (i) Read through the chapter learning objectives. Are there any gaps in your knowledge? If so, study the section again.

    (ii) Read and learn the defined terms.

    (iii) Read and learn the diagrammatic summary of each chapter.

    (iv) Do the self test questions again. If you know what you're doing, they shouldn't take long.

This approach is only a suggestion. You or your college may well adapt it to suit your needs.

Remember this is a **practical** course. Try to relate the material to your experience in the workplace or any other work experience you may have had.

Chapter summary

Chapter 1 – Insolvency Code of Ethics

The Insolvency Code of Ethics and Money Laundering regulations are introduced in this chapter. The principles of the legislation could easily be tested in any of the three JIEB exam papers.

Chapter 2 – Statements of Insolvency Practice

This chapter introduces Statements of Insolvency Practice (SIPs), what they are and who produces them and it lists what SIPs are currently in use. A good knowledge of the content of SIPs is required in order to pass the JIEB exam. Insolvency Guidance Papers are also introduced in this chapter.

Chapter 3 – Options for debtor and creditors

This chapter introduces the various options available to a debtor who becomes insolvent and the options available to a creditor who is seeking to recover his debt.

Chapter 4 – Introduction to voluntary arrangements

Individual voluntary arrangements are dealt with in more detail in this chapter, including matters to be dealt with at the initial meeting with the debtor and the content of a voluntary arrangement proposal.

Chapter 5 – Voluntary arrangement procedures

This chapter outlines the procedure to be followed to obtain approval for a voluntary arrangement, both with and without an interim order. Fast track voluntary arrangements are discussed and the effects of approval of a voluntary arrangement. These are popular topics for the JIEB exam.

Chapter 6 – Post approval matters

This chapter contains a lot of useful background information including the powers, duties and liabilities of the supervisor, how the supervisor is remunerated, how the arrangement may be varied, the circumstances in which an arrangement might fail and the consequences of failure. Completion of voluntary arrangements is also covered.

Chapter 7 – Introduction to bankruptcy

Bankruptcy is introduced in this chapter, the grounds for presenting a petition and the procedure to be followed. Also the circumstances in which an IP will look into the possibility of a voluntary arrangement and the appointment of an interim receiver or special manager.

Chapter 8 – Post bankruptcy order procedure

This is a very practical chapter dealing with many examinable topics including the consequences of a bankruptcy order being made, the functions, powers and duties of the OR, investigations into the bankrupt's affairs, creditors' meetings and the appointment of a creditors' committee.

Chapter 9 – The trustee

This chapter deals with the trustee in bankruptcy, his duties, powers and remuneration. These are popular JIEB exam topics.

Chapter 10 – Bankruptcy Estate

The bankruptcy estate is regularly tested in the JIEB exam. This chapter deals with what assets form the bankruptcy estate, the powers of the trustee to augment the estate and challenge antecedent transactions and how the trustee deals with the matrimonial home.

Chapter 11 – Proofs of debt

This chapter explains how creditors' proofs are dealt with in bankruptcy and the procedure for making dividend payments to creditors. Creditors' claims are tested regularly in each of the three JIEB exam papers.

Chapter 12 – Closure of bankruptcy

This chapter deals with closure of bankruptcy, release of the debtor and vacation of office by the trustee. Bankruptcy Restriction Orders and annulment are also covered in this chapter. Closure is regularly tested in the JIEB exam.

Chapter 13 – Partnership Law

In this chapter the options for creditors and partners of insolvent partnerships is introduced and the procedure for partnership voluntary arrangements is explained. Whilst partnership law has not been tested in detail in the JIEB exam, it is important to have an overview of the options available.

Chapter 14 – Administration of the estate of insolvent deceased individuals

This chapter outlines the effects of death of the debtor on an IVA or bankruptcy and also details how to deal with the insolvent estate of a deceased debtor. Whilst these topics are not regularly tested they did form the basis of a question in the 2007 exam.

Chapter 15 – Numbers questions

This is a very practical chapter detailing how to produce financial statements such as:

- Statement of Affairs
- Estimated Outcome Statements
- Receipts and payments accounts.

At least one numbers question has appeared in every JIEB exam paper to date.

Insolvency Code of Ethics

Contents

Introduction
Examination context
Topic List
    1   Insolvency Code of Ethics
    2   Money laundering
Self-test
Answers to Self-test

Introduction

Learning objectives

- Identify fundamental principles
- Apply the Code of Ethics in practice in relation to appointments as trustee in bankruptcy or supervisor of a voluntary arrangement
- Understand the implications of money laundering regulations for an office holder

Tick off
☐
☐
☐

Working context

When deciding whether to accept an insolvency appointment all office holders must adhere to the Code of Ethics. A new Code of Ethics was issued on 1 January 2009. The Code provides a framework within which office holders work. All aspects of insolvency work are governed by the Code of Ethics so a practical understanding of it is a necessity.

Stop and think

What are the fundamental principles? Why is a Code of Ethics required? What is money laundering? Why are regulations required concerning money laundering?

Examination context

The Insolvency Code of Ethics is not a very examinable topic in respect of the Personal Insolvency JIEB exam paper, however it may appear as a question in any of the three exam papers so is relevant in terms of the JIEB exam.

Money Laundering Regulations came into force in 2003 and therefore in terms of the exam this is relatively new material for the examiner. It appeared as an exam topic in the 2005 Administrations, CVAs and receiverships paper and the implications of money laundering for the office holder could easily be tested in any of the three exam papers.

Exam requirements

Past questions to look at include:

2008   Question 2 (a)
2000   Question 5 (c) (d)

1 Insolvency Code of Ethics

Section overview

The Code of Ethics governs the conduct of practitioners. All practitioners should be guided by the fundamental principles contained in the Code of Ethics. It sets out to assist the Insolvency Practitioner (IP) in the application of legislation and also in matters not covered by legislation. Failure to observe the code may not, of itself, constitute professional misconduct, but will be taken into account in assessing the conduct of an IP. An IP should not engage in any business, occupation or activity that impairs or might impair integrity, objectivity or the good reputation of the profession and as a result would be incompatible with the fundamental principles.

1.1 Fundamental principles

The Code identifies five fundamental principles with which the IP is required to comply:

1. **Integrity** – an IP should be straightforward and honest in all professional and business relationships.
2. **Objectivity** – an IP should not allow bias, conflict of interest or undue influence of others to override professional or business judgements.
3. **Professional competence and due care** – an IP has a continuing duty to maintain professional knowledge and skill at the level required to ensure that a client or employer receives competent professional service based on current developments in practice, legislation and techniques.
4. **Confidentiality** – an IP should respect the confidentiality of information acquired as a result of professional and business relationships.
5. **Professional behaviour** – an IP should comply with relevant laws and regulations and should avoid any action that discredits the profession.

1.2 Threats

The Code requires the IP to identify, evaluate and address threats to the fundamental principles. Many threats fall into five categories:

1. **Self interest threats** – these may occur as a result of the financial or other interests of a practice or an IP or of an immediate or close family member of an individual within the practice.
2. **Self review threats** – these may occur when a previous judgement made by an individual within the practice needs to be re-evaluated by the IP.
3. **Advocacy threats** – these may occur when an individual within the practice promotes a position or opinion to the point that subsequent objectivity may be compromised.
4. **Familiarity threats** – may occur when, because of a close relationship, an individual within the practice becomes too sympathetic to the interests of others.
5. **Intimidation threats** – these may occur when an IP may be deterred from acting objectively by threats, actual or perceived.

1.3 Safeguards

IP's should ensure that safeguards are in place to reduce the level of any threat. These may include:

- Leadership that stresses the importance of compliance with the fundamental principles.
- Policies and procedures to implement and monitor quality control of engagements.
- Documented policies regarding the identification of threats to compliance with the fundamental principles, the evaluation of the significance of these threats and the identification and the application

of safeguards to eliminate or reduce the threats, other than those that are trivial, to an acceptable level.

- Documented internal policies and procedures requiring compliance with the fundamental principles.
- Policies and procedures to consider the fundamental principles of the Code before the acceptance of an insolvency appointment.
- Policies and procedures regarding the identification of interests or relationships between individuals within the practice and third parties.
- Policies and procedures to prohibit individuals who are not members of the insolvency team from inappropriately influencing the outcome of an insolvency appointment.
- Timely communication of a practice's policies and procedures, including any changes to them, to all individuals within the practice, and appropriate training and education on such policies and procedures.
- Designating a member of senior management to be responsible for overseeing the adequate functioning of the safeguarding system.
- A disciplinary mechanism to promote compliance with policies and procedures.
- Published policies and procedures to encourage and empower individuals within the practice to communicate to senior levels within the practice and/or the IP any issue relating to compliance with the fundamental principles that concerns them.

Safeguards specific to an appointment may include:

- Involving and/or consulting another IP from within the practice to review the work done.
- Consulting an independent third party, such as a committee of creditors, a licensing or professional body or another IP.
- Involving another IP to perform part of the work, which may include another IP taking a joint appointment where conflict arises during the course of the appointment.
- Seeking directions from the court.
- Obtaining knowledge and understanding of the entity, its owners, managers and those responsible for its governance and business activities.
- Acquiring an appropriate understanding of the nature of the entity's business, the complexity of its operations, the specific requirements of the engagement and the purpose, nature and scope of the work to be performed.
- Acquiring knowledge of relevant industries or subject matters.
- Possessing or obtaining experience with relevant regulatory or reporting requirements.
- Assigning staff with the necessary competencies.
- Using experts where necessary.
- Complying with quality control policies and procedures designed to provide reasonable assurance that specific engagements are accepted only when they can be performed competently.

Where a threat cannot be eliminated the IP should evaluate the significance of such a threat and apply necessary safeguards to reduce them to an acceptable level.

In situations where no safeguards can mitigate a threat, the IP should conclude that it would not be appropriate to accept the insolvency appointment.

The IP should always be aware of how his actions will be perceived by others. Sometimes the mere perception of risk or conflict will undermine confidence in the practitioner's objectivity. In such circumstances, acceptance of an insolvency appointment would be unwise.

IPs should document their consideration of the fundamental principles and the reasons behind their agreement or otherwise to accept an insolvency appointment.

1.4 Fees and other types of remuneration

The special nature of insolvency appointments makes the payment or offer of any commission for, or the furnishing of, any valuable consideration towards the introduction of insolvency appointments inappropriate. This does not, however, preclude an arrangement between an IP and a bona fide employee whereby the employee's remuneration is based in whole or in part on introductions obtained for the practitioner through the efforts of the employee.

1.5 Significant professional and personal relationships

The environment in which IPs work can lead to threats to the principle of objectivity and integrity. The most common threats arise from ongoing and previous relationships.

- **Self review threats** – where the practitioner has had a significant professional relationship with the company or individual in relation to which or whom an appointment is taken.
- **Self interest threats** – threats which refer to personal relationships which may affect the reasoning the practitioner applies.

The IP should identify and analyse the significance of any professional or personal relationship which may affect compliance with the fundamental principles. The IP should consider whether any individual within the practice, or the practice itself, has or had a professional or personal relationship with a principle or employee of an entity for which an insolvency appointment is being considered, or any business controlled by or under the same control as the entity or part of it.

A professional relationship includes where an individual within the practice is carrying out or has carried out audit work or any other professional work. A professional relationship may also arise from an individual within the practice having an interest in an entity.

An IP should not accept an insolvency appointment in relation to an entity where any personal, professional or business connection with a principle is such as to impair or reasonably appear to impair the IP's objectivity.

In assessing whether a relationship is significant the IP should consider:

- How the relationship will be viewed by others.
- How recently any work was carried out.
- Whether the fee received for the work by the practice is or was significant to the practice itself or is or was substantial.
- The impact of the work conducted by the practice on the financial state and/or the financial stability of the entity.
- The nature of the previous duties undertaken by a practice or an individual within the practice during an earlier relationship with the entity.
- The extent of the insolvency teams familiarity with the individuals connected with the insolvency appointment.

If there is a significant relationship, the IP should consider whether that relationship gives rise to any particular threat. In situations where no threat arises, an IP will be able to undertake or continue the insolvency appointment.

Where a threat arises from a significant relationship and the threat cannot be overcome by safeguards, the professional work cannot be undertaken or continued.

1.6 Audit work previously undertaken for a company or individual to which an appointment is being sought

Where the IP or a practice has previously carried out audit work within the previous three years for a company or individual to which the appointment is being considered, the IP should not accept an appointment.

Where the audit work was conducted over three years ago, the IP should still consider whether any self review threats may arise and impose any necessary safeguards before the appointment is accepted.

1.7 Professional work undertaken by an individual within the practice for an entity or any principle of an entity to which an insolvency appointment is being considered

Where an individual within the practice is undertaking professional work (eg tax work) for an entity or any principle of an entity to whom an insolvency appointment is being considered, this will give rise to a threat to independence. The nature of the professional work will have to be considered. For example, basic tax work for the director of an entity may not be regarded as so significant as tax planning work undertaken for the entity.

1.8 Appointment as nominee and/or supervisor on an IVA, trustee in bankruptcy or trustee under a Deed of Arrangement

Where there has been a significant professional or personal relationship with an individual, no individual within the practice should accept appointment as nominee or supervisor of a voluntary arrangement or as trustee in relation to that individual.

1.9 Bankruptcy following appointment as Supervisor of an IVA

Where an individual within the practice has been supervisor of an IVA in relation to a debtor, the IP may, subject to giving careful consideration to the principles set out in the Code, accept appointment as trustee.

1.10 Personal relationships

An IP should not accept an insolvency appointment in relation to an individual where any personal connection with the individual is such as to impair or reasonably appear to impair the IP's objectivity.

1.11 Purchase of the assets of an insolvent debtor

An office holder, or any individual within the practice, or any close relative of the office holder, should not acquire any of the assets of the insolvent debtor.

1.12 Joint appointments

When accepting joint appointments, office holders should apply the Code of Ethics as they would to an individual appointment. Where an office holder is specifically precluded by the guidance from accepting an insolvency appointment as an individual, a joint appointment will not render the appointment acceptable.

2 Money laundering

Section overview

There are a number of Acts that contain law relating to money laundering. The main ones are:
- Money Laundering Regulations 2007.
- Part 7 Proceeds of Crime Act 2002 (Money Laundering) (POCA 2002) (as amended by The Serious Organised Crime and Police Act 2005 (SOCPA)).
- S18 and s21A Terrorism Act 2000 (TA 2000) (as amended by the Anti-Terrorism and Crime and Security Act 2001 and The Terrorism Act 2006).

Compliance with the 2007 Money Laundering Regulations is a legal requirement. The regulations came into force on 15 December 2007 and apply to all appointments held by an IP at that date. IPs should follow guidance published by the Consultative Committee of Accountancy Bodies (CCAB).

Definition

Money Laundering: a number of offences involving the proceeds of crime (including tax evasion and fraud) or terrorist funds. It is the process by which the identity of dirty money (ie The proceeds of crime and the ownership of those proceeds) is changed so that the proceeds appear to originate from legitimate sources. It includes possessing, dealing with or concealing the proceeds of any crime or similar activities in relation to terrorist funds, which includes funds from legitimate sources which are likely to be used for terrorism, as well as the proceeds of terrorism.

2.1 Money laundering process

Money laundering is conventionally described as being a three stage process:

- **Placement** – where cash (literally money in the form of coins and banknotes) is deposited into the banking system. Serious and organised criminals need access to the international banking system due to the practical difficulties in using cash to settle large transactions.
- **Layering** – a series of transactions designed to disguise the audit trail.
- **Integration** – whereby the now apparently cleaned funds are invested in the legitimate economy.

An Insolvency Practitioner can be targeted at any of the three stages, for instance:

- **Placement** – A potential purchaser of a business who wishes to pay for assets in cash.
- **Layering** – A criminal sends a cheque made payable to a liquidator of a company purporting to be in payment of a debt owed to the company which is being wound-up. The liquidator pays the cheque into an account maintained in the name of his firm in compliance with SIP 11. The debtor ledger is then checked and when it becomes apparent that the debt in question does not exist a cheque in the name of the firm is sent to the criminal. The funds appear legitimate.
- **Integration** – A criminal acquires a business through an office–holder using funds which have already passed through a money laundering process and now appear to be legitimate.

2.2 Offences

There are a wide range of offences under POCA 2002, TA 2000 and 2007 Regulations. The main ones relate to where a person:

- Conceals, disguises, converts or transfers criminal property from the UK.

- Enters into or becomes concerned in an arrangement which he knows or suspects facilitates the acquisition, retention, use or control of criminal property by or on behalf of another person.
- Acquires, uses and/or possesses criminal property.

A second tier of offences relate to the regulated sector and relate to where a person:

- Fails to disclose knowledge or suspicion of money laundering to the nominated officer or Serious Organised Crime Agency (SOCA).
- Tips off any person that such a disclosure has been made (s333A POCA).

This offence arises where a person in the regulated sector discloses either that a disclosure has been made to a MLRO or that investigations into allegations of money laundering have been carried out.

2.3 IP's obligations re money laundering

IP's are required to:

- Obtain verification of the identity of the person or entity over which he is appointed. Acceptable evidence or verification includes a court order, a court endorsed appointment or an appointment made by a debentureholder or creditors' meeting supported by a company search or similar.
- Establish procedures to identify customers and verify their identities.
- Carry out ongoing monitoring of business relationships.
- Consider the way the business has been operated and assess the risk of assets being tainted by crime. The IP may consider it necessary to apply to the SOCA for consent to perform the normal range of duties of collection, realisation and distribution of assets.
- Appoint a nominated officer called a 'Money Laundering Reporting Officer' (MLRO) to whom principals and employees must make money laundering reports. (This does not apply to sole practitioners who do not employ any staff or act in association with any other parties.).
- Establish internal systems, procedures, policies and controls to forestall and prevent money laundering.
- Provide relevant individuals with training on Money Laundering.
- Maintain records of client identification and of business relationships for at least five years.
- Report suspicions of money laundering to SOCA.

2.4 Identification procedures

Reg 5 Money Laundering Regulations 2007 details identification procedures which IP's must have in place for identifying the customer and verifying their identity on the basis of documents, data or information obtained from a reliable and independent source.

Identification procedures are required when:

- Entering a business relationship.
- Carrying out an occasional transaction.
- Where there is suspicion of money laundering or terrorist financing.
- Where there are doubts concerning the validity of previous identification evidence.

Definition

Occasional transaction: a transaction amounting to 15,000 euros or more. (This would include the sale of assets of an insolvent involving the paying of 15,000 euros or more to the IP).

Personal Insolvency

Identification procedures for an individual would include the IP seeing and taking copies of evidence establishing the applicants full name and address ie Passport, photo driving licence, recent utility bill, HMRC tax notification, Benefits Agency benefits book.

Identification procedures for a company may also involve identifying the controllers of the company. Suitable evidence for a company includes:

- Certificate of incorporation.
- Evidence of company's registered address.
- Copy of company's annual return.

2.5 Reporting suspicions of money laundering

Internal reports of money laundering should be made to the MLRO who is required to decide whether to report the matter on to the SOCA. If in doubt, the MRLO should seek legal advice. Reports should be made as soon as possible, irrespective of the amounts involved.

There are two types of form for reporting to the SOCA:

- Standard Disclosure Form
- Limited Intelligence Value Report Form

Care must be taken that a money launderer is not tipped off (this constitutes an offence under POCA 2002 and TA 2000).

Having made the report, no action that would assist the launderer or otherwise constitute money laundering by the IP may take place for seven working days, unless SOCA gives consent for it to go ahead. This may impact on a potential sale in which case reports to SOCA may be marked urgent.

2.6 High Value Dealers

High value dealers are required to register with the Commissioners of HM Revenue & Customs.

Definition

High value dealer: the activity of dealing in goods whenever a transaction involves accepting a total cash payment of 15,000 euros or more in one operation or several if they are linked.

Self-test

Answer the following questions.

1. You have been acting as the supervisor of the voluntary arrangement of Fred Jones. Due to the failure of the arrangement a bankruptcy petition has been presented. Are you able to act as Fred's trustee in bankruptcy?

2. For the last three years you have provided tax advice to Sarah Brown. She has now approached you and asked you to assist her in putting forward proposals for a voluntary arrangement to her creditors. Are you able to act in this regard?

3. What are the fundamental principles?

4. How can professional competence be maintained?

Now, go back to the Learning Objectives in the Introduction. If you are satisfied that you have achieved these, please tick them off.

Answers to Self-test

1. Appointment as trustee may be accepted, subject to consideration to the principles set out in the Code of Ethics.

2. Where there has been a significant professional relationship with an individual, appointment as nominee or supervisor should not be accepted. In order to determine whether the tax advice given was significant we would have to consider matters such as:

    - The nature of advice given and the impact of the advice on Sarah's financial position.
    - The significance of the fees received for the work.
    - The likelihood of having to take action in respect of any advice given.

    Advice from RPB could be sought however it is likely that the appointment should not be accepted.

3. Integrity
   Objectivity
   Professional competence and due care
   Confidentiality
   Professional behaviour.

4. By having a continued awareness and understanding of relevant technical and professional developments. This would include:

    Developments in insolvency legislation.
    Regulations of the licensing body.
    Technical issues being discussed within the profession.
    Guidance issued by licensing bodies or the Insolvency Service.
    Statements of Insolvency Practice.

2

Statements of Insolvency Practice

Contents

Introduction
Examination context
Topic List
1 Statements of Insolvency Practice and Technical Releases
2 List of SIPs
3 Insolvency Guidance Papers

Appendix 1 Insolvency Guidance Paper – Control of cases

Appendix 2 Insolvency Guidance Paper – Succession planning

Appendix 3 Insolvency Guidance Paper – Systems for control of accounting and other business records

Self-test
Answers to Self-test

Personal Insolvency

Introduction

Learning objectives

- Understand what a Statement of Insolvency Practice (SIP) is, who produces them and why they are important
- Learn relevant SIP numbers and names
- Understand what a Technical Release is
- Understand what an Insolvency Guidance Paper is

Tick off
☐
☐
☐
☐

Working context

SIPs outline best practice and basic principles which must be followed by insolvency professionals. A good knowledge of the SIPs is therefore fundamental to ensure that all areas of your work are carried out with the appropriate levels of competence and skill.

Stop and think

Why is a uniform approach to insolvency issues required?

STATEMENTS OF INSOLVENCY PRACTICE 2

Examination context

It is unlikely in the exam that a question will appear testing your knowledge of a particular SIP in its own right. However, a good detailed knowledge of the SIPs are required in order to pass the exam, for example a question regarding remuneration will require a detailed knowledge of SIP 9 and a question regarding voluntary arrangements will require a detailed knowledge of SIP 3.

Exam requirements

Past questions to look at include:

2006	Question 1 (a)
2000	Question 5 (c) (e)
1999	Question 2 (b)
1998	Question 4 (c)
1997	Question 3 (c)
1995	Question 4 (a)
1992	Paper II, Question 5

1 Statements of Insolvency Practice and Technical Releases

Section overview

Statements of Insolvency Practice (SIPs) set out basic principles and essential procedures with which office holders are required to comply.

1.1 SIPs

Statements of Insolvency Practice (SIPs) are issued under procedures agreed between the insolvency regulatory authorities acting through the Joint Insolvency Committee. SIPs should be used as guidance only and should not be relied upon as definitive statements. The introduction to each SIP details who it is issued by and sets out the context in which it is to be used.

1.2 Technical Releases

SIP 5 and SIP 6 were withdrawn by the Society of Practitioners of Insolvency in August 1999 and replaced by Technical Releases. These apply in exactly the same way as the original SIPs.

2 List of SIPs

Section overview

The following is a list of SIPs in force at July 2009. Where a detailed knowledge of the content of the SIP is required reference is made to the relevant chapter in this text.

2.1 Summary of SIPs

SIP	Name	Chapter
1	An administrative receiver's responsibility for the company's records	
2	A liquidator's investigation into the affairs of an insolvent company	
3	Voluntary arrangements	4, 5
4	Disqualification of directors	
5	Non preferential claims by employees dismissed without proper notice by insolvent employers (replaced by Technical Release 5)	
6	Treatment of director's claims as employees in insolvency administrations (replaced by Technical Release 6)	
7	Preparation of insolvency office holder's receipts and payments	15
8	Summoning and holding meetings of creditors convened pursuant to s98	
9	Remuneration of insolvency office holders	6, 9
10	Proxy forms	
11	The handling of funds in formal insolvency appointments	9
12	Records of meetings in formal insolvency proceedings	5
13	Acquisition of assets of insolvent companies by directors	
14	A receiver's responsibility to preferential creditors	
15	Reporting and providing information on their functions to committees in formal insolvencies	8
16	Pre-packaged sales in administrations	

3 Insolvency Guidance Papers

Section overview

Insolvency Guidance Papers (IGPs) are issued to insolvency practitioners to provide guidance on matters that may require consideration in the conduct of insolvency work or in an insolvency practitioner's practice.

Unlike SIPs which set out required practice, IGPs are purely guidance and practitioners may develop different approaches to the areas covered by the IGPs.

IGPs are developed and authorised by the Joint Insolvency Committee and adopted by each of the insolvency authorising bodies.

3.1 Insolvency Guidance Papers

The following is a list of Guidance Papers issued up to July 2009:

- Introductory article to Guidance Papers
- Succession planning
- Control of cases
- Bankruptcy – family home (see Chapter 10 for more details)
- Systems for control of accounting and other business records

Appendix 1

Insolvency Guidance Paper – Control of cases

Introduction

Insolvency appointments are personal to an individual practitioner, who has an obligation to ensure that cases are properly controlled and administered at all times. However, issues can arise when an insolvency practitioner delegates work to others, or takes appointments jointly with other practitioners. In such circumstances, a practitioner's planning and administrative arrangements will need to consider how best to ensure that cases are properly controlled at all times and that proper regard is paid to the interests of creditors and other affected parties.

Delegation

Given the wide variation in the size of firms dealing with insolvency work, each practitioner will have different case loads and resources and thus a different requirement to delegate work. Delegation can take on a number of forms, including:

- Delegation of work to staff in the practitioner's own office or to sub-contractors.
- Delegation of work to staff within a firm but in another location.
- Taking a reduced role on an appointment taken jointly with an insolvency practitioner in the practitioner's office.
- Taking a reduced role on an appointment taken jointly with an insolvency practitioner within the same firm but in another location.
- Allowing a specialist insolvency practitioner within a firm to take responsibility for all work of a specific type.
- Allowing a specialist within a firm to handle work of a specific type (eg tax).
- Sharing work on an agreed basis on an appointment taken jointly with a practitioner from another firm.
- Employing another firm to give specialist advice (eg tax) or to undertake specific work (eg an investigation) and
- Allowing a practitioner in a former firm (following either the practitioner's move to another firm or retirement) to take responsibility for appointments for a short time pending the transfer of cases.
- For each of the above examples (and in other cases where delegation takes place) the practitioner must be satisfied at all times that work is being carried out in a proper and efficient manner, appropriate to the case.

Control

In determining the procedures to be put in place to ensure that an appropriate level of control can be established in relation to delegated work, it is recommended that a practitioner have regard to the following matters:

- The structure within a firm, and the qualifications and experience of staff.
- The need for the practitioner to be involved in setting case strategy at the outset, depending on the nature, size and complexity of the case.

STATEMENTS OF INSOLVENCY PRACTICE

- The procedures within a firm to ensure consultation by joint appointees, other practitioners and staff.

- The extent to which levels of responsibility are defined and the circumstances in which a reference to, or approval by, the practitioner is required.

- Whether there are clear guidelines within a firm to deal with the administration of cases at locations remote from the practitioner.

- The ways in which compliance and case progress are monitored and then reported to the practitioner.

- The frequency of case reviews, and who carries them out.

- The systems for dealing with correspondence received and, in particular, complaints.

- The process by which work is allocated on a joint appointment with a practitioner from another firm, the rationale for that split and the controls to be put in place, subject always to statutory requirements and

- The way in which specialist advisers (including agents and solicitors) and sub-contractors are chosen and engaged and how their work is monitored.

- Insolvency practitioners are aware that they may be required to justify their decisions and demonstrate that appropriate levels of control have been established. It is recommended that for firm wide procedures guidance is set out in writing and that on a case by case basis contemporaneous working papers or file notes are prepared.

Appendix 2

Insolvency Guidance Paper – Succession planning

Introduction

Insolvency appointments are personal to an insolvency practitioner, who has an obligation to ensure that cases are properly managed at all times and to have appropriate contingency arrangements in place to cover a change in the insolvency practitioner's circumstances. The over-riding principle is that the interests of creditors and other stakeholders should not be prejudiced.

Continuity

It is important for insolvency practitioners to consider on a regular basis the arrangements in place to ensure continuity in the event of death, incapacity to act, retirement from practice, or the practitioner otherwise retiring from a firm.

Sole practitioners

A sole practitioner should consider the steps necessary to put a workable continuity agreement in place, although there may well be considerations as to whether a sole practitioner's cases would be accepted by another insolvency practitioner. The full consequences, both practical and financial, of the relationship with another insolvency practitioner have to be recognised by both the office holder and the nominated successor, so that continuity can be achieved and the interests of creditors and other stakeholders safeguarded. In particular, the nominated successor would have to consider whether the obligations arising from a successor arrangement can be discharged properly and expeditiously, having regard to the number and nature of cases to be taken over.

A retiring office holder should normally make arrangements for the transfer of cases (including, where appropriate, an application to Court) in sufficient time to ensure that the cases are transferred before the retirement takes place.

The nominated successor may need to make an application to Court for the transfer of cases as soon as possible after the other office holder's death, incapacity or, if no other arrangements have been made, retirement.

The arrangements with the nominated successor will need to be reviewed as circumstances dictate, but preferably at least annually.

The principal matters that might routinely be dealt with in a continuity agreement are set out in the Appendix to this paper.

Firms

Every insolvency practitioner in a firm (whether a principal or employee) should consider the comments made above regarding sole practitioners and should discuss with the firm the arrangements for succession planning, to cover death, incapacity to act, retirement, or leaving the firm. It is recommended that this is reflected in the partnership agreement or in a separate insolvency practice agreement.

In a firm with other insolvency practitioners, it is likely that the arrangements would include, at the least, an understanding that another insolvency practitioner will take over open cases and make an application to court for the transfer of those cases, if the office holder is unable to do so. It will be the professional responsibility of the remaining partners (as insolvency practitioners) to take prompt action to safeguard the interests of creditors and other stakeholders.

When an office holder retires from a firm, it may be acceptable for the office holder to remain in office for a short period, with an insolvency practitioner in the firm dealing with the administration of cases. However, there the office holder needs to receive appropriate information on the progress of cases and be consulted when decisions are to be made; the office holder is likely to require unrestricted access to case files. Such an arrangement, however, is unlikely to be appropriate other than for cases that are clearly in their closing stages. In normal circumstances, the retiring office holder should be replaced within a reasonable period, likely to be within 12 months of retirement.

Where there are no other insolvency practitioners in a firm and in the absence of any contractual arrangements to deal with death, incapacity to act, or retirement, the remaining partners (presumably themselves members of professional bodies) should consider their own professional obligations to ensure the proper management of their practice, including making arrangements for another insolvency practitioner to step in as office holder. The firm may have to procure an application to court for the transfer of cases as soon as possible after the office holder's death, incapacity or retirement.

The principal matters that might routinely be dealt with in an insolvency practice agreement (or a partnership agreement) are set out in the Appendix to this paper.

Disputes

There can be disputes between firms and partners (and employees who are office holders) who leave the firm, principally arising from the personal nature of insolvency appointments. However, commercial disputes should not be allowed to obscure the over-riding principle set out at the beginning of this paper - that the interest of creditors and other stakeholders should not be prejudiced.

It is important therefore, that the contractual arrangements referred to above should provide for the (essentially) mechanistic and financial consequences of an office holder leaving the firm (or upon incapacity to act). There will be similar considerations when an office holder (either partner or employee) is suspended by a firm, or is otherwise excluded from the firm's offices.

Where there are no contractual arrangements, or where a dispute arises, both parties should consider their professional obligations and the standard of conduct required by their professional bodies. Further, an office holder must have regard to the statutory obligations of the offices held.

If there is a dispute, it is for the office holder to decide how best to ensure that the obligations of office can be discharged; an application to court may be the only means of finding a solution. It is always open to an office holder to consult with his or her authorising body.

As noted above, there may be professional obligations on remaining partners to arrange for the proper management of their practice and so ensure that they do not bring their own professional bodies into disrepute.

Appendix

Principal matters that might be dealt with in a continuity agreement:

1   A clear statement of the circumstances upon which the agreement would become operative and also the circumstances in which the nominated successor can decline to act.

2   The extent and frequency of disclosure to the nominated successor of case details and financial information.

3   Detailed provisions to provide for:
    – The steps to be taken by the nominated successor when the agreement becomes operative.
    – Ownership of, or access to, case working papers.
    – Access to practice records.
    – Financial agreements.

Principal matters that might be dealt with in an insolvency practice agreement (or in a partnership agreement):

1. Clear statements of what happens in the event of an insolvency practitioner (whether partner or employee):

    - Dying, or being otherwise incapable of acting as an insolvency practitioner
    - Retiring from practice
    - Being suspended or otherwise excluded from the firm's offices or
    - Leaving the firm.

2. Where the agreement provides for another insolvency practitioner (whether in the firm or in another firm) to take over appointments:

    - The time within which transfers of cases will take place and the arrangements for the interim period, including provisions for access to information and files.
    - The obligations placed on the practitioner, the firm and the successor practitioner, both in the interim period and thereafter.
    - Professional indemnity insurance arrangements and
    - Financial arrangements.

3. Where the insolvency practitioner is to remain as office holder following retirement or leaving the firm:

    - Ownership of, or access to, case working papers.
    - Access to practice records.
    - Professional indemnity insurance arrangements and
    - Financial arrangements.

Appendix 3

Insolvency Guidance Paper – Systems for control of accounting and other business records

Introduction

The existence and accuracy of an insolvent's accounting and other business records will affect the efficient realisation and distribution of an insolvent's assets. and may also be relevant in other circumstances, for example in disqualification proceedings or prosecution of criminal offences. An insolvency practitioner will also need to take account of the various statutory requirements for businesses to retain certain categories of records.

It is important that insolvency practitioners have satisfactory systems in place to record the receipt. and control of access to, movement, and eventual disposal of records. The guidance note looks at the parameters of these systems, although each case will be considered on its own merit. Some cases may need significantly more detail than is suggested here.

Formal recording systems can also assist an insolvency practitioner in the effective management of storage costs.

Control of records

It is likely that any system implemented by an insolvency practitioner would record:

- the practitioner's initial enquiries to establish the nature and location of records;
- the steps taken to safeguard records;
- requests made of directors and others to deliver up records;
- what records have been taken under the practitioner's control, and when and how this was done;
- the location of the records;
- whether third parties have had access to the records (and for what purpose); and
- the eventual disposal of the records, and when and how this was done.

It will be particularly important in cases where the insolvent's records are referred to in legal proceedings (whether for the purpose of civil asset recovery or in other circumstances) that a formal recording process has been followed. Accordingly, an insolvency practitioner should be able to show that any system is applied consistently and that staff are trained in its use.

Records in electronic form

An insolvency practitioner will need to consider how to deal with information held in electronic form. Retrieval and storage of such information may include as appropriate securing severs and personal computers (or hard drives), copying information from those sources, or obtaining hard copies. The system of control is likely to follow the principles set out above.

Joint appointments

Where an insolvency practitioner is appointed jointly with a practitioner from a different firm, responsibility for records should be included within the agreed division of duties. Where both practitioners receive records, each should implement a system of control.

Self-test

Answer the following questions.

1. Which SIP gives guidance on keeping records of meetings in formal insolvency proceedings?
2. What matters are dealt with by SIP 3?
3. Which SIP provides guidance on office holder's remuneration?
4. Which SIP provides guidance on the handling of funds in insolvency in insolvency appointments?
5. What matters are dealt with by SIP 15?
6. What matters are dealt with by SIP 7?

Now, go back to the Learning Objectives in the Introduction. If you are satisfied that you have achieved these, please tick them off.

Answers to Self-test

1. SIP 12
2. Voluntary arrangements.
3. SIP 9
4. SIP 11
5. Reporting and providing information on their functions to committees in formal insolvencies.
6. Preparation of insolvency office holders' receipts and payments accounts.

3

Options for debtor and creditors

▸ ▸ ▸ ▸ ▸ ▸ ▸ ▸ ▸ ▸ ▸ ▸ ▸ ▸

Contents

Introduction
Examination context
Topic List
1 Options for the debtor
2 Options for creditors
Summary and Self-test
Answers to Self-test
Answer to Interactive question

Personal Insolvency

Introduction

Learning objectives

▶ Understand the different options available to an insolvent individual and creditors.

Tick off ☐

Working context

Office holders are often asked to give advice to individuals facing insolvency and those who are affected by that insolvency, for example, creditors. It is important therefore to understand the options available and the advantages and disadvantages of each option so that the best advice can be given.

Stop and think

Why is bankruptcy not always the right option for an insolvent individual? What other options are available? Why might an informal agreement with a debtor be better for a creditor than pursuing bankruptcy?

OPTIONS FOR DEBTOR AND CREDITORS 3

Examination context

The JIEB exam is a very practical exam, it is likely therefore that questions are asked requiring you to give advice to an individual having been given relevant facts regarding their financial position.

Exam requirements

Past questions to look at include:

2008	Question 2 (b)
2008	Question 4 (d)
2006	Question 3
2004	Question 5
2001	Question 3
2001	Question 5 (b)
1996	Question 5 (b)
1989	Paper II, Question 3 (b)

Personal Insolvency

1 Options for the debtor

Section overview

Personal insolvency is defined as an inability to pay debts as they fall due (known as the cash flow test). The cash flow test is failed if a debtor owes a creditor £750 or more and the creditor issues a statutory demand which is neither complied with or set aside in accordance with the rules, within 21 days, or an execution for a judgement has been returned unsatisfied (s268 IA). There are a number of options for a debtor who has become insolvent both statutory and non-statutory.

1.1 Matters to consider when choosing the right option

When deciding which of the statutory and non-statutory options to take the individual should consider the following factors:

- Is the option binding on the individual's creditors?
- Does the option leave the individual free from all or part of the debts when completed?
- How long will it last?
- How will the option chosen affect the individual's employment?
- Will the individual's credit rating be affected?
- Will the individual's home be at risk?
- What fee will have to be paid and when?
- Can the individual meet the repayment requirements of the chosen option?

1.2 Do nothing

Many debtors may well choose to take this option but it should never be advised. Invariably this option will result in lots of stress and almost inevitably bankruptcy.

1.3 Negotiated agreement with creditors

This is where the debtor contacts his creditors and negotiates an agreement to repay all or some of his debts. This may involve making payments from income or from a lump sum, for example, an inheritance or from relatives. This option is most appropriate where the debtor has only a small number of creditors who are supportive of the debtor.

A third party is not required to make the negotiations on behalf of the debtor so costs are lower than in other options. Creditors may be willing to write off some of what is owed after a period of time if the debtor has made every effort to repay what is owed. There is no court involvement.

The main disadvantages of this option is that it is not binding on the creditors who may refuse the debtor's proposals and take action to recover their debt. Even if a creditor initially consents to the arrangement he may be at liberty to change his mind even after the arrangement has been in place for some time. Legal advice should be taken to ensure that any compromise reached between the debtor and creditors is legally binding.

The debtor remains liable to repay the full amount of the debt. If only small repayments are possible it may take a long time to clear the debts and interest charges may be accruing during this period. The debtor is responsible for negotiating with his creditors and keeping them informed of the progress of repayments, this may be stressful.

1.4 Debt reorganisation or consolidation loan

This is where the debtor applies for a loan to reorganise or clear his debts. The result should be that the debtor then makes only one monthly payment on one loan rather than many payments to different creditors.

A consolidation loan is only appropriate where the debtor has income from which to make the loan repayments. Care should be taken to ensure that the new repayments are lower than those made before the loan was taken out and consideration should also be given to how long the loan will last, what interest will have to be paid and what penalties and other charges there are.

A fee may have to be paid for arranging the loan and the lender may require that the loan is secured on the debtor's house.

This option may not be available to debtors with a poor credit rating.

1.5 Debt management plan

Where a debtor wishes to avoid the stigma of bankruptcy, a debt management plan may be another option. In this case, a debt management company will assess the debtor's financial situation to establish an affordable monthly repayment amount. The debt management company will then contact all of the debtor's creditors to negotiate a reduced monthly repayment. The debtor will thereafter pay the debt management company one sum and they in turn will pay the creditors a pro-rata amount. Plans can last for five years or more.

The individual or company chosen to manage the plan must be licensed and regulated under consumer credit law. Some companies will not charge a direct fee for their services, taking monies out of payments made to creditors instead. Other companies will require payment of an initial charge for preparing, negotiating and administering the plan.

Debt management plans have become very popular in recent years highlighted by the fact that interest on the debt will often be frozen.

As with all other pre-insolvency options however, there is the main disadvantage that there is no debt forgiveness and the debtor must pay the debt in full over time. Creditors cannot be forced to accept the proposed plan and can still take enforcement action against the debtor.

1.6 Debt relief orders

Debt relief orders (DRO) came into force on 6 April 2009. They are aimed at assisting over indebted individuals with relatively few liabilities, little surplus income and few assets who are currently unable to access other forms of debt relief. They offer an alternative to bankruptcy at a reduced cost.

The Tribunals, Courts and Enforcement Act 2007 introduced a new Part 7A into the Insolvency Act 1986, comprising ss251A – 251X and Schedules 4ZA and 4ZB.

Who is eligible for a DRO?

In order to apply for a DRO applicants must meet the following criteria:

- Be unable to pay their debts.
- Have total liabilities of less than £15,000.
- Have assets of less than £300 (but in addition may own a vehicle worth less than £1,000).
- Debtors must not own a house (even if it has no equity value).
- Have surplus income of less than £50 per month.
- Be domiciled in England or Wales, or for the last three years have been resident or carrying on a business there.
- Not have an existing bankruptcy order, bankruptcy restrictions order or current DRO or IVA or have had a DRO in the last six years.
- A current pending debtors petition in relation to the debtor but the debtor has not been referred to the DRO procedure by the court as a more suitable method of debt relief.
- A current pending creditors bankruptcy petition against the debtor but the debtor has not obtained the creditors permission for entry into the DRO procedure.

How is a DRO applied for?

DRO's are applied for online to the official receiver with an approved intermediary helping to complete the application.

The applicant must submit an application and fee (£90) to the official receiver.

The application must include:

- List of debts to which the debtor is subject at the date of the application giving details of amounts owed and to whom.
- Details of any security held in respect of those debts.
- Such other information re the debtor's affairs as may be prescribed.

If the requirements are met the official receiver can make the order without the involvement of the court. The official receiver will send a copy of the order to the applicant and will enter the order onto the Individual Insolvency Register.

Effects of a DRO being made

During the period for which the order is in force (12 months) the debtor will be:

- Protected from enforcement action by the creditors included in the application.
- Free from those debts at the end of the period.
- Obliged to provide information to and co-operate with the official receiver.
- Expected to make arrangements to repay their creditors should their financial circumstances improve.
- Subject to restrictions.

Restrictions imposed during period of the DRO

During the period of the order the debtor may not:

- Obtain credit of £500 or more, either alone or jointly with another person, without disclosing that they are subject to a DRO.
- Carry on a business (directly or indirectly) in a name that is different from the name under which they were granted a DRO, without telling all those with whom the debtor does business the name under which they were granted a DRO.
- Be involved with (directly or indirectly) with the promotion, management or formation of a limited company and may not act as a company director without the court's permission.
- Apply for a DRO more than once every six years.

Debt relief restrictions order (DRRO)

The official receiver will have the power to apply for a debt relief restrictions order which will extend the period of restriction for up to 15 years for debtors who have acted irresponsibly, recklessly or dishonestly.

Debts not included in a DRO

Court fines and confiscation orders.
Child support and maintenance.
Student loans.

Assets not included in £300

Household equipment such as bedding, clothing, furniture.

Tools, books and other items of equipment used in the debtor's employment or business.

A car which has been specially adapted because of a physical disability required to carry out every day activities.

Motor vehicle worth less than £1,000.

Effect when DRO ends

All debts listed on the order will be written off at the end of the period to which the order relates.

1.7 County Court Administration Order (s106 TCE 2007)

Where a debtor has at least two debts totalling less than £5,000 and one or more of the creditors has obtained a court judgment against them, the debtor can apply to court for an administration order (AO). An AO is a court based procedure whereby the debtor agrees to make regular payments to the court to pay towards what is owed to creditors.

There is no fee for an AO but the court will take 10% of the monies paid towards costs.

The court will inform the creditors of the AO and they then have 16 days to inform the court of any objections they have to the order. Creditors may ask to be left out of the order and separate repayments will then have to be made.

A debtor will need to be in receipt of a regular income in order to make the required repayments.

An AO cannot last for more than five years.

During the period for which the AO is in force:

- No bankruptcy petition may be presented by a qualifying creditor.
- No other remedies for the recovery of a qualifying debt may be pursued.
- Existing proceedings will be stayed.
- No interest may be charged.
- The debtor must provide the court with details of his earnings, income, assets and outgoings.
- The debtor must advise the court of any anticipated disposals of assets.

If payments under the AO are not made the order can be cancelled and the debtor will be subject to the same restrictions as someone who is bankrupt.

1.8 Individual voluntary arrangement (IVA)

Individual voluntary arrangements were first introduced by the Insolvency Act 1986. The purpose was to enable creditors to obtain relief from their debts outside bankruptcy. An IVA will enable an insolvent debtor to secure a moratorium on his debts. Once an arrangement is in place the creditors outstanding indebtedness will be settled wholly through the terms of the arrangement.

An IVA has many advantages namely:

- Debtor retains control of assets.
- Can exclude assets from the arrangement.
- It avoids bankruptcy and its associated disabilities, obligations and stigma. In particular it enables the debtor to keep better control over his assets and hopefully remain in business/employment. These disabilities and obligations will be discussed more fully later.
- Assets don't vest in supervisor (in bankruptcy they automatically vest in the trustee).
- It avoids the threat of prosecution for retrospective bankruptcy offences and prevents the making of a bankruptcy restrictions order (BRO).
- It will bind all creditors, even if they dissent, provided that overall more than 75% in value of the creditors voting in person or by proxy vote in favour.
- Realisations should be higher as there are lower costs than in bankruptcy, no automatic discharge and more chance that the debtor will retain his employment or business to produce income for the creditors.
- Mechanism for stay of all proceedings in setting up period.
- Interim order prevents creditors taking action to recover their debt.

Personal Insolvency

There are also disadvantages to an IVA namely:

- The debtor will have to pay the proposed nominee's costs and court fees.
- If the VA is not approved it is highly likely that his creditors will proceed to petition for bankruptcy.
- The debtor will need the support of more than 75% (in value) of his creditors.
- It will continue beyond the automatic discharge period for bankruptcy. The average voluntary arrangement usually lasts for five years whereas the maximum discharge period for bankruptcy is usually one year.
- The VA may fail resulting in the eventual bankruptcy of the debtor.
- Creditors will not receive benefit that trustee in bankruptcy would have to pursue antecedent transactions.

1.9 Deed of arrangement

A deed of arrangement is a formal agreement governed by the Deeds of Arrangement Act 1914. It is probable that an IVA will prove more attractive to debtors. The main reason for this is that a dissenting creditor (unlike in a VA) cannot be bound into the arrangement, leaving him free to pursue all his remedies against the debtor.

There are however some advantages namely:

- Long established mechanism with good precedents.
- Simple and speedy procedures.
- It requires only a simple majority of the creditors in number and value to bring it into effect.
- It will not be necessary to call a meeting of creditors, and
- No need to appoint a nominee.

As a consequence the costs of a deed of arrangement are likely to be lower.

1.10 Bankruptcy

Bankruptcy is a formal court procedure which may be commenced by the debtor or one or more of his creditors owed at least £750.

Bankruptcy has many disadvantages which explains why so many debtors try hard to avoid it (see Chapter 7). The worst of the disadvantages are in turn the advantages of an IVA namely:

- All assets vest in the trustee so the debtor loses control of his assets (in particular the main asset of the debtor's estate – his home or share in it).
- The debtor will become subject to the disabilities, obligations and stigma that arises in bankruptcy making it difficult to trade.
- Bankrupt cannot act as a director of a company or be involved in its management unless the court agrees.
- Potential liability for bankruptcy offences and the making of a bankruptcy restrictions order.
- The trustee will be able to challenge the validity of transactions already completed if they appear to be at an undervalue or a preference.
- Even after discharge the debtor will have a poor credit rating.
- A bankruptcy restrictions order may be applied for if the debtor has acted irresponsibly, recklessly or dishonestly.

Despite its disadvantages however, for some debtors bankruptcy may be the best option and it does have some advantages over an IVA:

- In bankruptcy (unlike an IVA) the debtor will enjoy an automatic discharge usually within a maximum period of one year (s279).

- The vast majority (if not all) debts will not survive the bankruptcy.
- The bankrupt will have no further contact with creditors and this should lead to less stress.
- Creditors cannot take further action unless the debts are secured on the debtors home or other property.

Interactive question: Barry Marsden

Barry Marsden has a small business manufacturing bicycles. Initially he traded profitably, although in the past few years he has found it more difficult to make ends meet and he is no longer able to pay his debts as they fall due. He trades from premises in Newbury which were originally owned by him personally but were sold to J Holdings Ltd three years ago for £25,000 at a time when he was finding it difficult to meet his debts. The premises were then worth £75,000 but are currently valued at £156,000. The majority shareholder of J Holdings Ltd is Anne Bell, Barry's long term partner. Although Barry's business picked up for a while after the transfer of the premises, Barry was of the opinion that things would worsen again shortly. With this in mind he gave his collection of antiques to Anne Bell 18 months ago.

Barry now wishes to enter into an arrangement with his creditors for the composition of his debts in order to avoid the stigma of being made bankrupt. His only remaining assets of value are his house worth £180,000, but which is subject to an outstanding mortgage of £120,000, his car worth £6,500 and unused stock valued at £7,500. He has unsecured liabilities of £156,000. He proposes to realise his remaining assets, distributing the proceeds among his creditors. He has also been promised employment by J Holdings Ltd and will make voluntary contributions from his income for the term of the arrangement.

Requirement

Advise Barry as to the relative advantages and disadvantages of entering into:

(a) A deed of arrangement under the Deeds of Arrangement Act 1914, or
(b) A voluntary arrangement under the Insolvency Act 1986.

See **Answer** at the end of this chapter.

2 Options for creditors

Section overview

There are a number of options available to a creditor to recover his debt from the debtor. These include:

- Compromise the debt.
- Sue and obtain judgement.
- Support a voluntary arrangement.
- Petition for bankruptcy.

2.1 Compromise

If at all possible (assuming that the debtor cannot genuinely afford repayment) compromise is the best option. However being able to establish the exact state of the debtor's financing and establishing liability may not be possible without court proceedings. If a compromise is achieved the terms of that compromise should be properly recorded (with the aid of legal advice if necessary). The creditor should also be aware that the compromise could (assuming that bankruptcy does follow at some stage) be challenged on the ground that it amounts to a preference (s340).

2.2 Sue and obtain judgement

The main advantage of such action is that it indicates to the debtor that the creditor is serious about recovery of the debt and it will put liability and quantum beyond doubt.

Taking court proceedings may however prove to be expensive and even if judgment is obtained recovery will only be possible if the debtor is good for the cash.

2.3 Support a voluntary arrangement

Creditors are concerned primarily about the amount that they are likely to receive from the estate in bankruptcy. Most creditors will support a voluntary arrangement that appears to offer a better return than bankruptcy and looks likely to be successful.

Clearly a creditor will have to be satisfied that the proposal is feasible and that all assets that would be available in bankruptcy will be in the arrangement. It may be possible to exclude such assets but creditors are likely to demand compensation for such exclusion, which is normally provided by way of third party funds.

One reason that creditors may choose not to support an arrangement, which, on paper at least, appears to offer a better return than bankruptcy, would be if there was a lack of trust in the debtor's integrity.

It should always be remembered when advising a creditor that a supervisor of a VA only has the power to investigate transactions defrauding creditors pursuant to s423. A trustee in bankruptcy can however investigate the whole range of antecedent transactions.

Voluntary arrangements are looked at in more detail in Chapter 4.

2.4 Serve a statutory demand and petition for bankruptcy

This option is often referred to as the 'nuclear deterrent' of debt collection. If it results in full payment prior to the petition being issued it will have achieved its objective quickly and cheaply.

Once a petition is issued however it is likely that other creditors may support the petition making bankruptcy much more likely. It should be remembered that there are disadvantages in bankruptcy for the creditor as well as the debtor, not least the likelihood of a low or zero dividend.

Bankruptcy is looked at in more detail in Chapter 7.

Summary and Self-test

Summary

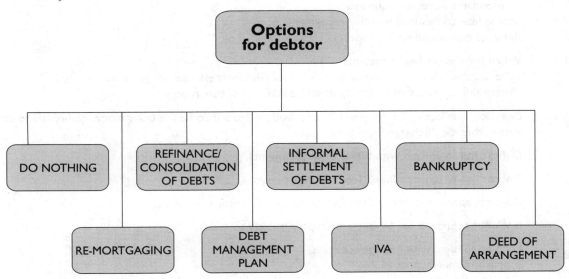

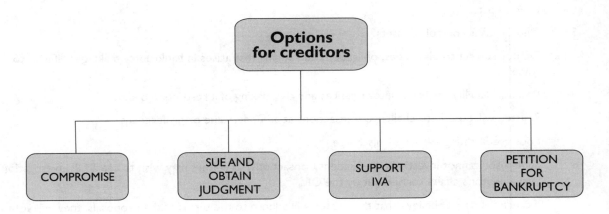

Self-test

Answer the following questions.

1. What are the advantages of re-mortgaging as an option for a debtor?
2. When would re-financing be appropriate as an option for a debtor?
3. What are the main disadvantages for a debtor of pursuing an IVA as an option?
4. What are the advantages of a Deed of Arrangement?
5. What are the main disadvantages of bankruptcy for a debtor?
6. Why would creditors sometimes choose bankruptcy of an individual over an IVA?

Now, go back to the Learning Objectives in the Introduction. If you are satisfied that you have achieved these, please tick them off.

Answers to Self-test

1. Mortgages have lower rates of interest than other debts.
   Repayments are made over a longer term.
   Consolidates debts into one loan.
   Should lead to reduced monthly repayments.
   Releases equity tied up in property.

2. When the debtor has an income.
   Where debtor has a large number of debts ie. High interest rate credit cards.
   Where debtor seeks to avoid stigma and disabilities of bankruptcy.

3. Duration may last up to five years if contributions from income are being made, compared to one year automatic discharge from bankruptcy.

   Debtor has to comply with terms of arrangement.

   Debtor has to pay nominee's fees and court costs.

   Requires approval of more than 75% (in value) of debtor's creditors.

   If VA not approved or VA fails, bankruptcy is likely to result.

4. Long established with good precedents.
   Simple and speedy procedure.
   Only requires approval of a simple majority of creditors in number and value.
   Don't have to call meetings of creditors.
   No need to appoint a nominee.
   No report to court.
   Lower costs.

5. Debtor loses control of assets.

   Debtor subject to disabilities, obligations and stigma that arises in bankruptcy making it difficult to trade.

   Potential liability for bankruptcy offences and the making of a restriction order.

   Trustee will be able to challenge transactions at an undervalue or preferences.

   Poor credit rating even after discharge.

6. Supervisor cannot investigate antecedent transactions. Creditors may wish to see a full investigation into a debtor's affairs carried out by the OR.

   If creditors do not believe that the debtor will adhere to the terms of the proposals, they will vote against it.

   If VA doesn't offer a substantially better return than bankruptcy creditors will be unlikely to accept it.

Answer to Interactive Question

Answer to Interactive question: Barry Marsden

(a) **Deed of Arrangement**

    (i) There is no court involvement.
    (ii) Long established mechanism, simple and speedy procedure.
    (iii) No meeting of creditors required.
    (iv) Costs likely to be lower than IVA.
    (v) Requires only majority in number and value of creditors to agree.

However, it does have some disadvantages:

    (i) No provision for a moratorium pending execution, no protection from creditors.
    (ii) Even after registration of the deed, dissenting creditors are not bound by it and may present bankruptcy petition against Barry.

(b) **Voluntary arrangement**

    (i) The main advantage is that Barry could apply for an interim order which would provide protection from creditors.
    (ii) If approved it binds all creditors.
    (iii) Avoids stigma and disabilities of bankruptcy (no investigation into Barry's affairs by supervisor, supervisor has no power to take action under s238 etc).
    (iv) Debtor retains control.

However it does have disadvantages:

    (i) Requisite majority for approval is higher than in the case of a deed of arrangement. A majority in excess of three quarters in value of the creditors present in person or by proxy at the creditors' meeting and voting in respect of the resolution is required.
    (ii) Duration is likely to be long, possibly five years to enable contributions from income to be made.
    (iii) Creditors will wish to be compensated for transfer of assets prior to arrangement.
    (iv) Creditors will only agree if it provides a substantially better outcome than alternatives.
    (v) Failure of the arrangement is likely to result in the bankruptcy of Barry.
    (vi) Barry will have to comply with the terms of the arrangement.
    (vii) Barry will have to pay proposed nominee's fees and court costs.

4

Introduction to voluntary arrangements

▸ ▸ ▸ ▸ ▸ ▸ ▸ ▸ ▸ ▸ ▸ ▸ ▸ ▸ ▸

Contents

Introduction
Examination context
Topic List
 1 Introduction to voluntary arrangements
 2 Initial meeting with the debtor
 3 The proposal
Appendix 1 Suggested letter from proposed nominee to debtor
Appendix 2 Suggested contents of letter from nominee to third party making voluntary contribution
Appendix 3 IVA Protocol
Summary and Self-test
Answers to Self-test
Answer to Interactive Question

Personal Insolvency

Introduction

Learning objectives

- List the statutory requirements re the content of the proposal
- The purpose and conduct of the initial meeting with the debtor
- Roles of nominee and supervisor

Tick off
☐
☐
☐

Working context

You may be asked to assist in putting together a proposal for a voluntary arrangement, it is important therefore to understand the statutory requirements regarding content of the proposal and matters to be considered by a debtor when considering a voluntary arrangement.

Stop and think

Why is an alternative to bankruptcy required? Why is it important that certain matters are dealt with in the proposal? Why isn't a voluntary arrangement suitable for everyone?

INTRODUCTION TO VOLUNTARY ARRANGEMENTS   4

Examination context

Voluntary arrangement proposals have been a popular exam topic, you are likely to be asked to comment on draft proposals given or what information you would require in order to draft proposals for a voluntary arrangement.

Exam requirements

Past questions to look at include:

1997	Question 3 (a) (b)
1996	Question 5 (b)
1995	Question 2
1995	Question 4 (a) (b)
1994	Question 2
1993	Question 5
1991	Paper I, Question 6

1 Introduction to voluntary arrangements

Section overview

The IA 1986 set out a procedure which enables a debtor to make a proposal for a voluntary arrangement (IVA) with his creditors as an alternative to bankruptcy. It should be remembered however that voluntary arrangement and bankruptcy are not mutually exclusive. A bankrupt may seek a voluntary arrangement and a debtor subject to a voluntary arrangement can be made bankrupt. The voluntary arrangement must take the form of a composition in satisfaction of his debts or a scheme of arrangement. The legislation concerning voluntary arrangements is found in s252 – s263 and r5.1 – r5.65. SIP 3 also gives guidance to office holders. The EA 2002 introduced a 'fast track' IVA for undischarged bankrupts.

Definition

Composition: an agreement under which creditors agree to accept a certain sum of money in settlement of the debts due to them.

1.1 Purpose of voluntary arrangement

The voluntary arrangement procedure envisages a debtor, with the assistance of his nominee, putting a proposal to his creditors for the satisfaction of his debts.

If the proposal is accepted by a majority (in excess of 75% in value) of creditors, the proposal will be implemented by the nominee who now becomes the supervisor.

The voluntary arrangement, once approved, will bind all creditors entitled to vote at the creditors' meeting, whether or not they had notice of the meeting, attended, or voted in favour.

1.2 Role of the IP

It is not possible for a debtor to act on his own to implement a voluntary arrangement. He must engage the services of an authorised practitioner to act. The role of the IP will change during the process of obtaining approval for the IVA. The IP has three roles:

- **Advisor**: the IP's role as an advisor is to consider the best course of action for the debtor in the light of his particular circumstances.
- **Nominee**: the IP has a duty to perform an independent, objective review and assessment of the proposal for the purposes of reporting his opinion to the court. The duty of the nominee is owed to the creditors and the court.
- **Supervisor**: his responsibility will be governed by the terms of the arrangement.

The overriding duty of the IP is to ensure a fair balance between the interests of the debtor, the creditors and any other parties involved.

Following the IA 2000, provision has been made so that the nominee and supervisor need not be a licensed insolvency practitioner (s389A). They will require to be authorised to act in such capacity (s389A(1)).

2 Initial meeting with the debtor

Section overview

Purpose of meeting

The purpose of the first meeting with the debtor is essentially to give and obtain information to enable:

- A proposal and statement of affairs to be drafted.
- Approaches to be made to strategic and pressing creditors.
- Information to be given to the debtor to explain:
  - The procedure to obtain a voluntary arrangement
  - His duties pursuant to legislation
  - The role of the nominee/supervisor and his duties.

2.1 Matters to be dealt with at first meeting

1. The IP should explain to the debtor the different roles he will perform during the conduct of the case and the different duties and responsibilities that they entail. He should point out the need for the nominee and supervisor to maintain independence.

   The proposed nominee must ensure that the debtor understands that he is acting as an officer of the court and as such his conduct is expected to be of the highest standard (ex parte James). The proposed nominee should also make it clear that pursuant to s262 (B) if it appears to the nominee or supervisor that the debtor has been guilty of any offence in connection with the arrangement for which he is criminally liable, he must report the matter to the Secretary of State.

2. Establish that a voluntary arrangement is the most appropriate way of dealing with the debtor's affairs.

   He should explain to the debtor the alternative procedures available to obtain a VA and advise of the relevant advantages and disadvantages of an IVA and other procedures available.

   The debtor must be provided with a copy of the booklet 'Is a voluntary arrangement right for me?' and he should be asked to confirm in writing that he has read and understood it.

3. Must ensure that the debtor is in a position to propose an IVA.

   There are various requirements regardless of whether the debtor intends to apply for an interim order. These are:

   - The debtor is either an undischarged bankrupt or able to petition for his own bankruptcy.
   - The practitioner is willing to act as nominee.
   - The debtor intends to propose a VA.

   If the debtor intends to request an interim order, it is also necessary to ensure that the debtor has not applied for interim order in the last 12 months.

   An initial assessment should also be made as to whether a VA is a viable alternative to bankruptcy.

4. Should consider whether the protection of an Interim Order is required or not.

5. The IP should require the debtor to provide details of all known or possible liabilities.

   It will be necessary to ascertain the status of the debtor's creditors and their attitude to any arrangement. This is so that they can be dealt with adequately within the proposal and approached to ascertain whether they will support a VA. The supervisor must give notice to all creditors of whom he is aware. However even if notice is not given any creditor who would have been entitled to vote at the creditors' meeting had he been given notice of that meeting, is bound by a VA once approved whether or not he did have notice of the meeting (s260). This overturns the position that previously applied and makes the VA stronger as such creditors will no longer be able to petition for bankruptcy.

He should also seek to identify creditors who have commenced execution or other legal processes or who have special rights which may require special consideration in the proposal.

6   The IP must take all necessary steps to familiarise himself with the debtor's financial circumstances.

It is of the utmost importance to ascertain how the voluntary arrangement is going to fund both the debtor and the creditors. If income is to be provided, the creditors will have to be satisfied that any offer is reasonable. It is likely that creditors will want to see details of the debtor's expenditure and this should be obtained prior to drafting the proposal.

If assets are to be provided, the creditors will be concerned to ascertain what is available and what is excluded. Details should be obtained, ready for drafting the proposal.

If assets are to be excluded, it is highly likely that creditors will not accept such exclusion unless such assets would have also been excluded in bankruptcy. Consequently, the extent to which compensation can be provided must be investigated at this stage.

Such compensation is frequently made available through funds provided by a third party, often a family member.

If third party funds are available, details and evidence of the funds will have to be provided in the proposal. As much information as possible should be obtained at this stage so that an initial approach can be made. The nominee should also ensure that the third party has the benefit of independent legal advice.

7   The debtor should be asked to provide a statement of affairs detailing the nature and amount of all of the debtor's assets and liabilities. The debtor should be advised that a misstatement in the statement of affairs could amount to a 'material irregularity', being a ground on which an approved voluntary arrangement may be challenged by a creditor.

If the debtor is an undischarged bankrupt and has already submitted a statement of affairs under s272, he need not deliver a further one unless required by the nominee.

8   The IP should take steps to satisfy himself that the value of the assets is appropriately reflected in the statement of affairs.

9   Many debtors proposing a voluntary arrangement are sole traders hoping for a survival of their business. The creditors will need to be convinced that the business is viable going forward. To this end the debtor will need to provide evidence of how the business got into trading difficulties and how it intends to trade out of them. Both the proposed nominee and the creditors will want to examine past trading accounts, a business plan and future projections. This documentation should therefore be obtained as soon as possible.

Ultimately the debtor will have to convince both the proposed nominee and the creditors that the business can generate sufficient income to support both the debtor and the VA creditors.

10   The IP should enquire as to:

- Possible transactions at an undervalue.
- Payments which may be preferences.
- Liabilities which may be extortionate credit transactions.

These must be disclosed in the proposal.

11   The debtor must be made aware of his duties pursuant to s262A. The Act, as amended by IA 2000 replaces the criminal offence previously contained in r5.30 and states that the debtor commits an offence if he makes any false representation or commits any other fraud for the purpose of obtaining the approval of his creditors to a proposal for an arrangement (s262A).

Any agreement between a debtor and a creditor, which is not disclosed in the arrangement and seeks to pay sums to the creditor in addition to those payable under the arrangement, is fraudulent and unenforceable by the creditor. This must be bought to the debtor's attention as a matter of course.

INTRODUCTION TO VOLUNTARY ARRANGEMENTS

It is not the duty of the IP preparing the VA proposal to challenge what the debtor and/or his agents assert to be fact *Hurst v BDO Stoy Hayward*. (Subject to rule arising from *Greystoke v Hamilton-Smith* below.)

The proposed nominee must also impress upon the debtor the importance of ensuring that the information provided is correct in all material facts and that such an obligation continues up to the date of the creditors' meeting and the meeting itself (*Cadbury Schweppes plc v Somji*).

R5.26 also requires the debtor on approval of the VA to do all that is required for putting the supervisor in possession of assets included in the arrangement.

12 The IP must consider:

- The credibility of the debtor.
- History of previous failures.
- The need for asset protection.

There is an overriding duty to ensure a fair balance between the interests of debtor, creditors and third parties.

13 The Insolvency Service ('Dear IP' Millenium Edition letter) has said that the IP must exercise professional judgment in respect of the proposed IVA, ensuring:

- It is feasible.
- Fair to debtors and creditors.
- Fit to be put to creditors, and
- Provides an acceptable alternative to bankruptcy.

In addition, case law now provides (*Greystoke v Hamilton-Smith*) that where the fullness and candour of debtor's information and property come into question the IP should check:

- That the true position re the debtor's assets and liabilities does not differ substantially from what has been represented to the creditors.
- The proposal in broad terms has a real prospect of implementation.
- That there is no unavoidable and manifest unfairness in the proposal.

14 *Cadbury Schweppes v Somji*

The practitioner should ask the debtor if he is aware of any negotiations or offers which have been made to any of his creditors. This is important because such information may materially affect the other creditors' attitude to the proposal. In *Cadburys Schweppes v Somji*, for instance, an associate of the debtor offered to buy some of the creditors' debts at a valuation far exceeding their likely IVA dividend value. If offers like this have been made:

- The proposal should say so.
- The practitioner should draw the creditors' attention to them.

Failure to make full disclosure of such offers/negotiations could constitute:

- Grounds for a default petition (s264(1)(c)) ...on the basis that there has been a material omission.
- Grounds for appeal probably on the basis of material irregularity (s262).

15 The IP should form an opinion of the appropriate method of dealing with the debtor's affairs, taking into account:

- The debtor's attitude.
- The likelihood of the debtor adhering to the terms of the proposal.
- The extent of control over the assets exercised by the debtor as opposed to the supervisor of the proposal.
- The removal/absence of the restrictions otherwise imposed by formal bankruptcy.

16 The IP should ensure that the proposal addresses all of the matters prescribed by the Rules.

17 The debtor should be made aware that it is an offence to make any false representations or commit any other fraud for the purpose of obtaining the approval of the creditors to the proposed arrangement.

18 Emphasise that the proposal is the debtor's proposal and that it is essential that full and accurate disclosure of all relevant matters be made.

If full disclosure is not made, the following potential consequences should be borne in mind:

- Creditors may find out the true position, demand adjournments, further and better particulars, modifications or simply reject the proposals altogether.
- A petition for bankruptcy may be presented by any creditor owed more than £750.
- The nominee may present a bankruptcy petition.
- If full disclosure of all liabilities is not made, the nominee will not be able to notify all creditors. Non-notified creditors will be bound but may later challenge the VA under s262.
- Indicting agreement to an IVA through fraud is a criminal offence.

Continuing obligations under the proposal must be complied with or again this will be grounds for the presentation of a default petition by the creditors/nominee.

Valuations in the proposal are the debtors, it is essential that these should be as accurate as possible (in the absence of professional valuations).

19 Outline the procedure to be followed (See Chapter 5 for more details):

Application to court for interim order may be made. Give a:

- Brief explanation of the effect of such an order.
- Fact that solicitors have been instructed to apply (if any).
- Requirement for debtor to attend at hearing (if any).

Creditors' meeting will be held at which nominee will preside and debtor will be required to attend and answer questions.

20 Issue an engagement letter to the debtor setting out the matters discussed and agreed upon.

Details of the staff who will be dealing with the matter should be provided so that the debtor can contact them if there are any problems.

Request that the debtor sign a copy of the engagement letter and return it to confirm that he has read and understood the content.

(See Appendix 1 for the suggested contents of an engagement letter).

3 The proposal

Section overview

The proposal is a contractual arrangement between the parties who are free to make whatever provision they see fit within the general law and the statutory framework set out within the Act and the Rules. The terms of the arrangement are contained in the proposal which is approved by the creditors. A comprehensive and accurately drafted proposal is therefore fundamental to the arrangement. The detailed content of the proposal is set out in r5.3 and SIP 3. R3 have now produced standard terms and conditions for inclusion in the proposal which it hopes the profession will adopt. Reference to these terms in the exam should gain some credit.

3.1 Contents of the proposal

What follows is a checklist of things that need to be borne in mind when answering questions on the exam paper in relation to the proposal. The checklist is an amalgamation of the requirements of r5.3, SIP 3 and the R3 standard terms and conditions. It should be remembered that pursuant to r5.3(3), provided the nominee has given his agreement in writing the proposal can be amended at any time up to the delivery of the nominee's report to court under s256(1)/256A.

1. A short explanation of desirability of VA and reasons why the creditors may be expected to concur with it should be included. This should include:

    - Some background and explanation of the present insolvency.

    - Extracts from trading accounts from previous years. This is so that:
        - If it is proposed that the debtor is to continue in business (and that the revenue from that business is to assist in paying creditors) some assessment can be made of how realistic this part of the proposal is.
        - The debtor can demonstrate the deteriorating situation which culminated in insolvency.

2. The Statement of Affairs, which should include full details of assets and liabilities (including both business and personal assets and liabilities).

    Assets

    - Should include all assets including assets outside jurisdiction.
    - Should include prospective or contingent assets with statement of likelihood of realisation.
    - Ideally professional valuation of assets (but remember time and cost constraints).
    - Value of dwelling house (realistic selling NOT asking price) and estimate of debtor's equity.
    - Motor vehicles should be valued using the industry guide to prices for second hand vehicles.
    - Nominee should ensure that values given are prudent especially in relation to book debts, work in progress and leases where valuation can be particularly problematic.
    - Costs of realisation should be shown.

    Assuming that there are assets to be sold the supervisor will have to come to a decision about how, when and for what price the assets will be sold. He will also need to consider the terms of the sale. If a sale is to be left to the debtor the supervisor will need to be mindful of his role in supervising that sale. If assets are jointly held then the co-operation of the co-owner will be vital and the creditors will want confirmation of the same. Clearly it will be of concern to creditors if an item of property does not achieve the value estimated in the proposal. To avoid problems arising the proposal itself should state what the consequences of such a failure would be.

    Note. Proposal may also contain disclaimer that failure to achieve stated values will not give rise to default (debtor) or liability (nominee).

    Debtors

    Proposal may deal with:

    - Whether any have been challenged by the debtor himself.
    - If any particular debt is unlikely to be paid, whether the cost of litigation would be justified in pursuing the claim.
    - Authority for supervisor to correspond with debtors seeking payment of sums due.
    - Supervisor to have full powers to compromise claims, employ solicitors etc.

3. Extent to which assets are charged. Look for details of mortgages, charges, HP, liens and reservation of title clauses in favour of creditors.

4   Any assets to be excluded from the VA.

The proposal may suggest the same exclusions as for bankruptcy (ie tools of trade and domestic equipment). Creditors are unlikely to object to such exclusions.

If it also excludes the main residence, the proposal should explain in what way creditors will be compensated, ie:

- Contribution by third party.
- Buy-out of debtor's share by spouse.

If the proposal excludes assets used in business, there should be provision for realisation in the event of ceasing to trade.

If an asset is to be excluded because realisation will be too expensive/difficult/impossible, proposal should say so.

5   Particulars of any assets (other than debtors) which are to be included, sources of such property and terms on which made available.

Eg cash contributions from spouse, family trust, parent, business partner or other wealthy philanthropist.

- Desirable for letter of confirmation from third party contributor to be annexed to proposal and for funds to be held by the supervisor in an account pending approval of the arrangement.
- Proposal may state that failure by a third party to contribute will constitute a default by the debtor.
- Nominee will wish to be satisfied that the third party has had opportunity to take independent advice.

See Appendix 2 re suggested contents of a letter to a third party

6   Nature and amount of debtor's liabilities, manner in which they are to be met/postponed/otherwise dealt with.

Reasonable enquiries should be made. Ideally, nominee should contact each creditor with a view to obtaining an up to date statement of liability. However:

- This is slow and increases costs.
- May precipitate enforcement action by creditors.

Where a liability (eg mortgage arrears) is increasing, proposal should state the rate of increase.

A liability (eg on a credit card which the debtor finds convenient for use in his business) can be excluded from the IVA but the proposal must say so and the IP should draw attention to the exclusion in his comments. (A credit card company is likely to withdraw the card and demand immediate repayment in full unless a deal can be arranged).

7   Treatment of preferential and secured creditors and associates.

Rights of preferential creditors may not be modified or excluded without their consent.

In bankruptcy sums owed to a spouse or civil partner are generally postponed to all other debts. It is likely that the creditors will want to see a similar provision in relation to a spouse or civil partner in VA. The nominee should, of course, be careful to ensure that the spouse or civil partner obtains independent legal advice. Other associates may also be wiling to postpone their debts and should be approached to ascertain their position.

If a secured creditor has agreed to postpone enforcing his security this should be explained in the proposal. A secured creditor's right to enforce its security cannot be postponed without its consent.

INTRODUCTION TO VOLUNTARY ARRANGEMENTS

8   The proposal should deal with the position regarding VAT during the period between the date of the interim order and the date of approval of the proposal (sometimes called the 'hiatus period'). This is because HM Revenue and Customs now take the view that if the proposal does not deal with the hiatus period:

- Such VAT does not fall within the arrangement and HM Revenue and Customs are therefore entitled to take the normal enforcement measures to collect it.
- Whereas if the proposal does cover the hiatus period VAT, HM Revenue and Customs are bound by the proposal (assuming the creditors approve it) and therefore will not be able to take enforcement action.

9   Claims or potential claims under s339, s340 and s343.

Claims or potential claims under s339, s340 and s343 will need to be detailed.

Remember that the supervisor has no power to challenge such transactions in an IVA. He only has the power to challenge transactions defrauding creditors.

Consequently where grounds for challenge are available, creditors may prefer bankruptcy.

Alternatively the recipient of a transaction at undervalue (commonly the spouse) or preference, may offer to compromise the claim.

10 Proposed duration.

Re A Debtor (No. 222 of 1990) – a certain period of time should be stated.

May be short (eg two years) where proposal is for rapid sale of assets and distribution to creditors. Even here, it may be longer before final dividend can be paid if:

- There is litigation.
- Depressed market conditions make immediate realisation of assets very difficult.

Where the proposal is based on payments to creditors out of income or from business revenues, creditors may demand a lengthy duration as price of assent. (Typically five years).

Provision may be made for extension of proposed duration in certain circumstances.

11 Proposed dates of distributions to creditors with estimates of their amounts.

- Interim and final?
- Final only?

12 Amount proposed to be paid to the nominee by way of remuneration and expenses.

Expenses should be quantified and described.

Remuneration of nominee does not include future remuneration once he becomes supervisor.

Proposal should state whether nominee's remuneration includes or excludes sums to be paid to the debtor's solicitor for legal work.

13 Manner in which it is proposed that the supervisor should be remunerated and his expenses defrayed.

As a minimum, proposal should provide for:

- Means of calculating and agreeing supervisor's remuneration (eg by resolution of creditors or a creditors' committee).
- Payment of solicitors, estate agents and other expenses.
- Payment of remuneration and expenses in priority to all other claims.

14 Whether:

- Any third parties are to provide guarantees.
- Unusual, third party should be advised to take independent advice.

15 The manner in which funds held for the purposes of IVA are to be banked/invested/dealt with pending distribution.

- All funds realised should be paid to the supervisor (not the debtor).
- Supervisor should be empowered to open bank accounts and invest (usually short term).

16 The manner in which funds held for the purpose of payment to creditors and not so paid on the termination of the arrangement are to be dealt with. For example, if a creditor disappears prior to receiving the final dividend (proposal could provide for this sum to be re-distributed amongst other creditors)

17 Manner in which the debtor's business is to be conducted.

Generally the debtor will continue to run the business, it would be unusual for the supervisor to do so.

A proposal that the business will generate funds for creditors is superficially attractive but:

- Failure of the business is often the reason why debtor is insolvent in the first place.
- The business will need to service ongoing liabilities and debtor's ongoing expenses before any surplus can go to creditors under IVA.

Some measure of supervision by the supervisor should be included, eg an obligation on debtor to provide the supervisor with information and to maintain proper accounts, records and banking arrangements.

Past trading accounts, realistic forecasts, cash flow statements and projections should be attached.

Problems in maintaining suppliers, staff etc. should be explained.

If any accounts or returns are outstanding (eg in relation to VAT) confirmation of when these will be completed.

18 Details of any further credit facilities which it is intended to arrange for the debtor and how the debts arising are to be paid – creditors will be reluctant but facilities may be necessary eg. to complete work-in-progress.

19 Functions of supervisor, details of supervisor and fact he is IP.

The Proposal should:

- Give the supervisor a general power to call meetings of creditors.
- Set out the supervisor's powers – incorporation of the powers of a trustee in bankruptcy would be appropriate (modified as appropriate).
- Set out rules re proofs, set-off, distribution in specie (perhaps by incorporating bankruptcy rules).
- Incorporate provisions re: Income Payments, eg £X per month to be paid into the VA by direct debit.
- Obligation on debtor to inform Supervisor of any change in personal circumstances and any change in income.
- Incorporate bankruptcy provisions re: windfalls.
- State how it is proposed to deal with the claims of any person who is bound by the arrangement by virtue of s260(2A) – non-notified creditor.

20 Bankruptcy

Although not mentioned specifically in r5.3, the proposal should make provision re: possibility of the debtor being subsequently made bankrupt.

- Why is this necessary?

    The law dealing with the effect of bankruptcy on IVAs is still developing and subject to some uncertainty. To avoid potential problems, express provision should be made. Bankruptcy may prejudice a creditor's preferential status. In bankruptcy the relevant date for preferential creditors is the date of the order. Any preferential creditors in an IVA (where the relevant date is the interim order or the s257 meeting, if no order,) are likely to lose their preferential status in bankruptcy.

▸ Provision of express trust

The debtor should declare a trust, where the debtor holds his 'assets' on trust for the purposes of the IVA for the creditors. Assets will include all rights attaching to the assets and all derivative property. Assets held on trust are excluded property for the purposes of bankruptcy and will therefore remain vested in the debtor.

It is usual for a well-drafted proposal to create an express trust of arrangement assets. However the supervisor will hold any funds that have been passed to him by or on behalf of the debtor for distribution under the arrangement on trust for the creditors whether or not an express trust has been created. If legal title is to be transferred to the supervisor steps to achieve the transfer should be taken immediately.

The effect of bankruptcy on the arrangement is dealt with fully in Chapter 6.

21 Default

The proposal should set out:

▸ What will constitute a 'default' by the debtor justifying the presentation of a bankruptcy petition by the supervisor.

▸ Some mechanism for ascertaining the wishes of the creditors. This may involve holding a meeting or circularising the creditors.

▸ Supervisor to retain sufficient funds to present a petition.

The proposal should also set out whether there are any circumstances falling short of 'default', which might result in 'failure' of the IVA. This might be a failure to realise a major asset for the stated value or the failure of a third party to make a promised contribution. The effect of failure should be stated. The IVA may be terminated, but no s276 petition may be presented although it is likely that debtor could be bankrupted on grounds that unable to pay debts.

22 Leases

Although not specifically mentioned in r5.3, leases are an asset which will require specific provision in the proposal. The provision made will depend on what is being proposed in relation to the lease. Broadly, there are three possibilities:

▸ The lease has premium value and the debtor proposes it should be sold, the proceeds being made available for dividend purposes.

▸ The lease has no or insignificant premium value and the debtor proposes that the lease should not be retained.

▸ The debtor proposes retaining the lease for the purposes of his or her business.

(i) Debtor proposes selling the lease

Proposal should state the premium value of the lease. Any professional valuation can be appended to the proposal.

Nominee should have obtained a copy of the lease to ascertain whether licence to assign is required (it will be).

If licence to assign is required the nominee will need to negotiate with the landlord.

It is particularly important to obtain the landlord's consent to the terms of the proposal if there are rent arrears. This is because rent arrears give rise to the following problems:

– Generally landlords must not unreasonably refuse the license to assign, but a landlord is acting reasonably if he refuses licence to assign until arrears are paid.

- Non-payment of rent will entitle a landlord to distrain against the goods of the debtor. Although following the interim order (if obtained) the leave of the court will be needed. Distraint reduces the value of assets in the estate.

- The landlord will be entitled to forfeit under the terms of the lease – again, this is subject to the court's consent following the interim order.

Ultimately, it may be necessary to agree to pay the arrears to obtain the landlord's consent to the proposal. Although application for relief from forfeiture can be made, the court will require the payment of arrears in any event, as a condition of granting relief. In this situation, it would be better to pay the arrears at the outset and avoid the costs and risks of litigation.

(ii) **Debtor proposes retaining the leased premises for use in the business**

As above, if there are arrears of rent, the potential problems of distress and forfeiture will arise. Again, the nominee will need to reach some agreement with the landlord or there is a risk that without equipment and premises, a proposal to trade on will simply not be viable.

In addition, the proposal will need to provide for the payment of future rent during the use of the premises, as an expense of trading to prevent new arrears arising. No leave would be required for a landlord to exercise his self-help remedies of forfeiture and distraint for post interim order arrears.

Payment of 'strategic creditors' such as landlords is not unfairly prejudicial to other creditors of the same class (*Cazaly Irving Holdings v Cancol*). This is important as it means there is no ground for an appeal against the decision of the creditors meeting under s262.

(iii) **Debtor does not wish to retain use of leased premises**

Nominee will need to ascertain whether the landlord will accept a surrender.

The landlord has potentially two valid claims in the IVA.

- Liquidated, unsecured claim for arrears of rent.

- An unliquidated claim for future rent (and possibly dilapidations). The proposal should deal with how this will be quantified. For voting purposes, the nominee will estimate the value of the claim (see Chapter 5). For dividend purposes the proposal should state that the supervisor shall estimate the value of the claim (the landlord having a duty to mitigate) applying the discount for early receipt as a trustee in bankruptcy would.

23 **Post acceptance amendments**

Thompson and Horrocks v John Lawson Broome 1998 held that a properly drawn clause giving a power of variation in a voluntary arrangement was valid. However, careful drafting of such a clause will be necessary.

In the absence of an express provision allowing variation of the proposal, approval of 100% of creditors affected by the proposed variation will be required for any change to be valid.

24 The nature of the arrangement ie. Whether it is a composition in full and final settlement of the debts or a scheme of arrangement.

25 A realistic comparison of the estimated outcome of the arrangement and bankruptcy including comparative costs.

26 Proposals regarding after acquired assets and windfall gains.

27 Whether a committee of creditors is to be appointed and if so, what will be its powers, duties and responsibilities.

28 Requisite majorities required to pass resolutions at the meeting of creditors.

29   Debtor's warrants, duty and obligations.

SIP 3 suggests additional matters to be considered:

- What will happen to surplus funds arising, for instance if the business trades more beneficially than originally envisaged?
- Confirmation of when the terms of the IVA have been successfully completed and confirmation that creditors will no longer be entitled to pursue the debtor for any balance of their claim.
- The position regarding unclaimed dividends or unpresented cheques.
- How to deal with creditors who have not made claims.
- In the event of the arrangement not being successful and the individual being declared bankrupt, clarification of the amounts for which creditors will be entitled to claim.
- The proposal must deal with maintenance orders in favour of the debtor's wife, and any fines. The case of Re M (a debtor) 1996 held that a wife who had received a lump sum under matrimonial proceedings was bound to accept a dividend under an IVA.
- Provision for the supervisor to be granted a charge over assets, or some other suitable form of security.
- The situation with regard to contingent creditors and overseas creditors.
- The situation with regard to tax liabilities arising on disposal of the debtor's assets.
- Inadvertently omitted creditors (who are now bound by the VA).

The following information should also be provided, either in the proposal or in the nominee's comments:

- The source of any referrals to the nominee or his firm in relation to the proposed voluntary arrangement.
- Any payments made, or proposed to be made, to the source of such referrals.
- Any payments made, or proposed to be made, to the nominee or his firm by the debtor whether in connection with the proposed arrangement or otherwise.
- An estimate of the total fee to be paid to the supervisor together with a statement of the assumptions made in producing the estimate.

IVA Protocol

Insolvency practitioners, bankers, the insolvency service and other interested parties have produced an IVA protocol for use in straight forward consumer debt cases. Whilst the protocol is not mandatory it has the backing and support of the creditor groups particularly those members of the British Bankers Association. These parties have agreed to be bound by the terms of the protocol. The protocol provides for agreed methods of dealing with aspects of an IVA which would be detailed in any relevant IVA proposal. The protocol has been produced at Appendix 3 to this chapter.

Cadbury Schweppes v Somji 1999

Associates of a debtor (with debts of £6 million) proposing an IVA approached some of the creditors and offered to buy their debts for less than their true value but for more than those creditors would have received under the terms of the proposed IVA. The IVA was approved and IVA creditors subsequently found out that some creditors had a better deal outside the IVA than if they had been a party to it. They appealed successfully on the grounds of material irregularity and unfair prejudice. The debtor should have disclosed the debt purchases in the proposal.

Personal Insolvency

Interactive question: Sarah Chapple

A client in Swindon seeks your advice with regards to documents he has received concerning a proposal by Sarah Chapple, who trades in the same area, to her creditors for a composition in satisfaction of her debts. Sarah Chapple has given written notice to the nominee accompanied by a copy of the proposal and the nominee has summoned a meeting of creditors for 16.30 hours on 5 September at his offices in Manchester. The notice is accompanied by a summary of the statement of affairs, a list of creditors showing amounts due and the nominee's comments, as filed in court, which state:

'I have interrogated the debtor and I am satisfied that she has submitted a satisfactory proposal. I recommend a meeting of creditors to approve the proposal'.

A summary of the proposal reads as follows:

My assets comprise stock of £45,000, work in progress of £2,500 and very good book debts of £2,500. Cash at bank is £2,000 and the house in which I reside is worth £180,000. A building society is owed £160,000 being the balance of money advanced for the purchase of the house and a bank is owed £20,000 on money advanced for my business. The business was clothing manufacture which in November 2003 I closed down as it was not successful and diversified into home furnishings which I believe to be successful. I propose to continue to trade in home furnishings and pay profits to the supervisor to be distributed over the next three years. All sums distributed in that time will be accepted by creditors in full and final settlement of their claims. My other creditors include £12,900 owed for PAYE/NIC, £6,890 for VAT and 25 other creditors are owed £94,000. I shall retain assets. I point out that the house in which I reside is owned by my husband and he will retain the liabilities to the building society and the bank.

Your client is owed £40,000 of which £38,000 arises from a loan made five years ago as a deposit on a house in Swindon, not mentioned on the list of assets and £2,000 shown in the creditors' list which is for supplies of materials made during 2005. Your client plans to attend the creditors' meeting and asks whether he should approve or reject the proposals, and whether he should bring up any matters.

Requirement

Draft a letter to your client commenting on the proposal and upon any other matter arising from your perusal of the documents and the information given.

See **Answer** at the end of this chapter.

Appendix 1

Suggested letter from proposed nominee to debtor

Note. The following assumes that instructions have been taken for drafting a proposal but that the proposal has not yet been drafted and approved by the debtor.

Introductory

Confirm practitioner willing to act in assisting in preparation of proposal and willing to act as nominee in due course.

Reiteration of reasons why VA appropriate.

Debtor will be sent draft proposal and

- Should read it carefully to ensure accurate and complete
- Getting in touch if any questions, amendments, deletions, corrections etc.

Debtor will be required to serve notice of proposal on nominee (if not already done).

Importance of full and accurate disclosure in the proposal

Emphasise that the proposal is the debtor's proposal and that it is essential that full and accurate disclosure of all relevant matters be made.

INTRODUCTION TO VOLUNTARY ARRANGEMENTS

If full disclosure not made, the following potential consequences should be born in mind:

- Creditors may find out the true position, demand adjournments, further and better particulars, modifications or simply reject the proposals altogether.
- A petition for bankruptcy may be presented by any creditor or creditors owed £750+.
- The nominee may present a bankruptcy petition.
- If full disclosure of all liabilities not made, the nominee will not be able to notify all creditors. Non-notified creditors will be bound but may later challenge a VA under s262.
- Inducing agreement to an IVA through fraud is a criminal offence.

Continuing obligations in the proposal must be complied with or again this will be ground for presentation of a default petition by creditors/nominee.

Valuations in the proposal are the debtors. Essential these should be as accurate as possible (in the absence of professional valuations).

Assets in the arrangement held on trust.

Brief explanation of further steps in the IVA procedure

Application to court for Interim Order will be made (if appropriate), and

- Brief explanation of effect of order.
- Fact that solicitors have been instructed to apply (if any).
- Requirement for debtor to attend at hearing (if any).

Requirement for nominee to file report – his duties.

Creditors' meeting will be held at which nominee will preside and debtor will be required to attend and answer questions.

Percentage required to approve.

Effect of approval of VA.

Practical matters

Members of practitioner's staff who will be dealing with the matter. Debtor to contact if any problems.

Cost of preparing proposal and nominee's report. Confirmation that debtor has paid £x on account.

Request that debtor sign copy letter and return to confirm has read and understood contents. In particular that he has been advised of the consequences of committing an offence under s262A (as amended).

Appendix 2

Suggested contents of letter from nominee to third party making voluntary contribution

Confirmation that practitioner is acting in relation to debtor's proposed IVA and enclose copy proposal.

Recitation that practitioner understands third party is willing to contribute £X in event that proposal approved.

State that the third party is under no legal obligation to make the payment. However failure to provide funds may result in debtor's bankruptcy.

Confirm (if this is the case) that the funds are being held in an interest bearing account pending approval of the proposal. If approved, the funds are made available for VA purposes, if not approved they are to be repaid to the third party. The funds should be held on trust in a separate account and any balance should be repayable to the third party in the event of bankruptcy terminating the IVA.

Insist third party to seek independent legal advice and provide proof of the same.

Personal Insolvency

Appendix 3

IVA PROTOCOL

Straightforward consumer individual voluntary arrangement

Purpose of the protocol

1.1 The purpose of the protocol is to facilitate the efficient handling of straightforward consumer individual voluntary arrangements (IVAs) (as described below). The protocol recognises that the IVA supports a valid public policy objective by providing debt relief for individuals in financial distress. It also recognises that at the centre of this process there is a person, who needs to understand the process and the associated paperwork and the impact that the IVA will have on their lives.

Scope of the protocol

2.1 The protocol is a voluntary agreement, which provides an agreed standard framework for dealing with straightforward consumer IVAs and applies to both IVA providers and creditors. By accepting the content of the protocol, IVA providers and creditors agree to follow the processes and agreed documentation that forms part of the protocol. IVA providers indicate their acceptance of the content of the protocol by drawing up a proposal based on the standard documentation and which states that it follows the protocol. Creditors are expected to abide by the terms of the protocol in relation to proposals drawn up on that basis.

2.2 Creditors who are members of the British Bankers' Association have indicated their support for the protocol process in a letter attached at annex 1. A list of BBA members can be found at www.bba.org.uk

2.3 It is accepted that an IVA is a regulated process under statute, which requires certain work to be undertaken, which may have a cost unconnected with the size of the IVA.

2.4 The protocol does not override the regulatory framework relevant to each party (Annex 2).

2.5 For the avoidance of doubt, IVA provider means both insolvency practitioners and IVA provider firms employing insolvency practitioners. References to creditor in this protocol refer to both creditors and the agents who vote on their behalf and act in accordance with their instructions in relation to an IVA.

2.6 The efficient operation of the protocol will be monitored and reviewed by a standing committee. The standing committee is a representative group, its membership reflecting the participants in the IVA process (debtor, creditor, IP, regulatory bodies and government). The terms of reference of the standing committee and details of its current membership are attached at (Annex 3). The committee's role will include communication and consultation, where necessary, on future developments on the IVA protocol.

The straightforward consumer IVA

3.1 Not all cases can be classified as a straightforward consumer IVA. A person suitable for a straightforward consumer IVA is likely to be :

- In receipt of a regular income either from employment or from a regular pension.
- Have three or more lines of credit from two or more creditors.

3.2 Age is not a consideration, nor is the debt level, though both factors will impact on the overall viability of the IVA.

3.3 The protocol is suitable for both home owners and non home owners. There should be no circumstances where the individual would be forced to sell their property instead of releasing equity. The only exceptions would be where this was proactively proposed by the individual.

3.4 For individuals whose circumstances do not meet the above criteria an IVA may still be the most appropriate means of dealing with their financial problems but their case is unlikely to be suitable for the full application of the protocol procedures. The following are indicators that a person's circumstances are unsuitable for the application of the protocol. If any of these factors are present in an IVA proposal under this protocol they should be specifically highlighted in the proposal and the accompanying summary sheet:

- Uneven/unpredictable income - people with more than 20% of their income coming from bonuses or commission or who are unemployed.
- Benefit income - a debtor with more than 20-25% of their income coming from benefits. For the avoidance of doubt, tax credit is not a benefit.
- Disputed debts - there should be no known material disputes in relation to the debt.
- Investment properties - those with investment properties would not be suitable for a straightforward consumer IVA.
- Possibility of full and final settlement - where a full and final settlement is possible in year 0 (of over 65% of the total debt).
- Low surplus income - if the consumer has a very small surplus income (i.e. five years of dividend payments amount to less than 20% of the outstanding debt) and there is significant equity in their home.

3.5 There is nothing to prevent this protocol being applied to individuals who are self-employed, when that self-employment produces regular income. This should be highlighted in the proposal and the accompanying summary sheet.

3.6 The protocol does not require that the debtor has to follow the protocol process, even though his or her situation may fit within the definition of a straightforward consumer IVA. Where this occurs, but elements of the protocol are still used, this should be highlighted in the proposal and the accompanying summary sheet.

Transparency and co-operation

Transparency

4.1 All parties should act openly and disclose all relevant matters.

4.2 The proposal should disclose any previous attempts to deal with the individual's financial problems (e.g. informal payment plans, re-financing, debt management plan, previous IVA or bankruptcy) together with an explanation of why these attempts were unsuccessful. Where the IVA provider or a company or individual connected with the IVA provider was involved in these attempts this should also be disclosed. If the IVA provider or a company or individual connected with the IVA provider is providing any additional services to the individual, for example mortgage brokerage, this should also be disclosed, as should any commission earned.

4.3 All parties to this protocol must publish their processes for dealing with complaints and details of relevant regulatory authorities, in accordance with current requirements. Any complaints should be dealt with in accordance with existing processes.

Cooperation with the standing committee

4.4 Only when provided with all relevant information will the standing committee be able to monitor and review the efficient operation or otherwise of the protocol. Information required for this purpose will be determined by the standing committee. Such information, other than that which is commercially sensitive or which needs to be withheld for reasons of confidentiality, will be provided by IVA providers and creditors at the request of the standing committee.

4.5 All parties may provide information to the standing committee which will enable it to determine the effectiveness or otherwise of the protocol. Similarly, behaviour which does not comply with the terms of the protocol may be reported to the standing committee. However, the standing committee does not override existing regulatory procedures.

Obligations on insolvency practitioners

Advertising

5.1 Advertisements and other forms of marketing should be clearly distinguishable as such and have regard to the OFT Debt Management Guidance and all relevant codes of practice, in particular to the principles of legality, decency, honesty and truthfulness. Any telemarketing should comply with the codes relevant to that activity.

5.2 The IVA provider should not promote or seek to promote their services, in such a way (e.g. by 'cold calling') or to such an extent as to amount to harassment or in a way that causes fear or distress.

5.3 Where an IVA provider advertises for work via a third party, the IVA provider is responsible for ensuring that the third party observes all applicable advertising codes and OFT guidance. Similarly, where an IVA provider accepts from or makes referrals to others, they should also comply with the advertising codes. Third party advertisements should declare any links to IVA providers.

Advice

6.1 When approached by an individual in financial difficulty, the IVA provider will ensure the individual receives appropriate advice in the light of their particular circumstances, leading to a proposed course of action to resolve their debt problem. Full information on the advantages and disadvantages of all available debt resolution processes should be provided. Non-financial considerations should be taken into account.

6.2 It is accepted that for some, bankruptcy is not a preferred option as it could lead to loss of employment or membership of a professional body, which then has other financial consequences. Others may wish to avoid the perceived stigma of bankruptcy.

Verification of information contained in the proposal

Assets

7.1 As required in any IVA, steps should be taken to ensure that the value of all realisable assets is appropriately reflected in the statement of affairs. This may require independent evidence of valuation to be obtained in the case of material assets.

Liabilities

7.2 Full details should be obtained from the debtor of all known and potential creditors. These should be verified by obtaining statements, letters or copies of agreements from each creditor dated within six weeks of the debtor's first approach to the IVA provider and updated as necessary to reflect any changes prior to the issue of the IVA proposal.

Income

7.3 Income should be verified by means of three months of pay slips, or a suitable equivalent for the self-employed, and bank statements (in the case of weekly pay slips, it is sufficient to check a selection to cover the three month period). In the absence of pay slips (e.g. if they have been lost), then bank statements should be checked.

7.4 If the debtor lives with any person aged 18 or over and there is reasonable expectation that this person will pay board and lodging to the debtor, this payment must be added to the debtor's income in full.

Expenditure

7.5 The expenditure statement should be forward-looking and in line with Consumer Credit Counselling Service (CCCS) guidelines or the Common Financial Statement (CFS). Generally, there should be no deviation from the expenditure guidelines. However, where additional expenditure is necessary, for example due to special dietary requirements or increased heating bills due to caring for elderly relatives or above average work-related travel costs, this should be clearly explained.

7.6 If the debtor wishes to continue to pay for health insurance, the proposal should contain a note stating why this is considered to be essential expenditure.

7.7 The expenditure elements that require formal verification are:

- Secured loan payments - verification by sight of relevant mortgage or bank statements.
- Rent – verification by sight of rent agreement or relevant bank statement entries.
- Council tax – verification by sight of council tax bill or relevant bank statement entries.
- Vehicle Finance – verification by means of relevant HP/Finance agreement.
- Other financial commitments such as endowment policies, life policies, pension contributions and health insurance – verification by reference to appropriate documentation.

7.8 Where information for verification purposes, which is readily available and is not excessive, is sought from creditors, this information will be provided free of charge whether the request is made by the IVA provider or the individual.

7.9 The Nominee's report will include a statement that the income and expenditure have been verified by the nominee in accordance with the protocol and provide details of the means used where the individual is self-employed.

Use of standard documentation

8.1 The use of standard documentation will streamline the IVA process and enable creditors to quickly identify those cases which are protocol compliant and also the key information contained therein.

8.2 For protocol compliant IVAs, IPs should use the agreed standard terms (Annex 4) and the summary sheet (Annex 5). There is no standard format for the IVA proposal.

8.3 All documentation should state clearly that the IVA follows the protocol and that the agreed format IVA documentation has been used. Similarly, any variation from the protocol (for example special dietary requirements, see paragraph 7.4) should be clearly identified in all relevant paperwork.

During the IVA

Home equity

9.1 Six months prior to the expiry of the IVA there should be an attempt to release home equity (this would normally be after month 54, unless the IVA has been extended for any reason). However, where the debtor is unable to obtain a re-mortgage, the IVA should instead be extended by up to 12 months.

9.2 The amount of the equity to be released will be based upon affordability from income and will leave the debtor with at least 15% of their equity in the property. Where it is appropriate to re-mortgage the property through a repayment mortgage (as opposed to interest only), the specific limits will be:

- Re-mortgages would be to a maximum of 85% LTV.
- The incremental cost of the re-mortgage will not exceed 50% of the monthly contribution.
- There will be a cap on the total equity release to not exceed 100% of the remaining outstanding debt.

This does not prevent the IVA Provider proposing a more suitable arrangement where the circumstances warrant it.

9.3 If the amount of equity available in the home at month 54 is under £5k, it is de minimis, and does not have to be released and there would be no adjustment to the IVA term.

9.4 The costs of re-mortgaging to release equity should be deducted from the mortgage proceeds and the monthly payments deducted from the contribution. If the increased cost of the mortgage means that dividends to creditors fall below £50 per month after fees, monthly contributions are stopped and the IVA is concluded.

9.5 A clause detailing the above is to be included, where appropriate in the individual's proposal and the summary sheet (Annex 5) will identify that this clause is included. The proposal should include a valuation of the freehold property based on current value inflated by 4% per annum for the period to when the debtor may be asked to remortgage the property [or] for the period to month 54 of the arrangement. This estimate should be shown in the outcome statement, together with the rate of inflation used and the date to which the estimate has been made.

9.6 As in any IVA, the debtor should be provided with a clear explanation of the effects of the IVA, in particular the possible effect that it will have on his/her home.

9.7 At the time the debtor is asked to release the equity in their property, the Supervisor or a suitable member of his/her staff, must advise them that they should seek advice from an independent financial adviser, such advice to include the most appropriate mortgage vehicle and the length of the proposed repayment term.

Use of discretion, variation and failure

10.1 The supervisor has the discretion to admit claims of £1,000 or less, or claims submitted that do not exceed 110% of the amount stated by the debtor in the proposal, without the need for additional verification.

10.2 The IVA provider should ensure that they are provided with copies of payslips (or other supporting evidence) every 12 months. The supervisor is required to review the debtor's income and expenditure once in every 12 months. The debtor will be required to increase his monthly contribution by 50% of any net surplus one month following such review. The supervisor will also be able to reduce the dividend by up to 15% in total relative to the original proposal (without referring back to creditors), to reflect changes in income and expenditure.

10.3 Where the individual has failed to disclose exceptional income, the term of the IVA may be extended by up to a maximum of six months to recover any sums due, without any modification being required.

10.4 Where the individual is unable to remedy any breach of the arrangement, the supervisor shall as soon as practicable report to creditors and obtain their agreement to do one of the following:

▸ vary the terms of the arrangement, or

▸ issue a certificate ("Certificate of Termination") terminating the arrangement by reason of the breach; and/or

▸ present a petition for the individual's bankruptcy.

Reporting to creditors

11.1 The annual report to creditors prepared by the IVA provider should include details of the individual's income and expenditure, based on information obtained including payslips and P60s. The individual should also be asked to provide verified details of their expenditure and any material changes to it. Where the supervisor has used his or her discretion to vary the dividend payment, in accordance with 10.3, that should also be recorded in the annual report.

Obligations on creditors

Treatment of customers

12.1 In all dealings with a customer proposing an IVA under this protocol, creditors will continue to treat the customer in accordance with the regulatory standards and codes of practice to which they are subject, as set out in annex 2.

12.2 Throughout the duration of a protocol compliant IVA, creditors will treat their customer as referred in 12.1. Furthermore, creditors will co-operate with the duly appointed nominee and supervisor in relation to the efficient operation of this protocol and providing their obligations are being met.

12.3 Lenders should take reasonable measures to avoid offering further credit to individuals known to have an IVA in place, unless this is in justifiable circumstances (e.g. for re-mortgage purposes). However, it should be recognised that relevant information is not always readily available to creditors and may sometimes be withheld by debtors.

Acceptance of protocol compliant IVAs

13.1 It is understood that one of the aims of the protocol is to improve efficiency in the IVA process and to this extent creditors and IVA providers will avoid the need for modifications of an IVA proposal wherever possible. This does not affect the right of creditors to vote for or against an IVA proposal.

13.2 Where a creditor or their agent on their behalf votes against a protocol compliant IVA proposal, their reason for so doing should be disclosed to the IVA provider.

13.3 By voting in favour of a protocol compliant IVA, creditors accept that the supervisor has discretion as referred to in section 10 above and in the standard terms and should not challenge the use of that discretion.

13.4 Creditors should make reasonable endeavours to provide a proof of debt (in the form required by the IVA provider) and proxy form within 14 days of receipt of an IVA proposal and if possible at least seven days before the date of the meeting called to approve the proposal.

13.5 Creditors not submitting claims within four months of the meeting to approve the proposal will be excluded from participating in dividend payments, unless a reasonable explanation is provided for why this delay has occurred. In cases where the supervisor accepts the explanation is reasonable, those creditors will be entitled to receive their full share of dividends, notwithstanding the fact that some distributions may have been made prior to the submission of the claim.

Income and expenditure

14.1 Creditors will normally accept income and expenditure statements drawn up on the basis of generally accepted standard financial statements and verified in accordance with this protocol, as the basis of a protocol compliant IVA proposal. For this purpose standard financial statements includes the CCCS guidelines and the CFS, once revised.

14.2 Creditors will follow the guidance in the Banking Code in relation to the use of standard financial statements and will have the right to challenge such statements as described in the guidance to use of the CFS (e.g. where the creditor is aware of a history of fraud or other information which would raise concerns about the validity of the information).

Use of agents

15.1 It will be the responsibility of creditors to ensure that any agents carrying out instructions or acting on their behalf in relation to a protocol compliant IVA, do so in accordance with this protocol and in accordance with applicable regulatory requirements.

15.2 Where a creditor requires communication regarding the debt due or the IVA proposal to be sent via its agent, the creditor should ensure that details of the appropriate contact are provided to relevant IVA providers.

Sale of debt

16.1 Where debt is sold when an IVA is proposed but before it has been approved, creditors should ensure that the debt buyer is a signatory to the Banking Code or follows the principles contained in the Banking Code and complies with OFT Debt Collection Guidance.

THE IVA PROTOCOL: UPDATE AND CHANGES

This note sets out the amendments to the Protocol agreed by the IVA Standing Committee. It also includes some clarification and guidance for IPs and creditors.

Guidance for all users

The name

Proposals prepared under the Protocol will be referred to as Protocol Compliant IVAs. This will reduce the risk of confusion created by the myriad of terms currently in use (SCIVA, Standard IVAs, Straightforward IVAs, SIVAS etc).

Unnecessary modifications

IPs have reported that they are still receiving modifications from creditors which are unnecessary because the subject matter of the modification is already covered by the Protocol Standard Terms and Conditions.

In particular, please note the Protocol STCs covering the following:

- Duration of the arrangement – STC 5 makes it clear that this must be stated on the face of the proposal.
- Death of the debtor – covered by STC 16.

Unnecessary modifications take time to resolve and therefore do not help to achieve the two key objectives of the Protocol; to streamline and increase the transparency of the process. Creditors are respectfully reminded to ensure that any proposed modifications are not already covered by the Protocol STCs or the proposal.

Interaction between the Protocol STCs and the R3 Standard Conditions

The Protocol STCs are designed to be used instead of the R3 Standard Conditions in Protocol Compliant IVAs. R3 Standard conditions would cause the proposal to be non compliant. IPs are reminded to paragraph 8.3 of the Protocol regarding Protocol STCs.

Pension contributions

Paragraph 7 of the Protocol already states that payment in respect of the Debtor's pension policy should be verified by the IP. The IVA Standing Committee has asked for guidance to be provided on when such payments should be allowable as essential expenditure. That guidance, agreed by the Committee is that where the debtor is below the age of *55 at the date of the arrangement*, only the minimum contribution allowed by the scheme should be made. Where the debtor is 55 years or older at the date of the arrangement, an average of the last six months pension contributions should be allowed, subject to a contribution limit of £75 above the minimum pension contribution allowed by the scheme per month.

The Standing Committee believes this is a fair approach and balances the interests of debtors and creditors. If the debtor wishes to include any pension contributions in essential expenditure, the proposal should contain a note to the effect that the sum included is within the guidelines or, if it is not, a note explaining why another sum is justified.

Payments made to the nominee pre IVA

Where any payments have been made by the debtor to the nominee, or any third parties, in relation to the original consultation or preparation of the proposal, any balance remaining (after deduction of the fee agreed by the debtor) should be paid into the arrangement. This would be in addition to the contribution offered by the debtor in the proposal. Where the debtor has paid such sums the proposal should clearly state how the balance has been dealt with.

Payment Protection Insurance (PPI)

PPI taken out prior to the agreement will not *usually* be allowed as essential expenditure. This is because, in most cases, the loan which was to be protected by the policy forms part of the agreement and the policy will either have paid out or will be cancelled by the creditor.

However, there may be circumstances when Pre IVA PPI *may* be allowable. For example, if the policy was to protect a car loan and the debtor needs the car to travel to work, it would be in the interests of the creditors to allow the PPI payments.

Where a debtor wishes to continue to make Pre IVA PPI payments as part of essential expenditure, the proposal must clearly state why this is the case.

It is now possible to take out PPI to protect the payments under the arrangement itself ("Post IVA PPI"). It may be argued that this is a benefit to creditors as it gives the arrangement a better chance of success. However, some creditors may prefer to accept the risk of failure in return for the higher commercial decision for creditors and for that reason, if a debtor wishes to make PPI payments as part of essential expenditure, full details of the policy should be provided in the proposal.

Equity release

A sub group of the IVA Standing Committee has considered the issue of how to arrive at an estimated value of the property at the time the proposal is prepared. Having considered a number of options, the Group has decided that to ensure consistency, we will adopt an assumed growth rate in property value of 4% per annum. Historically property growth has been around 7% per annum but it was felt that using this 7% figure ran the risk of seriously over estimating the possible returns to creditors. We do not want a situation where the assumption used is regularly changed, and therefore, to provide consistency, the 4% figure will be used. If market conditions are such that the use of the 4% figure will lead to a clearly misleading estimate, then reference can be made to this in the proposal, but the 4% figures should still be used.

The Group also considered the extent to which the debtor should be directed to a particular type of mortgage vehicle. It was agreed that IVA providers are not well place to offer such advice and that the debtor should be directed to Independent Financial Advisors.

The Group has approved a draft clause on equity release which may assist those drawing up proposals. This is now available as annex 6 to the protocol.

CHANGES TO THE PROTOCOL

Health insurance

If the debtor wishes to continue to pay for health insurance, the proposal should contain a note stating why this is considered to be essential expenditure. This has been added to paragraph 7 of the Protocol document under 'expenditure'.

Board and lodging

If the debtor lives with any person aged 18 or over, and there is reasonable expectation that this person will pay board and lodging to the debtor, this payment must be added to the debtor's income in full. This has been added to paragraph 7 of the Protocol under 'income'.

Equity release

Paragraph 9 has been amended to clarify how the property should be valued for the purpose of the outcome statement. This now states that the current value should be inflated by 4% per annum to the period to when the debtor will be asked to remortgage the property.

Paragraph 9 also states that the debtor should be advised to seek independent financial advice at the point at which they are asked to release the equity in their property.

CHANGES TO THE PROTOCOL STANDARD TERMS AND CONDITIONS

After due consideration, the Standing Committee has agreed to add the following to the Protocol STCs:

Obtaining credit

The debtor must not obtain any further credit greater than £500 without the prior written approval of the Supervisor, except for the public utilities and to refinance any balloon payment at the end of a vehicle Hire Purchase Agreement. Should credit greater than £500 be obtained without the prior written approval of the Supervisor, this will constitute a default of the arrangement. This clause does not apply to any remortgage or equity release under paragraph 9 of the Protocol.

Un-cashed dividend cheques

Paragraph 10(3) has been amended to change 'unpaid' to 'un-cashed'. This is simply to clarify the meaning.

CHANGES TO THE REGULATORY FRAMEWORK (Annex) 2

Addition to the first paragraph on page 2:

This allows debtors dealing with an Insolvency Practitioner or debt advice firm holding a standard licence, to bring an unresolved complaint to the Ombudsman relating to the advice they had received. Similar complaints about an Insolvency Practitioner covered by a Group licence held by their regulator could not be brought to the Ombudsman, but should be brought to the authorising body which had licensed the Insolvency Practitioner.

Summary and Self-test

Summary

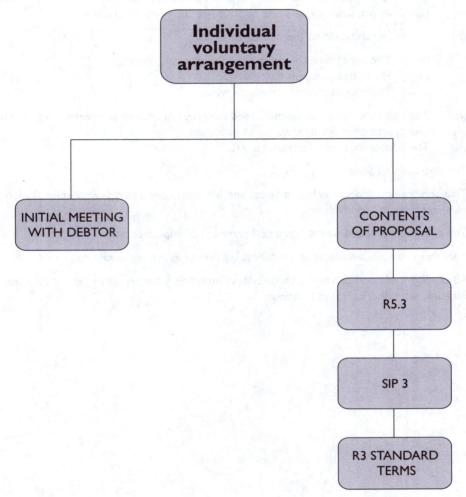

Self-test

Answer the following questions.

1. What is the purpose of the initial meeting with the debtor?
2. Three requirements must be met in order for a debtor to be able to propose a voluntary arrangement. What are these?
3. If the nominee or supervisor becomes aware that the debtor has been guilty of any offence in connection with the arrangement for which he is criminally liable, to whom should the matter be reported?
4. What matters are an IP required to check pursuant to *Greystoke v Hamilton-Smith*?
5. Who will be bound by an approved voluntary arrangement?

Now, go back to the Learning Objectives in the Introduction. If you are satisfied that you have achieved these, please tick them off.

Answers to Self-test

1. (a) To give and obtain information to enable:

    (i) A proposal and statement of affairs to be drafted.
    (ii) Approaches to be made to strategic and pressing creditors.

   (b) To give information to the debtor to explain:

    (i) The procedure to obtain a voluntary arrangement.
    (ii) His duties pursuant to legislation.
    (iii) The role of the nominee/supervisor.

2. (i) The debtor is either an undischarged bankrupt or able to petition for his own bankruptcy.
   (ii) The practitioner is willing to act as nominee.
   (iii) The debtor intends to propose a VA.

3. The Secretary of State.

4. That the true position re debtor's assets and liabilities does not differ substantially from what has been represented to creditors.

   The proposal, in broad terms, has a real prospect of implementation.

   That there is no unavoidable and manifest unfairness in the proposal.

5. All creditors entitled to vote at the creditors' meeting, whether or not they had notice of the meeting, attended, or voted in favour.

Answer to Interactive Question

Interactive question: Sarah Chapple

Letter format

A proposal for a voluntary arrangement is required to state or deal with a number of matters (r5.3, SIP 3, R3).

The proposal as it stands lacks sufficient information in key areas and the Nominee's comments on the proposal are of a general and limited nature:

- Sarah Chapple's proposal should give an estimate of the amount to be distributed to creditors and when the distribution will be made.
- How the business is to be conducted during the course of the arrangement should be detailed.
- Sarah states that she intends to retain her realisable assets and pay creditors out of profits generated by the business over the next three years. An estimate of the profits is not given. Creditors should be provided with information to assess past trading and future prospects, for example, management accounts, budgets, sales and cash forecasts.
- The proposal does not outline any arrangement for monitoring business trading and does not state how monies generated are to be banked or distributed.
- The proposal does not state the functions to be undertaken by the supervisor.
- The proposal does not state how the supervisor is to be remunerated or his expenses defrayed.
- The proposal does not state whether there are any circumstances which would give rise to the possibility of claims under the IA covering transactions at an undervalue, preferences or extortionate credit transactions should she be adjudicated bankrupt.
- Sarah Chapple's proposal does not give sufficient detail with regard to her husband's ownership of the house in which she resides. Her husband's acquisition of the house may be a transaction at an undervalue. There is no evidence of the house being professionally valued nor that the bank and building society advances are secured on the property. There is also no evidence that these advances are not the liability of Mrs Chapple and therefore competing with the claims of other creditors in the arrangement.
- There is no mention of the loan or property in relation to the £38,000 loan made by the client. The fact that neither are disclosed is a material irregularity.
- There are no details of any guarantees being given of Sarah's debts.
- The proposal makes no mention of how creditor's claims are to be dealt with and in particular how it is proposed to deal with creditors who are not notified of the proposal.
- The proposal does not state whether EC Regs are to apply.
- The proposal does not give sufficient information re the supervisor – name, address and qualification to act.

Sarah Chapple's proposal, as it stands, is incomplete and fails to comply with statutory requirements. In particular it is not possible to assess whether a better return would be achieved by her bankruptcy and immediate realisation of her assets rather than continued trading. The status of the matrimonial home and the other house needs to be established.

Suggest that creditors resolve to adjourn the meeting so that full explanations and information may be subsequently presented. The next and final meeting should be held no later than fourteen days after the date of the first meeting.

Point out that such meetings are required to start between 10.00am and 4.00pm on a business day and should be held at a location convenient for creditors (current meeting is timed for 4.30pm and located at a considerable distance from Swindon).

If further information is not satisfactory – client should reject proposals and take necessary steps to have Sarah Chapple adjudicated bankrupt.

5

Voluntary arrangement procedures

Contents

Introduction
Examination context
Topic List
1   Interim order
2   Procedure with interim order
3   Procedure without interim order
4   Fast track VAs (FTVA)
5   Effect of approval

Summary and Self-test
Answers to Self-test
Answers to Interactive Questions

Personal Insolvency

Introduction

Learning objectives

- The interim order: who may apply for it, on what grounds, the effect of obtaining an interim order
- The procedures to be followed to obtain agreement to a voluntary arrangement, both with and without an interim order
- Statutory requirements re nominee's comments on the proposal
- Statutory requirements re convening meeting of creditors to consider the proposal
- Fast track VAs: what they are and when they are appropriate
- Effect of approval of a VA on creditors
- Statutory requirements re Chair's report to court and Secretary of State

Working context

In a work environment you may be asked to advise a debtor on the process for obtaining approval of a voluntary arrangement or to assist in convening the creditors' meeting and making the necessary reports after the meeting. It is appropriate therefore that you are familiar with the statutory requirements and procedures to be followed to obtain approval for a voluntary arrangement.

Stop and think

What is an interim order? Why would one be required? To whom is the nominee required to send his comments on the debtor's proposal? What matters should he comment on?

VOLUNTARY ARRANGEMENT PROCEDURES

Examination context

The procedure to enter into a voluntary arrangement is a popular topic for the JIEB exam. The nominee's comments on the proposals and reports to court have also been regularly tested.

Exam requirements

Past questions to look at include:

2000	Question 4 (a)
1999	Question 2 (b) (c)
1997	Question 3 (c) (d)
1995	Question 4 (c)
1994	Question 2
1994	Question 3 (b)
1993	Question 2 (1)
1992	Paper I Question 7 (a) (b)
1992	Paper II Question 5

Personal Insolvency

1 Interim order

Section overview

The voluntary arrangement procedure envisages a debtor, with the assistance of his nominee, putting a proposal to his creditors for the satisfaction of his debts. The IA 1986 made the application for an interim order compulsory, however, since the IA 2000, a debtor may make a proposal to his creditors without first seeking an interim order (s256A). The relevant procedure for IVAs can be found in Part V of the Insolvency Rules 1986 (as amended). Part V is broken down into the following chapters:

- Chapter 1 – preliminary/introduction
- Chapter 2 – preparation of the debtor's proposal
- Chapter 3 – cases in which an interim order is applied for
- Chapter 4 – cases where no interim order obtained
- Chapter 5 – creditors' meeting
- Chapter 6 – implementation of the arrangement.
- Chapter 7 – fast track voluntary arrangements

1.1 Effect of an interim order

An interim order protects the debtor from all proceedings and enforcement action whilst his proposal is being prepared and put before his creditors.

Where the debtor has only a few creditors who are willing to support a voluntary arrangement, it is likely that the debtor will save time and money and not apply for an interim order. Undischarged bankrupts are also unlikely to need the protection of an interim order.

Pursuant to s252(2), an interim order has the effect that, during the period in which it is in force:

- No bankruptcy petition in respect of the debtor may be presented or proceeded with, and
- No landlord or other person to whom rent is payable may exercise any right of forfeiture by peaceable re-entry in relation to premises let to the debtor in respect of a failure by the debtor to comply with any term or condition of his tenancy, except with leave of the court, and
- No other proceedings and no other execution or other legal process, may be commenced or continued against the debtor or his property except with the leave of the court.

This means that judgement creditors for example, will need leave to enforce their security. However, no leave is required to take action that does not involve court proceedings for example, a secured creditor can appoint a receiver under the terms of a charge.

Exceptions to the rule are:

- Enforcement action pursuant to Proceeds of Crime Act 2002 (formerly the Drugs Trafficking Offences Act 1986) is not prevented (*Re: M 1992*) nor is enforcement of fines or compensation orders made in connection with criminal offences.

- If a landlord wants to exercise his self help remedies of distress and forfeiture leave of the court will be required even though no court proceedings are usually required to exercise these remedies (s252(2)(aa) and s252(2)(b) as amended by IA 2000)

1.2 Who may apply for an interim order?

S253(3) provides that application may be made by:

- An undischarged bankrupt, his trustee or the OR.
- The debtor.

S253(5) provided that an application can't be made if the debtor has petitioned for his own bankruptcy and the court has appointed an IP to enquire and report.

1.3 Grounds for granting an interim order

An interim order will be made provided that the application is in order and the four conditions for the court to make an interim order are satisfied (s255).

- Willing nominee who is authorised to act.
- Debtor has not applied for an interim order in the last 12 months.
- Debtor is an undischarged bankrupt or could petition for his own bankruptcy.
- Debtor intends to propose an IVA.

The court is also required to take account of any representation made by any person entitled to notice of the hearing.

1.4 Duration of the interim order

Unless an application for an extension is made, an interim order will cease to have effect at the end of 14 days from the date it is made (s255(6)).

Provided that the nominee's report recommends that a creditors' meeting be summoned, the court will further extend the interim order to enable the proposal to be considered (s256(5)). Otherwise, the court may discharge the interim order in force s256(6).

If a concertina order was requested, the interim order will be made for such period as to enable proposal to be considered.

It is not unusual for extensions to the interim order to be requested. Often, the initial 14 day period is insufficient to enable the proposal to be put together and the report made. In addition, it is possible that the creditors' meeting may have to be adjourned.

When hearing an application to extend the interim order, the court will consider whether there is support from the creditors. If there is strong opposition from 25% of the creditors, the court should not continue the interim order *Re Cove (a debtor) 1990*.

There is no need for a formal court order to discharge the interim order. It will automatically be discharged 28 days from the date that the decision of the creditors' meeting was reported to court (s260). If the meeting rejects the arrangement, the court can make an order to discharge the interim order before the expiration of the 28 day period (s259(2)).

The court may discharge the interim order if it is satisfied, on the application of the nominee (s256(6)):

(i) that the debtor has failed to comply with his obligations under s256(2), or

(ii) that for any other reason it would be inappropriate for a meeting of the debtor's creditors to be summoned to consider the debtor's proposal.

1.5 Concertina order

Although the Act and Rules envisage that two hearings will need to be held, a practice direction permits the court to make an interim order at the first hearing and an order that the creditors' meeting be summonsed. This is referred to as a 'concertina order'. The interim order will continue until after the creditors' meeting. This practice direction also provides for an order to be made without attendance. It is not appropriate to seek a concertina order where the proposal is likely to require amendment and/or the support of creditors has not been ascertained. (A copy of the practice direction can be found in Part VI of Butterworths).

2 Procedure with interim order

Section overview

It is not possible for a debtor to act on his own to implement a voluntary arrangement. He must engage the services of an authorised practitioner who will act as his nominee and later the supervisor.

2.1 Summary of the procedure

Debtor prepares proposals for a VA and sends them to the nominee who accepts the appointment.

Within seven days the debtor sends the nominee a Statement of Affairs (unless one has already been delivered in bankruptcy proceedings).

Debtor applies to court for an interim order (to obtain the moratorium). At least two days' notice of the hearing must be given to the nominee and any creditors petitioning for bankruptcy. Court makes the order (lasting 14 days).

At least two days before the expiry of the interim order the nominee submits a report on the debtor's proposal to court (see 2.2 for details).

Nominee summons a creditors' meeting (see 2.3 for details).

The creditors' meeting is held which may approve the proposal, or approve with agreed modifications or reject the proposal. A resolution to this effect is passed by 75% in value of those attending and voting subject to the right of dissidents to apply to the court on the basis of unfair prejudice or material irregularity.

If approved the nominee becomes the supervisor and all the creditors entitled to vote at the meeting are bound by the terms of the VA.

S260(2)(b) (as amended by IA 2000) states that the approved arrangement:

- Binds every person who in accordance with the rules was entitled to vote at the meeting (whether or not he was present or represented at it), or
- Would have been so entitled had he had notice of it, as if he were a party to the arrangement.

Pursuant to IA 2000, a creditor is now bound to a voluntary arrangement even if he did not receive notice of it. It is however still important that those entitled to notice receive it as a creditor who was not notified will be entitled to challenge the decision pursuant to s262. The fact that notice was not given will support such an application.

The IVA is then implemented.

2.2 Nominee's report

The nominee's report must be delivered to court not less than two days before the expiration of the interim order. (The interim order ceases to have effect at the end of 14 days beginning on the day after the order is made). It is possible, however, for the nominee to apply to court for an extension of time both to file his report and to extend the duration of the interim order (s256(4)).

If the nominee fails to submit a report, the debtor can apply to court requesting the replacement of the nominee and/or an extension of the interim order. It will be necessary for the nominee to receive seven days notice of the application.

The purpose of the report is to state (s256(1)/s256A(3)):

- Whether in the opinion of the nominee the voluntary arrangement has a reasonable prospect of being approved and implemented and whether a meeting of the debtor's creditors should be summoned to consider the debtor's proposal:

- If the report recommends a meeting, the nominee will annexe to the report his comments on the debtor's proposal.
- If the report does not recommend a meeting, the nominee is obliged to give reasons for his opinion (r5.11).

▸ The date on which, and time and place at which, he proposes the meeting should be held.

The nominee should take care to ensure that his report is as comprehensive and accurate as it can be. As the nominee is acting as an officer of the court it is fundamental to the integrity of the voluntary arrangement process that the creditors have faith in the scrutiny of the nominee. They should feel satisfied that they are voting on a proposal that has been scrutinised on their behalf. The nominee should also remember that he can compel the debtor to provide information (r5.6). The nominee will be expected to have examined the debtor's financial records before reporting to court.

Criticism of the quality of a nominee's report was made by Harman J in *Re A Debtor (no 222 of 1990) exp Bank of Ireland*. In that case an IP was criticised for '... bringing no critical eye whatever to bear upon the debtor's statements of asset and liabilities...' Following this criticism, the Insolvency Service provided guidance to IP's in 'DEAR IP' No 33 (March 1995) now incorporated into the Dear IP Millennium Edition. This guidance stressed that nominees should exercise their professional judgment when considering proposals and reporting to the court. At the very least, nominees are instructed to consider whether an arrangement is:

▸ Feasible.
▸ Fair to creditors.
▸ Fair to debtors.
▸ Provides an acceptable alternative to bankruptcy.
▸ Fit to be considered by the creditors.

SIP 3 provides that the nominee should comment on the following matters in their report to court:

▸ **Investigation** – extent of nominee's investigation of the debtor's circumstances.

▸ **Valuations** – basis of asset valuations.

▸ **Attitude** – information on debtor's attitude with particular reference to instances where he has failed to co-operate with the nominee.

▸ **Realistic values** – extent to which nominee considers reliance can be placed on the debtor's estimate of the liabilities to be included in the IVA.

▸ **Secured and third party talks** – result of any discussions between nominee and secured creditors or other interested parties upon whose co-operation the performance of the IVA will depend.

▸ **History** – of previous failures.

▸ **Other options** – estimate of result for creditors if IVA approved explaining why it is more beneficial for creditors than any alternative insolvency proceedings.

▸ **Rejection** – likely effect of rejection of proposal by the creditors.

▸ **Transactions a trustee can challenge** – details of any claims which might be better pursued by a trustee in bankruptcy than by a supervisor.

Pursuant to s256A the nominee must also explain why he considers that the arrangement has a reasonable prospect of approval and implementation.

Greystoke v Hamilton Smith

This case provided a three part test determining whether an IP can generally provide a positive report to the court. The nominee must be satisfied:

▸ That the true position re values of assets and liabilities is not materially different to that represented by the debtor.

▸ The IVA has a real prospect of approval and implementation.

Personal Insolvency

▶ Not manifestly and unavoidably unfair.

SIP 3 provides that where these conditions are not met and the nominee none the less recommends that meetings should be held to vote on the IVA, the nominee should explain in his comments why the IVA is being recommended.

2.3 Creditors' meeting

Once the interim order has been granted the creditors' meeting must be convened by the nominee (s257(1)). The purpose of the meeting is to decide whether or not the proposed voluntary arrangement should be approved with or without modifications. Modification to the proposal is permitted but with certain restrictions.

All modifications must be consented to by the debtor and no modifications can be made that would affect the rights of secured or preferential creditors without their consent. Care must be taken to ensure that the modifications are not such that would result in the proposal ceasing to be a composition or scheme of arrangement. It is however possible to propose a modification that will result in the appointment of a new nominee.

2.3.1 Calling the meeting

On receipt of the nominee's report the court will decide whether or not a meeting of creditors should be summoned to consider the debtor's proposal. Provided the court is satisfied with the nominee's report it is likely to follow the nominee's recommendation. The Interim Order (if sought) will then be extended until after the creditors' meeting has taken place.

R5.18 directs that in fixing a venue for the meeting the nominee should have regard for the convenience of creditors and that the meeting should be summoned to commence between 10.00 and 16.00 hours on a business day.

Where an interim order is in place the date of the meeting must be not less than 14 days from the filing of the nominee's report and not more than 28 days from the date of consideration by court of that report. Where there is no interim order r5.17 provides that the meeting must not be less than 14 days and not more than 28 days from that on which the nominee's report is filed in court under r5.14.

2.3.2 Notice of the meeting

Pursuant to s257(2) every creditor of the debtor of whose claim and address the nominee is aware must be summoned.

Each creditor is entitled to 14 days notice (r5.17), which must include a copy of the proposal, the statement of affairs or summary of it, a proxy form and the nominee's comments on the proposal. The creditors must also be given information about the requisite majorities required pursuant to r5.23.

2.3.3 Agreement of creditor claims

In an ideal situation the nominee will normally seek to agree creditors' claims prior to the creditors' meeting however this is not always possible. Consequently where documentary proof of claims has not been provided this should be obtained as soon as possible.

Claims should also be discussed and agreed with the debtor.

In circumstances where the nominee decides not to admit a claim for the amount claimed, notice should be given in writing to both the debtor and creditor. If either the debtor or creditor is unhappy with the decision they can apply to court to have the decision modified or reversed.

Proxies and statements of claim to be used at the meeting may be lodged at any time, even during the course of the meeting.

2.3.4 Role of the chair

The chair of the meeting will normally be the nominee. If for some reason the nominee is unable to attend he can delegate his duties but delegation must be to a member of staff experienced in insolvency matters.

VOLUNTARY ARRANGEMENT PROCEDURES

The chair will conduct the meeting and make decisions about the rights of creditors to vote and for what amount. The chair of the meeting will usually cast proxy votes but r5.20 provides that without specific direction from the proxy the chair shall not use proxy votes held by him to increase or reduce the amount of remuneration or expenses of the nominee or supervisor. Any proxy cast by the chair contrary to r5.20 will not count towards the requisite majority under r5.23.

2.3.5 Who is entitled to vote?

R5.21 establishes that every creditor who was given notice of the creditors' meeting is entitled to vote. Despite the fact that r5.21 envisages notice being given by the nominee, if a creditor who was not given notice by the nominee can establish a debt due and owing he will also be entitled to attend and vote *Re a Debtor (No 400 of 1996)*. Written notice of a creditor's claim must be given and r5.23 envisages this being given before or at the meeting.

The chairman may admit or reject any claim in whole or in part.

If there is any doubt about the validity of a claim the creditor should be admitted to vote but his vote marked as objected to. This is subject to such votes being subsequently declared invalid if the objection to the claim is sustained.

The entitlement of a creditor to vote is not limited to those claims where the value can be ascertained. For the purposes of voting (but not otherwise) the debt shall be valued at £1 unless the chairman agrees to put a higher value on it (r5.21). There is no need for bilateral agreement provided that the chair makes a genuine good faith attempt to value. It would be good practice to notify the creditor of any value before the meeting but there is no obligation to do so.

2.3.6 Majority required to approve a VA

For any resolution to approve any proposal (or modification) there must be a majority in excess of three-quarters in value of the creditors present, in person or by proxy, who do in fact vote on the resolution (r5.23).

The value of debts is ascertained (pursuant to r5.21) as follows:

- Where an Interim order is in force the date of the interim order.
- Where there is no interim order the date of the meeting.
- Where the debtor is an undischarged bankrupt the date of the bankruptcy order.

It should be noted however that when calculating the value of a debt (as at the date of the meeting) some claims (or part thereof) are left out of account as follows (r5.23):

- Written notice of the claim not given either at the meeting or before it to the chairman or the nominee. Note that *IRC v Conbeer 1996* has established that faxed proxies are valid for the purposes of insolvency legislation.
- Part or all of claim secured. **Note.** A part secured creditor can vote with the unsecured balance *(Calor Gas v Piercy 1994)*.
- It is in respect of a debt wholly or partly secured on a current bill of exchange or promissory note. Exception – where creditor willing to treat the liability to him of persons liable antecedently to the debtor on the bill or note as a security. The value of that security will then be estimated and deducted from the creditor's claim for voting purposes.

The legislation is drafted so as to ensure that a VA cannot be forced through by a majority of creditors who are associated with the debtor. In order to secure approval the vote must in effect be counted twice. Firstly all the votes will be counted. Assuming that a majority in excess of 75% is in favour a second count will then take place but this time counting only those:

- To whom notice was sent (subject to comments above).
- Whose votes are not to be left out of account under r5.23(3) (ie as secured, secured on a bill of exchange or as having failed to give written notice of claim).
- Who are not to the best of the chair's belief associates of the debtor.

Personal Insolvency

On this second count any resolution is invalid if those voting against it include more than half in value of the creditors. The practical effect of the rule is that a simple majority of valid, notified, independent creditors can veto an arrangement which would otherwise be approved by the use of associates.

2.3.7 Procedure at Meeting

The chairman presents his report to the creditors' meeting. He should then allow creditors an opportunity to make comments, ask questions or propose modifications.

The meeting may be adjourned if there is a failure to reach the requisite majority, however adjournment cannot be for more than 14 days. If a series of adjourned meetings are held the last meeting may not be more than 14 days from the original meeting.

The chair must give notice of adjournments to the court.

If following the final meeting the proposal is not agreed to it is deemed rejected.

2.3.8 Considerations in respect of proxy votes

Proxy forms must be properly completed.

If a nominee obtains proxy votes in favour of a proposal he must be careful when deciding how to deal with these proxies if new information becomes available at the meeting. He should not cast these votes without further reference to the creditors unless he is sure that it would be right to do so. If the new information is significant the nominee will have to adjourn the meeting for the purpose of relaying this information back to the creditors. This may give rise to a need to seek an extension of the interim order.

Faxed proxy forms are acceptable.

Interactive question 1: Simon Hedge

At a meeting of creditors to consider proposals for a voluntary arrangement put forward by Simon Hedge the following votes are cast:

	Amount of claim £
In favour of accepting the proposals	
John Dunne	25,000
ABC Ltd	30,000
Jo Anthony	95,000
Miscellaneous creditors	55,000
	205,000
Against accepting the proposals	
Satby Bank plc	200,000
Dick James	10,000
Miscellaneous creditors	5,000
	215,000

John Dunne is the trustee of a trust fund, the beneficiaries of which include Simon's girlfriend Debbie and their son Paul. The claim by John Dunne is for £20,000 due by Simon to the trust fund and £5,000 due to John personally.

The claim of Satby Bank plc does not take account of a mortgage worth £150,000 which it holds over Simon's house.

Dick James is the brother of Simon's former business partner, Harold.

ABC Ltd is a company in which Simon holds 25% of the voting shares, the remaining 75% of which is held equally by:

(1) Simon's brother, Barry Hedge.
(2) An institutional investor, and
(3) Paul.

Requirement

Advise the nominee whether or not Simon's proposals have been duly approved, giving reasons for your answers.

(It may be assumed that all creditors who voted gave written notice of their claim to the nominee either at or before the meeting).

See **Answer** at the end of the chapter.

3 Procedure without interim order

Section overview

The IA 2000 introduced s256A which made it possible for a debtor to propose an IVA without an interim order being in place first. This will be appropriate where a debtor is an undischarged bankrupt. He will be required to give notice to the OR and his trustee if one has been appointed. There are no court hearings involved in the procedure although documents must still be filed at court.

3.1 Summary of procedure

The debtor prepares a proposal and sends it to the nominee who accepts the appointment.

Within seven days the debtor sends to the nominee a Statement of Affairs (unless one has already been delivered in bankruptcy proceedings).

If the nominee is satisfied that the debtor is able to apply for a VA he has 14 days from the receipt of the proposal to submit a report to court (s256A). The report should state:

(a) whether, in his opinion, the voluntary arrangement which the debtor is proposing has a reasonable prospect of being approved and implemented.

(b) whether, in his opinion, a meeting of the debtor's creditors should be summoned.

(c) if, in his opinion, such a meeting should be summoned, the date on which, and time and place at which, he proposes the meeting should be held.

A creditors' meeting is held at the time, date and place proposed in the nominee's report to approve or object to the arrangement. The voting rules are the same as those where an interim order is in place.

3.2 Nominee's report

The court will not consider the nominee's report unless an application for an interim order is made (r5.14). Consequently in the absence of any application the court will assume that everything is in order. With his report the nominee must deliver to court:

- A copy of the proposal.
- Statement of affairs.
- Nominee's consent to act.

These documents must be served on the OR and trustee in the case of an undischarged bankrupt. If the debtor is not bankrupt but has a petitioning creditor the petitioning creditor must also be served.

The relevant court is either the court in which the bankruptcy order was made or the court in which the debtor could petition for his own bankruptcy depending on whether the debtor is an undischarged bankrupt or not. Any further application to court in connection with the VA will be made to this relevant court.

4 Fast track VAs (FTVA)

Section overview

The Enterprise Act 2002 introduced a fast track regime from 1 April 2004 which is only available to undischarged bankrupts. The procedure is contained in s263A – s263G and r5.35 to r5.50. The OR must act as nominee and no interim order is available. Note: the examiner has stated that candidates need only have an 'awareness' of fast track voluntary arrangements.

4.1 Procedure

The procedure is commenced by the bankrupt submitting his 'fast track proposal' and statement of affairs to the OR who, following receipt, must consider whether it has a reasonable prospect of being approved. The proposal must amongst other items contain:

- details of the debtor's assets.
- the assets available to be sold.
- payments the debtor is willing to make to creditors.
- the duration of the FTVA.
- details of the fees and costs of administering the FTVA.

Full details are contained in R5.37(2).

The OR will charge a fixed fee of £315 for acting as nominee. For acting as supervisor, the OR's fee will be 15% of the amount raised from the sale of assets and monies received from the debtor.

In addition, half of the OR's bankruptcy administration fee (£857.50) will be paid from realisations under the FTVA.

If the bankruptcy was made on a creditors' petition, the creditors' costs must also be paid.

A £15 registration fee for registering the FTVA must also be paid to the Secretary of State.

Making any false statements or fraudulently doing or omitting anything to get creditors' approval is a criminal offence.

The OR must consider whether or not he is willing to act as nominee and whether or not the proposal should bind all creditors and not just bankruptcy creditors.

If the OR takes the view that the proposal has a reasonable prospect of success (and provides a significantly better return for creditors than bankruptcy) he will issue the proposal to creditors and ask them to decide whether or not to accept it. The Rules envisage that this will be done by correspondence. There is no provision for modification as in a creditors meeting under s257.

The percentage in value to approve the VA is more than 75% as in the normal VA procedure (r5.43).

Effect of approval

Subject to approval, the VA takes effect and binds the creditors and debtor from the date on which the OR reports the outcome to the court.

R5.51 to r5.59 provide for an application for annulment of the bankruptcy order by either the OR or the bankrupt. Such application cannot be made before the expiry of 28 days commencing with the day upon which the report of the creditors meeting was made to court (S262(3)(a)). During this period appeals against the decision under s263 can also be made.

Where an IVA is proposed following the appointment of a trustee in bankruptcy, the trustee, acting as such is still required to pay the proceeds of asset realisations into the ISA under Regulation 20 Insolvency Regulations 1994. These proceeds will attract the Secretary of State fee which will not be rebated when the bankruptcy is subsequently replaced by an IVA (Dear IP No 35).

5 Effect of approval

Section overview

Once approved the voluntary arrangement will bind all creditors entitled to vote at the creditors' meeting, whether or not they voted in favour s260(2)(b).

5.1 Chair's report to court

S259(1) '...the chairman of the meeting shall report the result of it to the court and immediately after so reporting, shall give notice of the result of the meeting to such persons as must be prescribed.'

(If report states that proposal for a VA rejected the court may discharge the interim order (s259(2)).

SIP 12 reminds IPs of this statutory obligation. The report may state (r5.27(2)):

- Whether proposal approved (with or without modifications – and if with, what those modifications were) or rejected,
- Resolutions taken at the meeting and the decision on each one,
- List the creditors (with their respective values) who were present or represented at the meeting and how they voted on each resolution,
- Whether the EC Regulation applies to the voluntary arrangement and if so whether the proceedings are main proceedings or territorial proceedings,
- Any further information as chair thinks appropriate.

Must be filed with court within four days of meeting (r5.27(3)). As well as filing his report in court, the chair must give notice of the outcome of the meeting to those who received the notice of the meeting.

5.2 Report to Secretary of State

The Secretary of State maintains a register of VAs which is open to inspection within office opening hours.

R5.29 provides that immediately after the chair has filed in court a report that the meeting has approved the voluntary arrangement, he shall report to the Secretary of State the following details of the arrangement:

- Name and address of debtor
- Date of creditors approval
- Name and address of supervisor
- The court in which the chairs report has been filed

The supervisor (or a later replacement supervisor) must give Secretary of State written notice of appointment or vacation of office.

A £15 fee is payable on registration of the IVA.

5.3 Discharge of interim order

No attendance is needed for the final order. The final order records the effect of the chair's report and discharges the interim order.

5.4 Appeals

Appeals may be launched either under r5.22/23, which is an appeal from the decision of the chair at the meeting and/or pursuant to s262. Under s262 the appeal is against the decision of the meeting. An appeal under the Act and Rules can be brought together.

5.4.1 Appeal pursuant to r5.22/23 against chair's decision at the meeting

Creditors of the debtor can appeal to the court against decisions of the chair on:

- Entitlement to vote.
- Leaving out of account all or part of claim on basis of lack of written notice or security or a debt on, or secured, on a bill or note.
- Identifying a person as an associate of the debtor.

Application to the court must be within 28 days of the chair's report to the court.

If the decision on entitlement to vote gives rise to unfair prejudice or a material irregularity the court can:

- Make such order as it thinks fit.
- Including ordering another meeting to be summoned.

The chair will not be personally liable for costs of appeal.

5.4.2 Appeal pursuant to s262 against the decision of the meeting

The grounds (s262(1)) are that the VA unfairly prejudices the interests of a creditor or that there has been a material irregularity at or in relation to the s257 creditors' meeting.

Unfair prejudice appeals will only succeed where the prejudice arises from the unfairness of the proposal itself *(Re A Debtor No: 259 of 1990)* eg treating different types of ordinary creditor differently in regard to payment of dividend. For there to be prejudice this must have affected the rights of the creditor in some way. Material irregularity on the other hand involves procedural matters, eg a complaint that the chair rejected a valid claim for voting purposes. As to whether the irregularity is material the court will take a practical approach, ie it must have affected the outcome of the meeting.

Pursuant to s262(2) applicants may be either:

- The debtor.
- A person entitled to vote at the creditors' meeting.
- The nominee or his replacement
- The trustee or Official Receiver if the debtor is an undischarged bankrupt

The time limit for applications is within 28 days of the filing of chair's report on any meeting with the court (s262(3)).

If the court is satisfied that the ground is made out, it can revoke or suspend approval, or direct that a further meeting of creditors be held to consider revised proposals or reconsider original proposals. The court can extend the interim order accordingly and make supplemental directions.

The applicant serves a sealed copy of the court order on the debtor and supervisor and the debtor gives notice of the court order to all creditors. The applicant gives written notice of the court order to the Secretary of State within seven days of hearing.

Cazaly Irving Holdings v Cancol

It will not be unfairly prejudicial to pay strategic creditors in an IVA, for example payment of creditors to ensure continued trading. The proposal provided that the landlord would be paid arrears in full and ongoing rent on due dates. A creditor claimed this was unfair. The debtor argued that the landlord was a key creditor on whose support the IVA depended and therefore it was acceptable to give the landlord preferential treatment.

5.5 Protection for creditors not given notice

A creditor who was not given notice of the meeting is still bound by its decision. However such a creditor is protected by s262. This permits a creditor to apply to court to challenge the approval within 28 days from when he became aware of the meeting. Challenge is by court application.

It should be noted that a creditor without notice of the meeting is still entitled to receive a dividend.

Interactive question 2: Mr Hytche

You have been contacted by Mr Hytche t/a Motor Supply Services, who for many years has been supplying tools and car parts to Mr Brown.

The last four months' invoices sent to Mr Brown have not been paid and Mr Hytche has received notification from Mr Brown that he is seeking to enter into a voluntary arrangement with his creditors.

Mr Hytche decides to vote against Mr Brown's proposals at the meeting, however despite this, sufficient approval for the arrangement is obtained and the voluntary arrangement goes ahead.

Requirement

Write a letter to Mr Hytche advising him of his position following the approval of the arrangement. If he is unhappy with the voluntary arrangement what, if anything, can he do?

See **Answer** at the end of this chapter.

Personal Insolvency

Summary and Self-test

Summary

Summary of procedure to apply for an interim order:

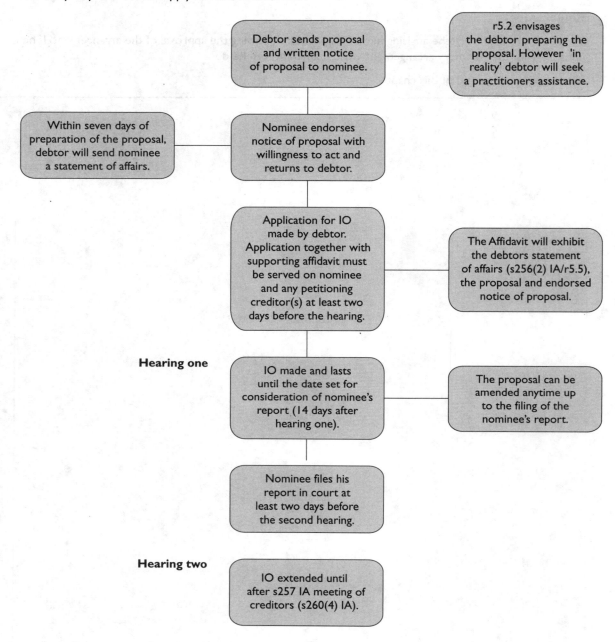

Summary of procedure where no interim order applied for:

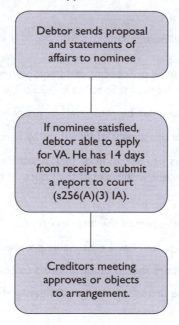

Self-test

Answer the following questions.

1. What is the effect of an interim order?
2. Within how many days of the proposal being sent to the nominee must the debtor send a statement of affairs to the nominee?
3. The nominee must submit a report on the debtor's proposal to court. When must it be submitted?
4. What is the purpose of the nominee's report to court?
5. How many days' notice must be given to the creditors of the meeting to consider the debtor's proposals?
6. What information should accompany the notice to creditors?
7. What is the required majority for a resolution to be passed approving a voluntary arrangement?
8. Within what time period must the Chair report to the court on the outcome of the meeting?
9. SIP 12 lists matters to be included in the report to the court. What are these?
10. An appeal against the decision of the creditors meeting must be made within what period?

Now, go back to the Learning Objectives in the Introduction. If you are satisfied that you have achieved these, please tick them off.

Answers to Self-test

1. The debtor is protected from all proceedings and enforcement action whilst the proposal is being prepared and put before his creditors. Specifically (s252(2)):

    - No bankruptcy petition may be presented or proceeded with.
    - No landlord may exercise a right of forfeiture by re-entry.
    - No other proceedings or execution or legal processes may be commenced or continued against the debtor except with leave of the court.

2. Within seven days.

3. At least two days before the expiry of the interim order.

4. To state whether the arrangement has a reasonable prospect of being approved and implemented.

    Whether a meeting of creditors should be summoned to consider the debtor's proposal.

    Date/time/place at which the proposed creditors' meeting should take place.

5. 14 days notice (r5.17).

6. A copy of the proposal.
    The statement of affairs or a summary of it.
    A proxy form.
    Nominee's comments on the proposal.
    Information re requisite majorities required under r5.23.

7. For any resolution to approve any proposal or modification, there must be a majority in excess of three-quarters in value of the creditors present, in person or by proxy, who do in fact vote on the resolution r5.23.

    The value of the creditor's debts are ascertained as follows:

    - Where an interim order is in force - as at the date of the interim order.
    - Where there is no interim order in force - the date of the meeting.
    - Where the debtor is an undischarged bankrupt - the date of the bankruptcy order.

    When calculating the value of a creditor's claim, the following should be left out of account:

    - Where written notice of the claim was not given either at the meeting or before it.
    - Where part or all of the claim is secured.
    - Where it is in respect of a debt wholly or partly secured on a current bill of exchange or promissory note.

    If a 75% majority votes in favour, a second vote is taken, this time only counting those:

    - To whom notice was sent.
    - Whose votes are not to be left out of account as above.
    - Who are not, to the best of the chair's belief, associates of the debtor.

    On this vote the resolution is invalid if those voting against it include more than half in value of the creditors.

    So a simple majority of valid, notified, independent creditors can veto an arrangement which would otherwise be approved by the use of associates.

8. Within four days of the meeting.

9   SIP 12: The report must state:
    - Whether the proposal was approved (with or without modifications – and if with, what those modifications were) or rejected.
    - The resolutions taken at the meeting and the decision on each one.
    - List the creditors (with their respective values) who were present or represented at the meeting and how they voted on each resolution.
    - Whether the EC Regs apply to the voluntary arrangement and if so, whether the proceedings are main proceedings or territorial.
    - Any further information as the chair thinks appropriate.

10 Within 28 days of the chair's report to court.

Answers to Interactive Questions

Interactive question 1: Simon Hedge

R5.17 – every creditor who was given notice of the creditors' meeting is entitled to vote at the meeting or any adjournment thereof.

Votes are calculated according to the amount of the creditor's debt as at the date of the meeting.

R5.18 – at the creditors' meeting, for a resolution to pass approving the proposals or any modification thereof, there must be a majority in excess of three-quarters in value of the creditors present in person or by proxy and voting on the resolution.

A claim or part of a claim will, however, be left out of account for voting purposes, where the claim or part of it is secured. Therefore, the claim of Satby Bank plc must be reduced by the amount of its security for voting purposes, leaving it with a £50,000 vote.

Total admissible votes against the proposals therefore amount to £65,000.

£65,000 represents less than 25% of the admissible votes cast and accordingly the proposals would prima facie appear to have been approved.

The resolution will be deemed to be invalid however if those who voted against it include more than half in value of the creditors:

- To whom notice of the meeting was sent.
- Whose votes are not to be excluded.
- Who are not, to the best of the chairman's belief, associates of the debtor.

Associate has technical meaning as set out in s435.

John Dunne

A person in his capacity as trustee of a trust, other than a pension scheme or employee's share scheme, is an associate of another person if the beneficiaries of the trust include, or the terms of the trust confer a power that may be exercised for the benefit of, the other person or an associate of that other person.

A person is an associate of his relative and relative includes an illegitimate child.

Paul is therefore a relative and associate of Simon.

Since Paul is a beneficiary under the trust, John Dunne is an associate of Simon insofar as he is claiming as trustee.

However, insofar as John Dunne is claiming in a personal capacity, he is not an associate.

Barry Hedge

A 'relative' is deemed to be an associate.

'Relative' includes a brother and therefore Barry is deemed to be an associate.

ABC Ltd

A company is an associate of another if that person has control of it or if that person and persons who are his associates together have control of it.

A person is to be taken as having control of a company, inter alia, if he is entitled to exercise, or control the exercise of, one third or more of the voting power at any general meeting of the company or another company which has control of it.

In the present case, Simon and two associates (Paul and Barry) have between them 75% of the votes, and therefore control ABC Ltd.

ABC Ltd is therefore an associate of Simon.

Dick James

A person is an associate of any person with whom he is in partnership and of the husband and wife or a relative of any individual with whom he is in partnership.

Therefore, Dick is a former associate of Simon, but is no longer an associate.

Conclusion

Non-associates who voted for the proposals total £155,000.

Non-associates who voted against the proposals total £65,000.

Since more than half, in value, of all non-associates who actually voted were for the proposals, the resolution is deemed to be valid and the proposals are deemed to have been accepted.

Interactive question 2: Mr Hytche

Letter format

All creditors are bound by an arrangement if they were entitled to vote at the meeting (whether present or represented) or if they would have been entitled to vote had they had notice of it (s260(2)(b)).

Mr Hytche had notice of and voted at the meeting to approve the VA and therefore is bound by it.

He cannot take enforcement action in respect of the debt outstanding prior to the VA and he will receive a dividend under the terms of the VA in respect of that debt.

75% in value of those attending and voting in favour of the arrangement is required to approve a VA.

Mr Hytche (as a person entitled to vote at the creditors' meeting) could challenge the decision of the meeting under s262 on the grounds that the VA unfairly prejudices the interests of the creditor or there was a material irregularity at or in relation to the s257 creditors' meeting.

Application under s262 may also be made by the debtor or the nominee.

Application must be made within 28 days of filing of the chair's report on the meeting with the court.

If satisfied, the court can revoke or suspend approval or direct that a further meeting of creditors be held to consider revised proposals or reconsider original proposals.

During the term of the arrangement, if the debtor fails to comply with obligations under the arrangement, a default petition may be presented by the supervisor or any creditor bound by the VA. The effect will be to bring the VA to an end. VA assets will be held on trust for VA creditors.

Mr Hytche could also apply to court under s263(3) on the grounds that he is dissatisfied by any act, omission or decision of the supervisor. The court may:

- Confirm, reverse or modify any act or decision of the supervisor.
- Give him directions.
- Make such order as it thinks fit.

Personal Insolvency

6

Post approval matters

Contents

Introduction
Examination context
Topic List
1. Duties, powers and liabilities of the supervisor
2. Remuneration
3. Statutory returns
4. Variation of the proposal post acceptance
5. Failure of the voluntary arrangement
6. Completion

Summary and Self-test
Answers to Self-test
Answers to Interactive Questions

Personal Insolvency

Introduction

Learning objectives

- Understand the duties, powers and liabilities of the supervisor
- Understand how a supervisor is remunerated
- Identify when an arrangement has failed
- Effect of bankruptcy on a voluntary arrangement
- Procedures on completion of a voluntary arrangement

Tick off
☐
☐
☐
☐
☐

Working context

You may be asked to assist in the ongoing administration of a voluntary arrangement ensuring that the terms of the arrangement are met. It is important to understand the implications of an arrangement not progressing as planned and what should happen if the arrangement fails.

Stop and think

What powers does the supervisor have? Do these differ to a trustee in bankruptcy? What happens if the debtor doesn't adhere to the terms of the proposal? How is the arrangement completed?

POST APPROVAL MATTERS

Examination context

Identifying circumstances where an arrangement has failed and how an arrangement may be varied to avoid failure are popular JIEB exam topics. The implications of bankruptcy for an arrangement has also been tested.

Exam requirements

Past questions to look at include:

2007	Question 1
2007	Question 2
2004	Question 2
2001	Question 4
2000	Question 1 (a)
2000	Question 5
1999	Question 3
1998	Question 4
1998	Question 5
1996	Question 4 (a)
1993	Question 2 (2)

Personal Insolvency

1 Duties, powers and liabilities of the supervisor

Section overview

The supervisor's role is to implement the arrangement and the terms of the arrangement will dictate what steps the supervisor takes.

1.1 Duties of the supervisor

The supervisor's main duty is to ensure that the arrangement proceeds in accordance with the terms of the agreed proposal. In order to do this he should maintain regular contact with the debtor.

There is little in the Act and Rules regarding the supervisor's duties given that the proposal document essentially forms the basis of the relationship between the debtor, supervisor and creditors. In addition to the proposal and statutory provision, the supervisor should also be aware of the professional guidance given by the SIPs and 'Dear IP' notices.

S263(4) contains the general statutory provision relating to the implementation and supervision of an approved arrangement. It is supplemented by the Rules.

The most important requirement is contained in r5.31, which imposes a duty on the supervisor to keep all those with an interest in the arrangement informed as to its progress.

Where the supervisor is required in the arrangement to:

- Carry on the debtor's business or trade (unusual in practice as the debtor will normally carry on his own trade).
- Realise assets of the debtor.
- Otherwise, administer or dispose of any of the debtor's (or estate's) funds.

He must, once in every twelve month period (counting from appointment), prepare an abstract of receipts and payments together with his comments on the progress and effectiveness of the arrangement. This must be sent to the court, the debtor and all bound creditors.

If, in any period of 12 months, he has made no payments and no receipts, he must, at the end of the period, send a statement to that effect to those parties to whom he should have sent an abstract.

If the supervisor is not obliged to prepare accounts and records, he must, not less than once in every period of 12 months beginning with the date of his appointment, send to the court, the debtor and all bound creditors, a report on the progress and efficiency of the arrangement.

R5.32(1) provides that the Secretary of State may, at any time during the course of the voluntary arrangement or after its completion, require the supervisor to produce for inspection:

- his records and accounts in respect of the arrangement.
- copies of abstracts and reports prepared in compliance with r5.31.

The Secretary of State may require production either at the premises of the supervisor or elsewhere, and he may cause any accounts and records produced to him to be audited.

The supervisor must give him such further information and assistance as he needs for the purposes of his audit.

1.2 Powers of the supervisor

The supervisor will obtain his powers from the arrangement. He can protect his interest in land by way of notice where land is registered.

The Act gives very limited powers namely:

- S424 – power to apply to court for an order in respect of transactions defrauding creditors.
- S264(1)(c) – power to present a bankruptcy petition.

- S263(4) – power to apply to court for directions.
- S263(5) – power to apply to apply to court for the transfer of cases.

Given the limited statutory powers it is important that when drafting the proposal the supervisor ensures that he has sufficient powers to put the arrangement into effect. (The detailed requirements of the proposal are contained in Chapter 4). As a guide however the supervisor should be given similar powers as a trustee in bankruptcy albeit that those powers may need to be modified.

If the supervisor finds that he has insufficient powers to deal with any issue post approval of the arrangement, there are steps that can be taken to rectify the situation. He should firstly call a meeting of creditors. (The proposal should have set out the mechanism for so doing). Pursuant to the decision in *Raja v Rubin and Goodman 1999* provided that all the creditors agree it will be possible to amend the arrangement. Alternatively, if there is a variation procedure, provided this is followed amendment will be possible. (See section 4 later in this chapter for more details.)

1.3 Liabilities of the supervisor

The supervisor must be careful because he does not enjoy statutory protection. If he trades on behalf of the debtor he will be liable under general law in respect of any contracts and will need to be careful to avoid liability for tax, trade and business rate debts. The supervisor is also under a duty to exercise reasonable care and skill in the conduct of the voluntary arrangement.

S263 makes it clear that in circumstances where the debtor, creditors or any other person who is dissatisfied by any act, omission or decision of the supervisor they have the power to apply to court. The court has the power to:

- Conform, reverse or modify any act or decision of the supervisor.
- Give directions, or
- Make such other order as it think fit.

Given that s263 gives an effective method of enforcing the duty of a supervisor, no private action can be brought against the supervisor for breach of duty, (*King v Anthony (1999)*). It should, however, be noted that the Human Rights Act 1998 may give rights of action as the supervisor in complying with the directions of the court is arguably a public authority.

As already stated, it is reasonably rare for a supervisor to run a debtor's business, but if a supervisor does get involved it should be noted that he may incur personal liability. If there are employees the arrangement will not terminate the employer/employee relationship (unless there is express provision to that effect either in the proposal or employment contract).

1.4 Removal of the supervisor

It is envisaged that the proposal itself will make provision for the removal of a supervisor and his replacement. There is, however, a fallback provision in IA 1986 if so required. S263 provides for the court to have a general power to appoint a supervisor.

1.5 Bonding

The nominee and supervisor are required to have in force a bond in a form approved by the Secretary of State.

They must hold:

(1) A general penalty sum of £250,000.

(2) A specific penalty sum equal to at least the value of those assets subject to the terms of the arrangement (whether or not those assets are in his possession) including, where under the terms of the arrangement the debtor or a third party is to make payments, the aggregate of any payments to be made.

The minimum specific penalty bond is £5,000 (even where the debtor's assets are less than £5,000) and the maximum specific penalty bond is £5,000,000 (even where the debtor's assets exceed this sum).

Where the nominee subsequently acts as supervisor, there is no requirement for the supervisor to obtain a new specific penalty bond unless there has been an increase in the value of the asses.

2 Remuneration

Section overview

There is no statutory criteria for fixing the remuneration of the nominee and supervisor. The terms of remuneration will be set out in the arrangement as agreed by the creditors. The fees, costs, charges and expenses which may be incurred for the purposes of a voluntary arrangement are set out in r5.33. SIP 9 provides guidance to the nominee and supervisor when seeking agreement to their fees.

2.1 R5.33

The fees, costs, charges and expenses which may be incurred under r5.33 are:

- Any disbursements made by the nominee prior to the arrangement coming into effect, and any remuneration for his services as such agreed between himself and the debtor (or the OR or trustee as the case may be).

- Any fees, costs, charges or expenses which:
    - are sanctioned by the terms of the arrangement, or
    - would be payable, or correspond to those which would be payable, in a bankruptcy.

2.2 R5.3

The proposal must state:

- The amount proposed to be paid to the nominee by way of remuneration and expenses.
- The manner in which it is proposed that the supervisor of the arrangement should be remunerated and his expenses defrayed.

The nominee must be prepared to disclose the basis of his fees to the meeting if called upon to do so.

The supervisor's remuneration is thus a matter for creditors' approval at the meeting. The creditors' meeting has the power to modify any of the terms of the proposal including those relating to the fixing of remuneration.

The terms of the proposal may provide for the establishment of a committee of creditors and may include amongst its functions the fixing of the supervisor's remuneration. Such a committee should be provided with the same information as if it were fixing remuneration in administration.

2.3 SIP 9

Whether the basis of the supervisor's remuneration is determined at the meeting which approves the arrangement or by a committee of creditors, the supervisor should provide details of the charge out rates of all grades of staff, including principals, which are likely to be involved in the case.

Where the supervisor's remuneration is to be agreed by a committee of creditors during the course of the arrangement, the supervisor should provide sufficient supporting information to enable the committee to form a judgement as to whether the proposed fee is reasonable having regard to all the circumstances of the case. An up to date receipts and payments account should always be provided.

Where the fee is to be charged on a time basis, the supervisor should disclose the amount of time spent on the case and the charge out value of the time spent, together with such additional information as may reasonably be required having regard to the size and complexity of the case and the functions conferred on the supervisor under the terms of the arrangement.

Where the basis of the remuneration of the supervisor as set out in the proposal does not require any further approvals by the creditors or any committee of creditors, the supervisor should specify the amount of remuneration he has drawn in accordance with the provisions of the proposals in his subsequent reports to creditors on the progress of the arrangement. Where the fee is based on time costs he should also provide details of the time spent and charge out value to date and any material changes in rates charged for the various grades since the arrangement was approved.

2.4 Expenses and disbursements

Where the supervisor proposes to recover costs which, whilst being in the nature of expenses or disbursements, may include an element of shared or allocated costs (such as room hire, document storage provided by the supervisor's own firm) they must be disclosed and be authorised by those responsible for approving his remuneration.

2.5 SIP 9 Appendix C – creditor's guidance notes

The creditors should be provided with the SIP 9 explanatory note 'A creditor's guide to IP's fees in voluntary arrangements' or the equivalent information in some other suitable format.

The SIP 9 Appendix C contains the following information:

- Explanation that costs are payable out of assets, therefore creditors have a direct interest in cost/remuneration levels. Consequently legislation provides a mechanism for creditors to fix fees.
- Brief description of the nature of the insolvency appointment.
- Brief description of the constitution and function of committees (if appropriate).
- Explanation of:
    - Basis of fees
    - Criteria to be applied
    - Who is responsible for deciding on basis and amount of remuneration.
- Information which should be provided by the IP.
- Rights of creditors if dissatisfied.
- Any other matters relating to fees.

3 Statutory returns

Section overview

The supervisor is required by r5.31 to submit an account of his receipts and payments within two months after the end of 12 months from the date of appointment and every subsequent 12 month period.

Receipts and payments accounts should be sent to:

- Court.
- The debtor.
- Bound creditors.

Interactive question 1: Duties

You are the supervisor of a voluntary arrangement. Outline the nature of your statutory obligation to keep accounts and explain the circumstances in which those accounts may be the subject of an audit.

See **Answer** at the end of this chapter.

4 Variation of the proposal post acceptance

Section overview

It is possible that the arrangement creditors may want to vary the terms of the proposal post acceptance. Most commonly this would be to avoid having to present a default petition where there has been a failure of the arrangement in strict accordance with its terms, but where the creditors want to continue with the arrangement. Another common reason for amendment will arise if a third party comes forward to offer a lump sum in full and final settlement of the debtor's obligations, or there is a change in the debtor's circumstances.

4.1 Procedure where proposal provides for variation

The proposal may expressly provide for post-acceptance amendments and this situation was considered in the case of *Thompson and Horrocks v John Lawson Broome*. The court held that a properly drawn clause giving a power of variation in a voluntary arrangement is valid. Doubts had previously been expressed as to whether it would be necessary for all of the creditors to vote in favour of such variation, or whether a majority in excess of three-quarters in value of the creditors present in person or by proxy and voting on the resolution would suffice (the proportion necessary to approve a proposal).

In *Thompson and Horrocks v John Lawson Broome* approximately 96% in value voted in favour and 4% voted for rejection. Mr. Justice Hart held that the variation could take effect, but made it clear that careful drafting of a variation clause would be necessary. It is advisable that any such clause should incorporate a provision to allow minority creditors to appeal against an amendment (eg on the basis that the variation is unfairly prejudicial to them).

Where the IVA Protocol is used, point 10.2 provides for the supervisor to reduce dividends by up to 15% from the original proposal without reference to creditors and to reflect changing income and/or expenditure.

4.2 Procedure where proposal makes no provision for variation

If the proposal does not contain any provision for amendment, it is a matter of some debate as to the extent to which the proposal can be modified. If an application is made by the debtor or supervisor under s263, it is likely that the court will direct that a creditors' meeting be held. Once again, there is some debate as to the percentage of creditors necessary to approve such a modification. In the case of *Raja v Rubin & Goodman 1999* it was held that, in the absence of a variation clause, 100% of the affected creditors must be in favour of a proposed amendment.

The question also arises as to the remedy available to an aggrieved minority creditor. A creditor could apply under s263(3) on the basis that he is dissatisfied by the decision of the supervisor (but not s262 which only applies to the original s257 meeting). The court would be likely to treat the application as it would if it were under s262.

Alternatively the existing voluntary arrangement could be brought to an end and a new proposal put before creditors. (If an interim order had been sought within the last 12 months the debtor would have to proceed without the protection of an interim order).

5 Failure of the voluntary arrangement

Section overview

To ascertain whether or not a voluntary arrangement has failed it will be necessary to look at the terms of the arrangement. A well drafted proposal will have made it clear what will have amounted to failure and the consequences of such. The proposal must be carefully drafted or even trivial defaults may result in failure.

5.1 Bankruptcy and the voluntary arrangement

The grounds for petition are set out in s276(1):

- Failure to comply with obligations under the voluntary arrangement.
- Giving false or misleading material information or making a material omission in any document at the creditors' meeting.
- Failure to comply with the supervisor's reasonable requests.

Re Keenan

The case provided that default by a debtor does not need to be culpable. A debtor therefore who fails to make income payments because she lost her job through no fault of her own is as much in default as a debtor who wilfully and deliberately flouts the terms of the arrangement. Either way the supervisor can petition the court for bankruptcy. The supervisor has an obligation to petition where the creditors are not prepared to vary the terms of the arrangement.

The court will retain discretion as to whether or not to make the order. An example of when the court may seek to exercise that discretion in favour of the debtor would be when the majority in value of the creditors are in favour of the VA continuing.

The petition is in prescribed form. The supervisor (or creditor) must ensure that there are sufficient details about the ground(s) of the petition to enable the court to make the order.

A well-drafted proposal should create an express trust of all voluntary arrangement assets. It would appear however that even if no express trust is created one will be created by implication: *Re Bradley Hole (1995): NT Gallagher & Son Ltd (2002)*.

Case law (prior to 2002) took the view that whether or not the VA trust survived bankruptcy depended upon whether the petition had been presented by a non-bound creditor (s264(1)(a)) or the supervisor/bound creditor (s264(1)(c)). (Petitions presented under s264(1)(a) resulted in survival of the VA, those under s264 (1)(c) failure).

Whether or not the trust survives is important. If the trust survives the assets subject to the arrangement remain available for the voluntary arrangement creditors. If the trust fails the assets fall into the bankruptcy estate to be distributed amongst those creditors within the VA (who can prove in bankruptcy) **and** those excluded from it.

The present position is now governed by the C/A judgment in *NT Gallagher & Son Ltd 2002*. The Court held:

- Where a CVA or IVA provides for monies or assets to be paid to or transferred or held for the benefit of arrangement creditors a trust is created.
- The effect of (liquidation or bankruptcy) on the trust depends upon the provisions of the VA.
- By default if no express provision is made in the VA the trust will survive.
- The arrangement creditors can prove in (liquidation or bankruptcy) for so much of their debt as remains after payment of what has been or will be recovered under the trust.

Personal Insolvency

The advice therefore should be to create an express trust of VA assets and to provide for the effect of failure of the VA in the proposal.

The trustee in bankruptcy will take possession of non-arrangement assets, realise such assets and distribute on behalf of all creditors. Credit will have to be given by arrangement creditors for sums received under the VA.

The supervisor must notify the Secretary of State that the VA has failed and give details of what further action the supervisor intends to take (ie petition for bankruptcy).

Interactive question 2: Peter Daly

Peter Daly entered into a voluntary arrangement with his creditors fourteen months ago. You have been acting as supervisor of the arrangement.

The basis of the arrangement was as follows:

(1) The matrimonial home was to be sold, realising equity of £84,000, half of which was to be paid into the arrangement. The other half represents Mrs Daly's share of the property.

(2) The couple's two children were to be moved to the local comprehensive school, saving school fees of £15,000 per annum which were to be paid to the supervisor.

(3) Mr Daly, being 56 years of age, was to realise a pension policy, paying the lump sum, estimated to be £47,000, into the arrangement. His other two pension policies were to be excluded from the arrangement.

(4) Whilst no regular payments from income were to be made by Mr Daly, any bonuses received from his employment were to be paid into the arrangement.

To date the matrimonial home has yet to be realised. In fact, Mrs Daly is now saying that she didn't agree to the house being sold and that she will resist any attempts to sell it.

She is also refusing to move the children from their current schools so no payments in lieu of school fees have been made into the arrangement.

Mr Daly has realised a pension policy, however the lump sum received was only £8,500. You believe that Mr Daly has realised a different policy to that disclosed to his creditors, however he is refusing to co-operate with your requests for further information.

No monies have been received in respect of bonuses. You believe that Mr Daly has instructed his employers to withhold bonus payments due until the term of the arrangement expires in 18 months time.

The arrangement contained a clause instructing the supervisor to petition for the bankruptcy of Mr Daly in the event of default or failure of the arrangement. Funds have been accrued for that purpose.

Mr Daley has incurred credit card debts during the period of the arrangement. These creditors are threatening to take bankruptcy proceedings against Mr Daley.

Requirement

Write a letter to Mr Daly outlining the current position and detailing what will happen to the arrangement in the event of Mr Daly being made bankrupt and the effect on his creditors.

See **Answer** at the end of this chapter.

6 Completion

Section overview

When the arrangement has been fully implemented the supervisor should conclude the administration as expeditiously as possible.

Pursuant to r5.34 the supervisor must send to all creditors the following information within 28 days of completion:

- Notice of completion or notice of non completion.
- Report to summarise all receipts and payments. It should explain any difference between the actual position and the voluntary arrangement projection.

Supervisor must send copies of all notices and reports to Secretary of State and the court. The supervisor will not be discharged until he has done so.

On receiving notice of the completion, termination or revocation of the VA, the Secretary of State will remove details of the arrangement from the register.

Dissatisfied creditors or the debtor can apply for directions under s263.

Summary and Self-test

Summary

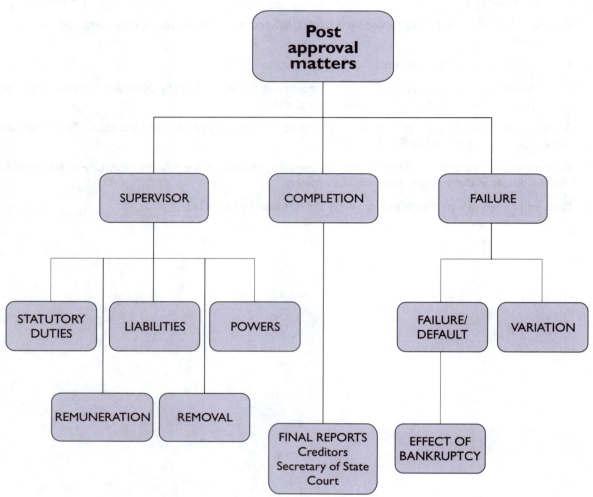

Self-test

Answer the following questions.

1. How often must the supervisor send a progress report to creditors?
2. What powers does a creditor have if he is dissatisfied ~~with any~~ with any decision of the supervisor?
3. Who may present a default petition?
4. What are the grounds for the presentation of a default petition?
5. What matters regarding remuneration must be stated in the proposal under r5.3?
6. What are the duties of the supervisor on completion of the arrangement?

Now, go back to the Learning Objectives in the Introduction. If you are satisfied that you have achieved these, please tick them off.

Answers to Self-test

1. Once in every twelve month period (counting from appointment).

2. Under s263 he may apply to court. The court has the power to:
   - Confirm, reverse or modify any act or decision of the supervisor.
   - Give directions.
   - Make such other order as it thinks fit.

3. The supervisor and any bound creditor.

4. Failure to comply with obligations under the voluntary arrangement.

   Giving false or misleading material information or making a material omission in any document at the creditors' meeting.

   Failure to comply with the supervisor's reasonable requests.

5. The amount proposed to be paid to the nominee by way of remuneration and expenses.

   The manner in which it is proposed that the supervisor of the arrangement should be remunerated and his expenses defrayed.

6. R5.34 – the supervisor must, within 28 days, send to all creditors, the Secretary of State and the court:
   - Notice of completion or notice of non-completion.
   - Report to summarise all receipts and payments. It should explain any difference between the actual position and the voluntary arrangement projection.

Answers to Interactive Questions

Interactive question 1: Duties

R5.31 provides that where the voluntary arrangement authorises or requires the supervisor to:

- Carry on the debtor's business or to trade on his behalf or in his name, or
- Realise assets of the debtor (where an undischarged bankrupt) belonging to the estate, or
- Otherwise to administer or dispose of any funds of the debtor or the estate.

He must keep accounts and records of all receipts and payments of money.

He must, not less often than once in every 12 months beginning with the date of his appointment, prepare an abstract of such receipts and payments and send copies of it accompanied by his comments on the progress and efficiency of the arrangement to:

- The court.
- The debtor.
- All those of the debtor's creditors who are bound by the arrangement.

If, in any period of 12 months, he had made no payments and no receipts he must at the end of the period send a statement to that effect to those parties to whom he should have sent an abstract.

An abstract of receipts and payments must relate to a period beginning with the date of the supervisor's appointment or (as the case may be) the day following the end of the past period for which an abstract was prepared and copies of the abstract must be sent out within two months of the end of the period to which the abstract relates.

If the supervisor is not obliged to prepare accounts and records, he must, not less than once in every 12 months beginning with the date of his appointment send to the Court, the debtor and all bound creditors, a report on the progress and efficiency of the arrangement.

R5.32(1) provides that the Secretary of State may at any time during the course of the voluntary arrangement or after its completion require the supervisor to produce for inspection:

- His records and accounts in respect of the arrangement.
- Copies of abstracts and reports prepared in compliance with r5.31.

The Secretary of State may require production either at the premises of the supervisor or elsewhere, and he may cause any accounts and records produced to him to be audited.

The supervisor must give him such further information and assistance as he needs for the purposes of his audit.

Interactive question 2: Peter Daly

Arrangement appears to have failed and there are many examples of default:

- Non-payment of funds into VA from house, school fees, bonuses, pensions.
- Debtor has failed to co-operate with the supervisor's requests for information.
- Wife would appear to be preventing arrangement from continuing.
- Debtor has incurred further credit – this may be contrary to the terms of the VA.

Mr Daly could be made bankrupt in two ways:

1. Creditors' petition presented by a non-bound creditor arising since the start of the arrangement on grounds of inability to pay debts s264(1)(a).

2. Default petition presented by the supervisor or any creditor bound by the VA. The grounds of the petition could be as follows s264(1)(c):

    - Failure to comply with obligations under the arrangement.
    - Giving false or misleading material information or making a material omission in any document or at the creditors' meeting.
    - Failure to comply with the supervisor's reasonable requests.

The effect of a bankruptcy petition on the VA is the same whoever presents the petition.

The assets will be held on trust for the arrangement creditors. This will either be an express trust (contained in the proposal itself) or an implied trust (*NT Gallagher & Sons Ltd 2002*).

The voluntary arrangement assets will be held for arrangement creditors and will not form part of the bankruptcy estate. Any assets excluded from the arrangement will form part of the bankruptcy estate.

VA creditors may prove for any shortfall on their debt in the bankruptcy.

Personal Insolvency

7

Introduction to bankruptcy

▸ ▸ ▸ ▸ ▸ ▸ ▸ ▸ ▸ ▸ ▸ ▸ ▸

Contents

Introduction
Examination context
Topic List
1   Bankruptcy procedure
2   Creditor's petition
3   Debtor's petition
4   Supervisor's petition
5   Investigation into possible IVA
6   Interim receiver
7   Special manager

Summary and Self-test
Answers to Self-test
Answer to Interactive Question

Personal Insolvency

Introduction

Learning objectives

- Identify who may present a bankruptcy petition
- Understand the procedure for obtaining a bankruptcy order
- List the grounds for presenting a bankruptcy petition
- Understand when an interim receiver may be appointed

Tick off
☐
☐
☐
☐

Working context

Many individuals are declared bankrupt each year, it is likely therefore that you will be asked to assist with bankruptcy cases in a work environment. IP's are often asked to advise creditors on the steps they can take to recover a debt. One option is to present a petition for the bankruptcy of the debtor. It is important therefore to understand the relevant procedure to follow in this regard.

Stop and think

Why would an individual wish to declare themselves bankrupt? How can a creditor show that an individual is insolvent? What does an interim receiver do?

INTRODUCTION TO BANKRUPTCY 7

Examination context

Whilst the procedure for bankruptcy is not a very examinable topic in the JIEB exam this chapter does provide essential background information.

Exam requirements

Past questions to look at include:

1996   Question 5 (b)

Personal Insolvency

1 Bankruptcy procedure

Section overview

Bankruptcies are commenced by the court making a court order. A petition for a bankruptcy order may be presented to court by either:

- A creditor
- The debtor
- The supervisor (or bound creditor) of a VA

The legislation governing bankruptcies may be found in Part IX IA (s264 to s385) and Part 6 and 6A of the Rules (r6.1 to r6A.8).

1.1 Commencement

A bankruptcy is deemed to commence on the date of the bankruptcy order (note it is not back dated to the date of the petition as in compulsory liquidation).

1.2 Advantages and disadvantages of bankruptcy

See 1.10 Chapter 3 for a list of the advantages and disadvantages of bankruptcy for a debtor.

For creditors, the costs of bankruptcy are generally higher than other insolvency options (due to Secretary of State fees etc) and therefore this will impact on the returns expected by creditors. However, bankruptcy will be favoured by a creditor where there is a need for a full investigation into the affairs of the bankrupt. (See Chapter 8 for more details).

2 Creditor's petition

Section overview

In order for a creditor to present a petition the debt must be:

- Owed to the creditor
- Exceed the bankruptcy level (currently £750)
- Be unsecured

The debt can be for a present or future debt.

2.1 Secured creditors

It is still possible to petition on a secured debt (s269) if:

- The petition contains a statement by the person having the right to enforce the security that he is willing, in the event of a bankruptcy order being made, to give up his security for the benefit of the bankrupt's creditors, or

- The petition is expressed not to be made in respect of the secured part of the debt and contains a statement by that person of the estimated value at the date of the petition of the security for the secured part of the debt.

2.2 Grounds of the petition

The grounds of the petition will be the debtor's inability to pay his debts. The creditor must be able to prove to the court that the debtor is unable to pay his debts or has no reasonable prospect of paying them.

INTRODUCTION TO BANKRUPTCY

This will be shown by:

- **Statutory demand (s268(1)(a))**: The petitioning creditor to whom the debt is owed:
  - Has served on the debtor a demand in the prescribed form requiring him to pay the debt or to secure or compound for it to the satisfaction of the creditor.
  - At least 21 days have elapsed since the demand was served, and
  - The demand has neither been complied with nor set aside in accordance with the rules.

- **Unsatisfied judgement execution (s268(1)(b))**: Execution or other process issued in respect of the debt on a judgement or order of any court in favour of the petitioning creditor(s) to whom the debt is owed, has been returned unsatisfied in whole or in part. (Obtaining a judgement on a debt and then levying execution which is unsatisfied).

2.3 Statutory demand

A statutory demand is a document prepared by a creditor in the prescribed form requiring the debtor to pay the debt referred to within 21 days. Alternatively, the debtor can provide some security for the debt or come to some other arrangement for the payment of the debt with the creditor.

A demand is deemed to be necessary as the creditor must prove that the debtor owed a debt of at least £750. The debt of £750 must be due at the date of presentation of the petition. Even if the debt is satisfied post presentation, the court still retains discretion to make a bankruptcy order on the petition.

There are three forms of statutory demands for a debt:

- Presently due but not based on a judgment.
- Presently due based on a judgment or order of the court.
- Due at a future time.

The creditor must do all that is reasonable to bring the demand to the debtor's attention and personal service is clearly preferable r6.3(2).

Under r6.3(3), where the creditor has reasonable cause to believe:

(a) That the debtor has absconded or is keeping out of the way with a view to avoiding service and
(b) There is no reasonable prospect of the sum being recovered by execution or other process,

The creditor may advertise the statutory demand in such manner as he thinks fit.

A debtor is deemed to be unable to pay his debts if at least 21 days have elapsed since a demand was served on him and he has not complied with it. Provided no application to set aside a statutory demand is made, at the expiration of the 21 day period the creditor can proceed to present a petition for bankruptcy.

An application to set aside a demand must be made within 18 days after service of the demand or advertisement under r6.3(3). The debtor must show sufficient cause for the setting aside for example, the:

- Debt is disputed in whole or part.
- Debt is secured.
- Debtor has a counter claim which is at least equal to the demand.

If the court is not satisfied that the demand should be set aside, it may make an order authorising the creditor to present a bankruptcy petition at a specified time (r6.5).

As an alternative, a petition can be based on an unsatisfied execution and a debt above the minimum level.

2.4 The petition

There are three conditions, which must be satisfied before the court will make a bankruptcy order. The:

- Debtor must be domiciled or personally present or carry on business in England and Wales on the day on which the petition is presented or at any time within the previous three years (s265(1)).

Personal Insolvency

- Debt owed by the debtor must be £750 or more and be a liquidated sum payable now or at some certain future time (s267).
- Debtor must be unable to pay the debt or have no reasonable prospect of being able to pay.

There are four forms of petition:

- Failure to comply with a statutory demand, debt payable immediately (Form 6.7).
- Failure to comply with a statutory demand, debt payable at a future time (Form 6.8).
- Unsatisfied execution of a judgment debts (Form 6.9).
- Default in connection with an IVA (Form 6.10).

The creditor must ensure personal service and lodge an affidavit of service at court. The petition is not advertised unless the court orders substituted service by this method.

Under the EU Regulation for the court to have jurisdiction to hear insolvency proceedings (which extends to a petition for bankruptcy) the debtor's centre of main interests must be in England and Wales.

'Centre of main interests' is not defined. Recital 13 provides that the centre of main interests should correspond to the place where the debtor conducts the administration of his interests on a regular basis and is therefore ascertainable by third parties.

Guidance on the meaning and application of the regulation can be found in case law *Shierson v Vlieland-Boddy 2005*.

- Debtor's main centre of interests to be determined at time court required to decide whether to open insolvency proceedings, ie at the hearing of the petition.
- Determination to be in light of facts as they are at the relevant time for determination. (Includes historical facts which led to position as it was at date of determination).
- Can only be one centre.
- Court must have regard to fact that centre of main interests must be ascertainable by third parties.
- No principle of immutability, a debtor is free to choose where he carries on his activities.
- Debtor free to choose his centre of main interests for self-serving purposes but if there is a suspicion that the centre has changed to avoid the application of the insolvency rules the court will need to be satisfied that the change is based on substance, not illusion and that it has the necessary element of permanence.

Once a request to lodge insolvency proceedings is made in a member state where a debtor has his centre of main interest the court in that member state will retain jurisdiction to hearing proceedings regardless of the debtor moving his centre before proceedings actually open.

The petition must contain the following information (r6.7):

- **Details of debtor** (so far as within the petitioner's knowledge).

  Name.

  Names, other than his true names in which he carries on or carried on business at the date of the debt or since and names of any others with whom he has carried on business.

  Place of residence.

  Occupation.

  Nature of business and address(es) which he carries on or was carrying on at the date of the debt or since.

  Whether the debtor has his centre of main interests or an establishment in another member state.

  If to the petitioner's knowledge the debtor has used any name other than his true name that fact shall be stated in the petition (r6.7(3)).

- **Details of the debt**

  Amount of debt and fact it is owed to the petitioner.

Consideration for the debt (or if none, the way in which the debt arises).

When the debt was incurred or became due.

Amount, rate and grounds of claim for any interest or other charge on the debt.

That the debt is unsecured.

If petition is based on a statutory demand the amount claimed cannot exceed that in the demand.

- **Grounds of petition**

    Petition on a present debt: That the debt is for a liquidated sum payable immediately and the debtor appears unable to pay it.

    Petition on a future debt: That the debt is for a liquidated sum payable at some certain future time (that time to be specified) and the debtor appears to have no reasonable prospect of being able to pay it.

    Petition on a judgement debt: Court from which the execution or other process was issued and particulars of the (unsatisfied) return must be given.

- **Details of statutory demand** (where appropriate)

    Date of demand.

    Manner of service.

    Statement that to best of creditor's knowledge and belief:
    - Demand neither set aside nor complied with.
    - No outstanding application to set aside.

2.5 Presentation and filing of the petition

R6.9 of the Insolvency Rules 1986 governs which court the petition should be presented in. Generally this will be the County Court for the district in which the debtor has resided or carried on business for the longest period in the last six months.

In four situations the petition must be presented in the High Court:

- Petitions presented by Crown Departments. Here the statutory demand must state that any subsequent petition will be presented in that court.
- Where the debtor has resided or carried on business for the greater part of six months prior to presentation of the petition in the London insolvency district.
- If the debtor is not resident in England and Wales.
- If the petitioner is unable to ascertain residence or place of business of the debtor.

The procedure to follow is:

- The creditor must deliver to the court:
    - The petition and copies:
        - For service on the debtor.
        - To be exhibited to the affidavit verifying that service.
        - For service on any IVA Supervisor in office and who is not the petitioner.
    - An affidavit verifying the petition in Form 6.13. The affidavit must:
        - Have a copy petition exhibited to it.
        - Be sworn by the petitioner or some other responsible person with knowledge of the requisite matters authorised by the petitioner.
        - Is prima facie evidence of the truth of the petition.

Personal Insolvency

- An affidavit of service of statutory demand in Form 6.11. The affidavit will have a copy of the statutory demand exhibited to it. The affidavit of service must be sworn by:
    - If service of demand acknowledged in writing by debtor/debtor's agent: creditor/creditor's agent swears and exhibits acknowledgement to the affidavit.
    - If no acknowledgement and service was personal service: affidavit sworn by server.
    - Where a judgement creditor has advertised the statutory demand, creditor (or anyone else with a direct personal knowledge of the circumstances) will swear, exhibiting copy advertisement to the affidavit.
    - In any other case anyone with direct personal knowledge of service swears using Form 6.12 which will explain attempts made to effect personal service.
- Receipt for the deposit payable on presentation of the petition (currently £430).
- The court fee (currently £190).

▸ The court will then:
  - Endorse date and time of filing on petition and copies.
  - Fix venue for hearing and again endorse on copies.
  - Send to the Chief Land Registrar notice of the petition together with a request that it may be registered in the register of pending actions (r6.13).

A sealed copy of the petition must now be served personally on the debtor by the petitioning creditor or his solicitor or by a person instructed by either of them, or an officer of the court.

The court can however order substituted service.

The affidavit of service must be filed in court along with:

▸ A sealed copy of the petition.
▸ (If appropriate) a sealed copy of the court order allowing substituted service.

If the debtor dies pre-service the court may order service to be effected on his Personal Representatives (PRs) or such other person as the court thinks fit (eg recently bereaved widow).

By r6.18(1) the hearing must not take place until 14 days have elapsed from the date of service of the petition.

The court may, on such terms as it thinks fit, hear the petition at an earlier date, if it appears that the debtor has absconded, or the court is satisfied that it is a proper case for an expedited hearing, or the debtor consents to a hearing within the 14 days (r6.18(2)).

If the creditor will not be able to serve in time he must apply to court for another venue giving reasons why the petition has not been served (r6.28(1)). However, the creditor will only get costs if the court so orders.

2.6 Effect of the petition

Once a petition is presented the court may stay any action, execution or other legal processes against the property or person of the debtor.

2.7 Responses to the petition

The debtor can do the following once a petition is served upon him:

▸ Nothing.
▸ Pay the debt.
▸ Request a Debtor Relief Order. If under r4A.25 the petitioner consents to the debtor making an application for a DRO then the court can refer the case to an approved intermediary, stay the bankruptcy proceedings and forward to the intermediary a copy order petition and statutory demand. If the DRO is made the petition can be dismissed.

INTRODUCTION TO BANKRUPTCY

- Offer to secure or compound the debt. Again the creditor should be warned in regard to s271(3) (dismissal of the application)
- Apply for an interim order under s252 (and make a proposal for a voluntary arrangement to nominee):
    - Once an interim order is made no bankruptcy petition may be presented or continued with (s252(2)(a)).
    - Even at the application stage the court has the discretion to stay any legal process (s254(1) and (2)).
- Oppose the petition (r6.21). Where the debtor intends to oppose the petition he must file in court, at least seven days pre-hearing notice of grounds of objection and serve a copy on petitioning creditor or his solicitor.

Note. Failure to comply with r6.21 does not prevent the debtor from defending himself at the hearing.

2.8 Pre-hearing steps

Petition can be amended with leave of the court (r6.22).

Where the petition is on a future debt then under r6.17 the debtor may apply to court for an order that the creditor give security for the debtor's costs.

Any creditors intending to attend the hearing must give the petitioner notice in Form 6.20 by 16.00 hours on the business day before the hearing date.

- A creditor failing to comply may only attend hearing with leave of the court.
- Notice states identity of creditor, amount and nature of debt, contact telephone number and whether creditor intends to oppose or support the petition.
- By r6.24 the petitioner must, on the date of the hearing, hand in a list of the creditors who have given notice in Form 6.20.

Note. There is no requirement for advertising the petition, unlike a compulsory liquidation.

2.9 The hearing

The following may appear at the hearing (r6.18.):

- The petitioning creditor.
- The debtor.
- A creditor who has given notice of intention to support the petition (r6.23) in Form 6.20.
- The supervisor of any voluntary arrangements in force.

By r6.26 if the petitioning creditor fails to appear at the hearing, he is then barred from presenting a petition in respect of the same debt again, unless the court gives leave.

For an order to be made, the petitioner must prove that:

- 14 days have elapsed since service of the petition.
- The conditions in s271(1) are satisfied. S271(1) requires that the debt is payable and has neither been paid or secured or compounded for. In the case of a future debt, the creditor must be able to show the debtor had no reasonable prospect of paying.

To satisfy s271(1), the creditor will have to provide an affidavit verifying the petition and a certificate that the debt is still outstanding as at the date of the hearing.

The court may:

- Dismiss the petition. Under s271(3) it may do this if satisfied:
    - Debtor able to pay all his debts (taking into account contingent and prospective liabilities) or
    - Creditor has unreasonably refused debtor's offer to secure or compound.

Personal Insolvency

- ▶ Stay the petition eg. Petition based on judgement debt and debtor intends to appeal.
- ▶ Permit petitioner (who must apply by affidavit) to withdraw petition.
- ▶ Court can replace a petitioner with another creditor who is present at the hearing (Substitution of petitioner or 'Change of Carriage 'of petition).
- ▶ Adjourn.
- ▶ Make a bankruptcy order. This:
  - Will require bankrupt to attend on the Official Receiver forthwith.
  - May include a provision staying any action or proceedings against the bankrupt.

2.10 Formalities on the making of the order

Court sends two sealed copies of the bankruptcy order to the Official Receiver (OR).

The OR keeps one copy and forwards the other to the bankrupt forthwith.

The OR will send notice of the making of the order to the Chief Land Registrar. This is for registration in the register of writs and orders affecting land.

The OR will also advertise the order in the Gazette and may also advertise the order in such other manner as he thinks fit.

The order itself will require the bankrupt to attend on the OR as soon as reasonably practicable.

3 Debtor's petition

Section overview

A debtor's petition may only be presented on one ground – that the debtor is unable to pay his debts (s272(1)). This is shown by the debtor filing with the petition a statement of affairs.

3.1 The petition

The petition must be in the prescribed form (Form 6.27) and contain the following information (r6.38 to 6.39):

- ▶ Name (and any other name he has at any time used), place of residence, occupation (if any).
- ▶ The name or names in which he carries on business, if other than his true name, and whether, in the case of any business of a specified nature, he carries it on alone or with others.
- ▶ Nature of his business and address(es) of his business(es).
- ▶ Any name or names, other than his true name, in which he has carried on business in the period in which any of his bankruptcy debts were incurred and in the case of any such business whether he carried it on alone or with others.
- ▶ Any address or addresses at which he has resided or carried on business during that period.
- ▶ Statement that petitioner is unable to pay his debts.
- ▶ Request that bankruptcy order be made.
- ▶ Particulars of any insolvency proceedings in respect of the debtor in the last five years.
- ▶ Name and address of supervisor of existing voluntary arrangement (where appropriate).

3.2 Filing of the petition

The debtor will file the following documents in court:

- Three copies of the petition:
    1. One is returned to the petitioner endorsed with venue of the hearing.
    2. One is sent to the OR.
    3. One is retained by the court to be given to any IP appointed to enquire and report into the possibility of a voluntary arrangement.
- Two copies of statement of affairs:
    - One is sent to the OR.
    - One is retained by the court (for IP as above).
- Affidavit verifying the statement of affairs.
- Receipt for deposit payable on presentation of petition (currently £360).
- Court fee (£190).

Court will now:

- Here the petition as soon as reasonably practicable or fix a venue and endorse on the petitions.
- Note: If an existing voluntary arrangement is in place, court will fix a venue and give the supervisor at least 14 days notice of it.
- Send to the Chief Land Registrar forthwith notice of the petition for registration in the register of pending actions.

3.3 Effect of filing the petition

The court may stay proceedings and appoint an interim receiver (see later in this chapter) as on a creditor's petition.

3.4 Statement of Affairs

The statement of affairs must be submitted in Form 6.28 and verified by affidavit.

R6.41 defines the content by reference to the prescribed Form 6.28 which requires details of the following:

- List of secured creditors (name, address of creditor, amount owed, nature and value of assets subject to security).
- List of unsecured creditors (name, address of creditor, amount claimed by creditor, amount debtor 'thinks' he owes).
- Inventory of assets, including bank and building society accounts (personal, joint and business), savings, motor vehicles, other assets.
- Name, age (if under 18) and relationship to debtor of any dependants.
- Details of any distress levied against the debtor.
- Details of any attempts made to come to any agreement with creditors. Debtor's opinion as to whether it is likely that a voluntary arrangement will be acceptable to creditors.
- Statement of means (income and expenditure).

3.5 Pre-hearing steps

If there is an existing voluntary arrangement and the petition requests the supervisor to become trustee that IP must, not less than two days before the hearing, file a report in court (r6.42(7)).

The report will give particulars of a date on which he gave written notification to the creditors bound by the arrangement of the intention to seek his appointment as trustee.

The date must be at least ten days pre the date of filing of the report.

Details of any response from the creditors must also be given.

3.6 The hearing

The court has discretion whether or not to make a bankruptcy order on the hearing.

If the debtor's debts are below £40,000 and he has a minimum level of assets of £4,000, the court must not make a bankruptcy order. The court should appoint an insolvency practitioner to prepare a report under s273. It then becomes incumbent on the practitioner to report back to the court on whether or not the debtor is willing to enter into a voluntary arrangement and on whether or not a meeting of the debtor's creditors should be convened. If the report does suggest that an arrangement would be appropriate, the court has the power to make an interim order of its own motion. If the report does not support an arrangement, the court will make the bankruptcy order.

Under s274A the court could refer the debtor to an approved intermediary to consider the merits of a Debtor Relief Order.

The court may also dismiss the petition – this would happen if the debtor fails to make out the grounds.

3.7 Formalities upon making of the order

Court sends two sealed copies of the bankruptcy order to the OR.

The OR keeps one copy and forwards the other to the bankrupt as soon as reasonably practicable.

The OR will send notice of the making of the order to the Chief Land Registrar. This is for registration in the register of writs and orders affecting land.

The OR will also advertise the order in the Gazette and may advertise the order in such other manner as he thinks fit.

4 Supervisor's petition

Section overview

The supervisor or any bound creditor may present a default petition pursuant to s264(1)(c).

4.1 Grounds

There are three grounds for presenting a default petition:

- Failure to comply with obligations under the VA.
- Giving false or misleading material information or making a material omission in any statement at the creditors' meeting.
- Failure to comply with the supervisor's reasonable requests.

See Chapter 6 for more information.

7 INTRODUCTION TO BANKRUPTCY

Interactive question: Mary Watts

Mary Watts entered into a voluntary arrangement 14 months ago.

As supervisor of the arrangement you have been very disappointed with Mary Watts' attitude. To date she has failed to comply with the terms of the arrangement and has repeatedly ignored your requests for further information.

You are also aware that she has incurred further credit, contrary to the terms of the arrangement and a number of creditors are in fact threatening bankruptcy proceedings against her.

Requirement

In what circumstances and by whom, can Mary Watts be made bankrupt?

See **Answer** at the end of this chapter.

5 Investigation into possible IVA

Section overview

The court may appoint an IP to enquire and report into the feasibility of a voluntary arrangement. The conditions are:

- The aggregate of unsecured bankruptcy debts are less than the small bankruptcies level (£40,000).
- The value of the estate is equal to or exceeds the minimum amount (£4,000).
- The debtor has not been adjudged bankrupt or entered into a composition or scheme in the last five years from the date of presentation of the petition.
- It would be appropriate to appoint a person to prepare a s274 report.

5.1 Appointment

The court will appoint an IP to prepare the report and ultimately to act as supervisor. A £360 fee is payable to the IP by the Insolvency Proceedings (Fees) Order 2009.

An application for the appointment of an interim receiver (see later) may be made at this stage by a debtor, a creditor or the IP.

Once the IP has been notified, the court will fix the venue for the hearing to consider the IP's report. The debtor will also be notified of the hearing.

5.2 IP's report

The IP must state the following matters in his report (s274):

- Whether the debtor is willing to make a proposal for a VA.
- Whether, in his opinion, a meeting of creditors should be held to consider the proposal.
- Date, time and place of the proposed meeting.

Personal Insolvency

6 Interim receiver

Section overview

An interim receiver may be appointed at any time after the presentation of a bankruptcy petition and before the making of the bankruptcy order. Generally the OR will be appointed as interim receiver, however, an IP may be appointed provided that they consent to act as such.

6.1 Procedure for appointment

A creditor of the debtor may apply to the court for the appointment of an interim receiver.

The application is made by way of an affidavit giving the grounds, the estimated value of the estate, whether a voluntary arrangement is in force and whether the OR has been given a copy of the application.

The grounds for an application are 'it is necessary for the protection of the debtor's property'.

The applicant sends the application and affidavit to the person proposed to be the interim receiver.

Before the court will make an order the applicant must deposit or secure such sum as the court directs to cover the remuneration and expenses of the interim receiver. The interim receiver cannot come back to the court for more funds if this initial amount proves insufficient.

The court will draw up the order appointing the interim receiver and two sealed copies will be sent to them. The interim receiver will send one copy to the debtor.

6.2 Functions and powers of the interim receiver

The function of an interim receiver is to take immediate possession of the debtor's property or part of it if the court has limited the scope of their powers.

The interim receiver has all the rights, powers, duties and indemnities of a receiver and manager.

The court can however direct that an interim receiver's powers are restricted in any respect.

If the OR is acting as interim receiver they may apply to the court under s370 for the appointment of a special manager.

6.3 Effect of appointment

The debtor must give the interim receiver an inventory of his property and provide such additional information and attend on the interim receiver at such times as he shall reasonably require (s286(5)).

Creditors may not commence any action or legal proceedings against the debtor without leave of the court (s285(3)).

6.4 Termination of appointment

The appointment of an interim receiver may be terminated by:

▶ An application by the OR, debtor or creditor.
▶ On the making of a bankruptcy order.
▶ On dismissal of the bankruptcy petition.

7 Special manager

Section overview

The court may appoint a special manager of the bankrupt's estate or business under s370 where an interim receiver has been installed and it appears that it is in the interests of creditors that such an appointment be made or where the OR has been made receiver of the bankrupt's estate on the making of a bankruptcy order.

7.1 Procedure

Application for appointment may be made by the OR or trustee of the bankrupt's estate where it appears that the nature of the estate, property or business, or the interests of the creditors generally, require the appointment of another person to manage the estate, property or business.

The application is accompanied by a report setting out:

- The reasons for the application.
- An estimate of the value of the estate, property or business which the special manager is to manage.

The court will make an order specifying the duration of the appointment (for a specified time or until the occurrence of a specified event) r6.167(2).

The powers of the special manager will be set out in the court order (may include any of the powers exercisable by the trustee).

The remuneration of the special manager will be fixed from time to time by the court r6.167(4).

7.2 Duties of the special manager

The special manager has a number of duties:

- Give security: The person making the appointment must give security before the appointment can take effect (r6.168). The amount of the security shall be not less than the value of the estate, property or business in respect of which the special manager is to be appointed. The appointer must file a certificate of adequacy of security in court.
- Prepare and keep accounts: The special manager must, every three months, prepare accounts containing details of his receipts and payments, for the approval of the trustee. When approved the special manager's accounts shall be added to those of the trustee.
- Produce accounts in accordance with the rules to the Secretary of State or to such other persons as may be prescribed.

7.3 Termination of appointment

The appointment will automatically terminate if the bankruptcy petition is dismissed or if, an interim receiver having been appointed, the latter is discharged without a bankruptcy order having been made (r6.171(1)).

If the OR/trustee are of the opinion that the employment of a special manager is no longer necessary or profitable for the estate, he may apply to the court for the appointment to be terminated (r.6.171(2)).

The OR/trustee must apply to court if creditors pass a resolution requiring that the appointment of the special manager be terminated (r6.171(3)).

Personal Insolvency

Summary and Self-test

Summary

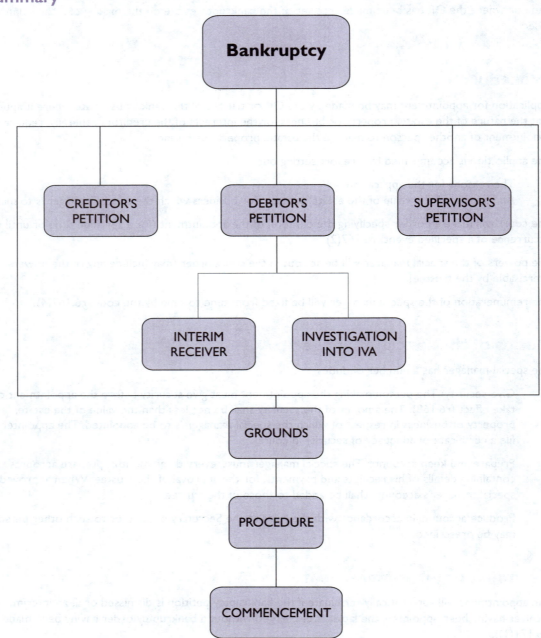

INTRODUCTION TO BANKRUPTCY

Self-test

Answer the following questions.

1. Who may present a bankruptcy petition?
2. How can a creditor prove to the court that a debtor is unable to pay his debts or has no reasonable prospect of paying them?
3. When does a bankruptcy commence?
4. How can a debtor prove that he is unable to pay his debts?
5. On what grounds may a supervisor present a default petition?
6. What can a debtor do if a petition is served upon him?
7. What documents must be filed in Court by a debtor when filing for his own bankruptcy?
8. Who may be appointed interim receiver?
9. What is the function of the interim receiver?
10. What is the effect of the appointment of an interim receiver?

Now, go back to the Learning Objectives in the Introduction. If you are satisfied that you have achieved these, please tick them off.

Answers to Self-test

1. A creditor, the debtor, the supervisor (or any bound creditor) of an IVA.

2. (a) By serving a statutory demand which is not complied with.
   (b) Obtaining judgement on a debt and levying execution which is unsatisfied.

3. On the date of the bankruptcy order.

4. By filing a statement of affairs with the petition and swearing an admission of Insolvency (r6.39(1)).

5. Failure to comply with obligations under VA.

   Giving false or misleading information to creditors to obtain consent to the VA.

   Failure to do all such things for the purpose of the VA as has reasonably been required by the supervisor.

6. Nothing.
   Pay the debt.
   Offer to secure or compound the debt.
   Apply for an interim order under s252 and make a proposal for a VA.
   Oppose the petition.
   If the criteria are met and with the consent of the petitioner seek a referral for a DRO.

7. Three copies of the petition.
   Two copies of a statement of affairs.
   Affidavit verifying statement of affairs.
   Receipt for deposit.
   Court fee.

8. Usually the OR, but an IP (who has consented to act) may be appointed.

9. To take immediate possession of the debtor's property or part of it.

10. Creditors may not commence any action or legal proceedings against the debtor without leave of the court.

    Debtor must give the interim receiver an inventory of his property and provide such additional information as may be required.

    Attend on the interim receiver at such times as he may reasonably require.

Answer to Interactive Question

Interactive question: Mary Watts

The arrangement would appear to have failed and Mary Watts is in default of the terms of the arrangement.

In this situation the supervisor, or a bound creditor, can present a default petition under s264(1)(c).

There are three grounds upon which a s264(1)(c) petition can be presented:

- Failure to comply with obligations under the VA.
- Giving false or misleading material information or making a material omission in any document or at the creditors' meeting.
- Failure to comply with the supervisor's reasonable requests.

Here, the supervisor could present a default petition since Mary Watts has failed to comply with the terms of the arrangement and has failed to comply with the supervisor's reasonable requests.

The proposal should set out terms for what should happen in the event of failure or default ie.

- Convening a meeting of creditors to ascertain their views.
- Presenting a bankruptcy petition.
- Making distributions to creditors prior to presenting a bankruptcy petition.

Since Mary Watts has incurred further credit, it is likely that these new creditors will not be bound by the terms of the arrangement and will therefore be able to petition for Mary's bankruptcy.

The grounds will be inability to pay debts (s264(1)(a).

Mary Watts could petition for her own bankruptcy on the grounds of inability to pay debts (s264(1)(b).

8

Post bankruptcy order procedure

Contents

Introduction
Examination context
Topic List
1 The bankruptcy order
2 Bankruptcy offences
3 Rights of the bankrupt
4 The Official Receiver
5 Checklist of matters to be dealt with immediately by trustee upon appointment
6 General meetings of creditors
7 Final meetings of creditors
8 Creditors' committee

Summary and Self-test
Answers to Self-test
Answer to Interactive Question

Personal Insolvency

Introduction

Learning objectives

Tick off

- Understand the consequences of a bankruptcy order being made ☐
- List the obligations and rights of the bankrupt ☐
- Identify bankruptcy offences committed by a bankrupt ☐
- State the functions, powers and duties of the OR ☐
- Advise on the formalities of convening meetings of creditors ☐
- Prepare a checklist of matters to be dealt with by a trustee upon appointment ☐
- State the functions and powers of the creditors' committee ☐

Working context

This is a very practical chapter which deals with matters that anyone involved in bankruptcy cases in a work environment should be familiar with: how a trustee is appointed, formalities to be dealt with upon appointment, obligations of a debtor, identifying offences committed by a debtor.

Stop and think

What does it mean for a debtor to be declared bankrupt? How are they affected? Why is a trustee not appointed in every bankruptcy case? What is the role of the OR? How does it differ to that of a trustee? What is a creditors' committee? What does it do?

POST BANKRUPTCY ORDER PROCEDURE

Examination context

The topics covered in this chapter are regularly tested in the JIEB exam, in particular the duties of the trustee, for example, in respect of creditors' meetings and creditors' committees.

Exam requirements

Past questions to look at include:

2004	Question 3 (iii)
2000	Question 3 (a)
1999	Question 1 (a) (d)
1995	Question 5 (a)
1993	Question 1 (a)
1992	Paper 1, Question 5 (a) (b)
1992	Paper 1, Question 6 (a) (b)
1991	Paper 1, Question 7
1990	Paper 1, Question 6

Personal Insolvency

1 The bankruptcy order

Section overview

At the hearing of the petition the court may make a bankruptcy order. The bankruptcy is deemed to commence on this date and until discharge the bankrupt will suffer the disabilities of bankruptcy and all its other consequences. It was the aim of the Enterprise Act 2002 to encourage enterprise however and to that end the Act sought to remove some of the stigma and hardship of bankruptcy.

1.1 Consequences of bankruptcy order being made

The official receiver (OR) will be appointed as the receiver and manager of the bankrupt's estate between the making of the order and the appointment of the trustee (s287).

Control of the debtor's estate passes to the OR.

Post petition dispositions by the debtor of his property are void (s284) (See 1.9 later in this chapter for more details).

Legal proceedings can only be commenced against the debtor with leave of the court and existing proceedings can be stayed (s285) (See 1.10 later in this chapter for more details).

Execution completed post commencement is void (s346) (See 1.11 later in this chapter for more details).

Landlords may only levy distress post bankruptcy order in relation to pre bankruptcy order arrears. This is further restricted to six months' rent accrued pre bankruptcy (See 1.11 later in this chapter for more details).

The bankrupt becomes subject to a number of obligations (See 1.3 later in this chapter for more details).

Bankrupt becomes liable for a number of bankruptcy offences (See 2 later in this chapter for more details).

Debtor must not obtain credit in excess of £500 without disclosing bankruptcy status (s360 (1)(a)).

Bankrupt has a duty to co-operate with the court.

Bankrupt must attend creditors' meetings if required.

1.2 Disabilities of the bankrupt

These restrictions apply to undischarged bankrupts and those bankrupts subject to a bankruptcy restriction order/undertaking.

Disqualifications under Enterprise Act 2002 (EA 2002).

One of the consequences of bankruptcy is to disqualify the bankrupt from holding various offices. There are also other professional disqualifications that may affect the bankrupt's ability to retain his employment or ability to trade. Such disqualifications continue until discharge (or annulment).

1.2.1 Political disqualification

MPs (including Devolved assemblies)

Following the commencement of the EA 2002 an individual is now only disqualified from membership of the House of Commons, sitting or voting in the House of Lords or sitting or voting in relation to a House of Lords or joint committee if subject to a bankruptcy restrictions order (BRO) (s426A).

The restriction also extends to include any of the devolved assemblies (s426B).

Vacation from office must occur on the making of the BRO. When the BRO is made the court will notify the Speaker of the relevant house of the Order. If the individual agrees to a BRU then the requirement to notify falls to the Secretary of State.

POST BANKRUPTCY ORDER PROCEDURE

JPs

Whereas a bankrupt was originally precluded from acting as a JP during the period of bankruptcy this rule has also been amended. It is now at the discretion of the Lord Chancellor as to whether the individual is disqualified from office.

Local Government

Again where an undischarged bankrupt was precluded from holding office this has now been amended. The disqualification only arises where the individual is subject to a BRO or if an 'interim' BRO has been made.

1.2.2 Professional disqualification

The effect of bankruptcy on professional status depends upon the professional body involved. However the bankrupt will not be able to act as an I.P. and The Law Society will suspend a solicitor's practicing certificate.

1.2.3 Restrictions on acting as a director

The restriction applies whilst an undischarged bankrupt or subject to a BRO.

- Automatically disqualified under Table 'A' Art.81.
- (S11 CDDA 1986) offence to act as director or directly or indirectly take part in the promotion formation or management of any company, except with leave of the court.

    Re McQuillam (1989) where the bankrupt had not made out the alleged need for his being allowed to act as director the court should not exercise its discretion to make an exception.

- (S15 CDDA 1986) bankrupt in breach of s11 CDDA 1986 is personally liable for the company's debt as is any person willing to act on his instructions.

1.2.4 Restrictions on partnership

By s33 Partnership Act 1890 a partnership will automatically dissolve on bankruptcy of a partner. S33 PA 1890 is subject to contrary provision in the partnership deed (if there is one).

The deed may provide for the:

- Firm to continue between the non-bankrupt partners.
- Expulsion of the bankrupt partner, and
- For the valuation and buying out of the bankrupt partner's share. Cash raised by the realisation of the partner's share would be available to the trustee in bankruptcy of that partner.

1.2.5 Restrictions on sole tradership

By s360(1)(b) an undischarged bankrupt or a former bankrupt subject to a BRO is guilty of offence if he:

- Engages (directly or indirectly) in any business under a name other than that in which he was adjudged bankrupt.
- Without disclosing to all persons with whom he enters into any business transaction the name in which he was so adjudged.

1.3 Obligations of the bankrupt

The debtor must:

- Deliver up to the OR all books, papers and other records of which he has possession or control (s291(1)).
- Give to the OR an inventory of the estate and such further information as the OR may reasonably require (s291(4)). Failure to comply will constitute contempt of court. This obligation continues after discharge (s291(5)).

Personal Insolvency

- Deliver possession of the estate to the OR (s291). If the property is not capable of delivery, it is the bankrupt's duty to do all that is reasonably required by the OR to protect the estate asset.
- Attend on the OR as the OR shall reasonably require.
- Provide accounts for the previous three years (when involved in running a business).
- Provide a statement of affairs within 21 days (see 1.4 for more details).
- Notify the OR within 21 days of property acquired by him after the commencement of bankruptcy (see 1.8 for more details).
- Notify the OR within 21 days of any increases in income (see 1.8 for more details).
- Comply with the directions of the court. Failure to comply will constitute contempt of the court (s364).

1.4 Statement of Affairs

Where a bankruptcy order has been made (other than on a debtor's petition) s288 provides that the bankrupt must submit a statement of affairs to the OR within 21 days of the bankruptcy order being made.

The time limit may be extended by the OR or he may release the bankrupt from the duty to submit.

The bankrupt may apply to court to be released from this duty.

The court may:

- Dismiss the application. It can only do this if the bankrupt has had an opportunity to attend an ex parte hearing on seven days notice, or
- Set a venue for a hearing – the court will give notice of it to the bankrupt, who in turn gives 14 days' notice to the OR. The OR can attend at the application or make a written representation (bankrupt must have been copied in at least five days pre-hearing).

The statement must be in the prescribed form, Form 6.33 (creditor's petition), Form 6.28 (debtor's petition) and must include the following details:

- List of secured creditors: name, address of creditor, amount owed, nature and value of assets subject to security.
- List of unsecured creditors: name, address of creditor, amount claimed by creditor, amount bankrupt 'thinks' he owes.
- Inventory of assets: including cash at bank or building society, household furniture and belongings, life policies, debtors, stocks in trade, motor vehicles and other property, and in each case, the value of the asset.

The debtor must:

- Verify the form by affidavit sworn before an officer of the Insolvency Service or the court.
- Deliver two copies to the OR (who files one in court).

The OR will provide the debtor with the forms and written guidance on how to complete them. The OR may employ someone to assist the bankrupt preparing the statement at the expense of the estate. The OR may, at the bankrupt's request, authorise an allowance so that the debtor may employ someone to assist him.

The OR may demand further written particulars from the bankrupt expanding on his statement of affairs and may require this information to be verified by affidavit.

The OR must send a report to the creditors containing a summary of the statement of affairs, a summary of any further particulars of it given by the debtor and any observations by the OR.

See Chapter 15 for details of how to prepare a statement of affairs.

POST BANKRUPTCY ORDER PROCEDURE

1.5 Provision of accounts

Upon the request of the OR the bankrupt must furnish the OR with accounts relating to his affairs of such nature, as at such date and for such period as he may specify. This is subject to a maximum period of three years pre-presentation but he may go back longer with permission of the court.

The bankrupt may receive assistance with the preparation of the accounts (as with statement of affairs).

The usual time limit for delivery of the accounts is 21 days from the request subject to extension by the OR The accounts should be verified by affidavit if the OR requires. Once received by the OR, a copy shall be filed at court.

1.6 Public and private examinations

At any time before discharge the OR may apply for the public examination of the bankrupt (s290(1)). The OR must apply for a public examination if requisitioned by half or more of the creditors in value.

A simple majority of creditors can requisition a public examination (r6.173) by sending a written request to the OR together with:

- List of requisitioning creditors and the value of their claims.
- Written confirmation from each creditor concurring with the request.
- Statement of reasons why examination requested.

OR must now apply to court within 28 days (unless he can show the court that the request is unreasonable).

Before the application to court the requisitionists deposit a sum as security for the costs of the examination before making the application.

Procedure before public examination (r6.172)

- OR applies to court for an order that bankrupt be publicly examined.
- Court makes order and sets venue.
- OR sends copy order to bankrupt.
- OR gives 14 days notice of examination to any trustee, special manager or creditor.
- OR may advertise (at least 14 days pre-hearing).

The following persons may attend and ask questions:

- The OR.
- The trustee (if appointed).
- A special manager (if appointed).
- Any creditor who has tendered proof.

Unfit Bankrupts (r6.174)

- This rule applies where the Bankrupt 'is suffering from any mental disorder, physical affliction or disability rendering him unfit to undergo or attend for public examination'.
- The OR, a friend, relative or court appointed representative may apply to the court.
- Court may stay the order or direct that the examination be conducted in such manner and at such place as it thinks fit.
- Applicants other than OR will have to provide medical evidence and give seven days notice of the application to the OR and any trustee.

Procedure at the hearing (s6.175):

Examination is on oath and the bankrupt must answer all such questions as the court may put, or allow to be put, to him.

OR, trustee, special manager and creditors may ask questions in person or (with court approval) through their lawyers or representatives appointed in writing.

Bankrupt can at his own expense employ a solicitor (with or without counsel) who may put to him such questions as the court may allow for the purpose of enabling him to explain or qualify any answers given by him and may make representations on his behalf.

A record of the hearing is made which the bankrupt must sign and verify by affidavit.

This record is only admissible in evidence in civil legal proceedings. It is not admissible in criminal proceedings *(Re Saunders)*.

Expenses of the hearing will be borne by the creditor's deposit (if a requisitioned examination) otherwise by the estate.

Non-attendance without reasonable excuse is contempt of court and may lead to a warrant being issued for the arrest of the bankrupt.

Please mark 'private examination' as an index entry.

Under s366 the trustee or the OR may apply to the court for the private examination of:

- Bankrupt.
- Bankrupt's spouse or former spouse.
- Any person known or believed to have any property comprised in the bankrupt's estate in his possession.
- Bankrupt's debtors.
- Any person appearing to the court to be able to give information concerning the bankrupt or the bankrupt's dealings, affairs or property.

The court may require persons in possession of the bankrupt's property or relevant information and the bankrupt's debtors to:

- Submit an affidavit accounting for their dealings with the bankrupt.
- Produce any documents in their control/possession relating to the bankrupt's dealings, affairs or property.

The court may issue a warrant for the:

- Arrest of any person summoned.
- Seizure of any books, records, money or goods in that persons possession.

1.7 Give attendance and assistance

Both before and after discharge, the Bankrupt is under a duty to give the OR (and trustee if appropriate) such attendance and assistance as the OR may reasonably require for the purpose of s283 to s291 IA, s333.

Failure to comply constitutes contempt of court. Note that committal for contempt of court is not the only way in which the duty may be enforced. The court may also grant an injunction in such terms as may be justified to enforce the duty.

The obligation of the bankrupt under s291(4) is now extended to information required for the purpose of an application for a BRO (s268 EA 2002).

1.8 Notify trustee of after acquired property or increase in income

The bankrupt has 21 days to give notice to the trustee of any property acquired by him/her after commencement (s333 and r6.200). It is for the trustee to then decide whether to claim such property for the estate.

S333 does not extend to situations where the bankrupt acquires property in the ordinary course of a business carried on by him. Pursuant to r6.200 such bankrupt must, at least every six months, provide the trustee with information in respect of the business. This must show details of goods/services sold, goods/services purchased and any profit or loss arising from the business.

The bankrupt has 21 days to give the trustee notice of an increase in his income arising since commencement (s333).

1.9 Post petition dispositions

Under s284 dispositions by the bankrupt from the presentation of the petition to the vesting of the estate in a trustee are void except to the extent that the court consents to or subsequently ratifies the disposition.

A disposition includes a payment in cash or otherwise and this rule applies even if the assets would not have formed part of the estate.

Third parties receiving payments from the bankrupt hold those payments as part of the bankrupt's estate. Payees suffering a loss as a result of this section are treated as a pre-bankruptcy creditor, unless they had notice of the petition as at the date the debt to them was incurred.

Persons acquiring interests through innocent third parties or payments received prior to the commencement of bankruptcy by a bona fide third party, for value, without notice are protected.

Following the case of *Mountney v Treharne 2002* it should be noted that in matrimonial cases where a property adjustment order is made an equitable interest will arise on the making of the order. However, the order may be timed to take effect at a later date. In which case the interest will arise when the order takes effect. For example, in *Mountney v Treharne* the order took effect at decree absolute. It is not necessary for a legal transfer to be executed. This could be an important point in determining timing for s284 purposes.

1.10 Restriction on legal proceedings against the debtor

S285(1) 'At any time when... an individual has been adjudged bankrupt the court may stay an action, execution or legal process against the property or person of the... bankrupt'.

Courts before whom proceedings against undischarged bankrupts are taking place are allowed to stay them or allow them to proceed with conditions.

After the making of a bankruptcy order creditors with provable debts have no remedy against the bankrupt and may not commence any action or legal proceedings against the bankrupt, ie their rights and remedies are limited to those in bankruptcy proceedings.

There are exceptions to the rule in s285(3) as follows:

- Permission of Court (which may impose conditions) (s283(3)(b)).
- Execution or attachment completed before Bankruptcy Order (s346 (1)).
- Distress levied by a landlord (but only in relation to rent for the six months prior to commencement) (s347(1)).
- Secured creditors may enforce their security. However s285(5) allows the OR on giving written notice to inspect the assets subject to the 'pledge, pawn or other security'.

Secured creditor cannot now realise security without giving OR/trustee reasonable opportunity to exercise the bankrupt's right of redemption.

1.11 Restriction on execution and distress

1.11.1 Execution completed pre-commencement of bankruptcy

The Rule (s346)

Where before the commencement of bankruptcy a judgment creditor issues execution against the debtor's goods or land or attaches a debt due to the judgment debtor... the creditor cannot retain the 'benefit of the execution' or any sum paid to avoid it unless it was completed or the sums were paid before bankruptcy commenced.

Personal Insolvency

When is execution complete? (S346(5))

Execution against goods – on seizure and sale or on the making of a charging order absolute under s1 Charging Orders Act 1979.

Execution against land – by seizure, appointment of receiver or making of charging order absolute.

Attachment of debts – on receipt by judgment creditor of the debt.

Effect of Rule

If prior to completion of execution the enforcement officer is notified of the making of a bankruptcy order he must, at the OR/trustee's request, deliver up goods, money seized or recovered in part satisfaction of the execution.

Enforcement officer's costs are a first charge on the proceeds and property taken.

If execution is levied for a sum of £1,000 or more (including costs) the enforcement officer must retain the balance (including monies paid to avoid seizure and sale) for 14 days and if during that time he is notified of a bankruptcy petition he must hand over that balance to the trustee after deduction of costs.

Third parties acquiring goods from the enforcement officer or other officer, in good faith, take a good title.

Court can set aside the rights of OR/trustee under these rules.

1.11.2 Distress

Generally the 'self-help' remedy of distress is available, during bankruptcy proceedings. This is available under s347(9) even after the trustee has been appointed and the bankrupt's assets have therefore vested in the trustee under s306.

There are however three restrictions on this general right to distrain.

- Where a creditor levies in the three months before the bankruptcy order (s347(3) and (4)):

    This rule applies to all creditors who have the right to levy distress and NOT just to landlords.

    The rule provides that the goods or effects distrained upon or the proceeds of their sale shall be charged for the benefit of the bankrupt's estate with the preferential debts of the bankrupt to the extent that the bankrupt's estate is for the time being insufficient for meeting those debts.

    The distress creditor will now rank as a preferential creditor for an amount equal to the value which was surrendered to the trustee in bankruptcy by complying with this rule. In effect the distress creditor forms his own separate class of creditor ranking behind the other preferential creditors but ahead of ordinary unsecured creditors.

- Where a landlord levies post-order in respect of pre-order rent arrears:

    Here although the landlord can distrain he is limited to distraining in relation to six months rent accrued due pre-order.

    The six months do not need to be consecutive.

    The landlord *can* distrain post-order in relation to new arrears (ie generated post order) without restriction.

    If a landlord distrains for more than six months worth of pre order arrears – the balance will have to be surrendered to the trustee.

- Where a landlord levies post petition and in the three months pre order:

    Here the rule in s347(1) should be applied first (see s347(2)). If the landlord has distrained for more than six months rent accrued due the balance will have to be surrendered to the trustee.

    Now the three month rule in s347(3) should be applied to the proceeds of distress still held in the landlord's hand after the application of s347(1). Again the landlord will rank as preferential in relation to the amount of any claw-back by the trustee pursuant to s347(3).

The landlord would then be entitled to retain any balance remaining after the application of the two rules.

2 Bankruptcy offences

Section overview

Whilst the EA 2002 abolished some bankruptcy offences there are still a number of offences which can be committed by the bankrupt, some of which are retrospective. The detailed provisions of IA 1986 are contained in s350 to s362.

2.1 Table of offences

The following table provides a summary of the main offences and defences.

Bankruptcy Offence	Defence	Penalty Schedule
S353. Non-disclosure of property/failure to inform of a disposal which might be set aside.	Innocent intent s352.	Seven years imprisonment, a fine or both.
S354. Concealment of property. If the Bankrupt fails to deliver up to OR or his trustee all his assets or if he conceals any debt due to or from him or any property with value £500+ commits an offence. Applies retrospectively to concealment within 12 months pre-petition.	Innocent intent s352.	As above.
S354(3). Offence if fails to account (to the OR, court, trustee) without reasonable excuse for loss of any substantial part of his property incurred in the 12 months before the petition was presented against him.	Innocent intent s352.	Two years imprisonment, a fine or both.
S355. Failure to deliver up books, papers, and other records or prevent production or conceal or destroy them or cause or permit false entries in them constitutes an offence. Retrospective liability if carried out 12 months before presentation of petition. In respect of trading records (defined in s355(5)) the 12 month period is extended to two years.	Innocent intent s352.	Seven years imprisonment, a fine or both.
S356. Offence if bankrupt makes any false statement.	Innocent intent s352.	As above.
S357. Offence committed if bankrupt makes any gift or transfer of property within five years of commencement. Further, concealment or removal of property within two months before or after judgment constitutes an offence.	Innocent intent s352.	Two years imprisonment, a fine or both.
S358. Offence if bankrupt leaves or attempts to leave or makes any preparation to leave England or Wales with property £1,000+ in value in six months prior to presentation of petition.	Innocent intent s352.	As above.

Personal Insolvency

Bankruptcy Offence	Defence	Penalty Schedule
S359. Offence if within 12 months pre-petition dispose of any property obtained on credit in respect of which money still owing.	Innocent intent s352.	Seven years imprisonment, a fine or both.
S360. Obtaining credit and engaging in business whilst an undischarged bankrupt or subject to a BRO without disclosing bankruptcy status.	No defence under s352.	Two years imprisonment, a fine or both
S11 CDDA 1986. Offence to be directly or indirectly involved in management of a limited company without court leave whilst an undischarged bankrupt or whilst BRO/BRU is in force.		As above.

Note. Note that following the changes introduced by EA 2002 it is **no** longer a criminal offence for a bankrupt to have:

▸ Failed to keep proper account records within two years of presentation of a petition, or

▸ To have materially contributed to insolvency by gambling or hazardous speculation within two years of presentation.

However, these are considerations that will be taken into account when considering whether or not to make a BRO.

2.2 Defence of innocent intention (s352)

A person is not guilty of an offence if he proves that, at the time of the conduct constituting the offence, he had no intent to defraud or to conceal the state of his affairs.

3 Rights of the bankrupt

Section overview

The bankrupt also has a number of rights.

▸ To challenge trustee's decision:

– if a bankrupt (or any creditor) is dissatisfied by any act, omission or decision of a trustee he may make an application to the court. The court will have the power to confirm, reverse or modify any such decision or act. The court may also give the trustee any direction as it thinks fit (s303).

– The court is only likely to interfere where the trustee has acted in bad faith or been fraudulent. It is unlikely to interfere with day to day administrative matters or where the trustee has acted in good faith.

▸ To complain to the relevant professional body of which the trustee is a member – the bankrupt may do this if he considers that the trustee is not complying with his ethical guidelines.

▸ To receive information – the bankrupt has a right to request that the trustee provide him with a statement or receipts and payments. The trustee must comply within 14 days of the receipt of any request. The statement should cover the period of one year, up to the last anniversary of the trustee's appointment which preceded the request.

▸ Right to apply to vary or discharge income payments order or agreement (r6.193).

8 POST BANKRUPTCY ORDER PROCEDURE

4 The Official Receiver

Section overview

The official receiver (OR) will be the receiver and manager of the bankrupt's estate between the making of the order and the appointment of the trustee (s287).

4.1 Role and function of the OR

The OR's main role is to protect the estate (s287(2)).

He has the same powers as a receiver or manager appointed by the High Court plus the power to dispose of goods which are perishable or likely to diminish in value.

The duties of the OR are to:

- Take all steps as he thinks fit for protecting the estate.
- As soon as practicable in the period of 12 weeks from the date of the bankruptcy order to decide whether to call a meeting of creditors.
- To investigate the conduct and affairs of the bankrupt (s289) unless he thinks an investigation is unnecessary (s289(2)). He has discretion to report to the court on the outcome of his investigation.

The OR may apply to the court for the appointment of a special manager under s370 (See Chapter 7 for details).

The OR does not have to do anything which involves expenditure (unless the Secretary of State so directs) s287(3)(b). He will not be liable for erroneous seizure and disposal unless he acts negligently.

4.2 Exceptions where the court will appoint a trustee (not OR) with immediate effect

Where, on a debtor's petition, an IP is ordered by the court to 'inquire and report' and no voluntary arrangement is made, the court may appoint the IP to act as trustee.

Where a bankrupt was previously subject to a voluntary arrangement, the court may appoint the supervisor to act as trustee.

In both cases:

- Trustee must file in court a statement to the effect that he is an IP and consents to act (r6.121).
- Trustee must give notice of his appointment to the creditors. The court may allow this to be done by advertisement (s297(7)).
- The trustee's notice will state whether he intends to summon a creditors' meeting to appoint a creditors' committee and will inform the creditors of their right to requisition a meeting (s297(8)).
- The OR will no longer have a duty to decide whether to call a meeting (s297(6)).

4.3 First meeting of creditors

As soon as practicable in the period of 12 weeks from the date of the bankruptcy order the OR must decide whether to call a meeting of the bankrupt's creditors.

The function of the meeting is to:

- Appoint a trustee (s293(1)).
- To establish a creditors' committee (s301(1)). (See later for details.)

If the OR decides not to call a meeting, he must give notice of his decision to the Court and to all creditors known to him or appearing in the bankrupt's statement of affairs.

Personal Insolvency

The OR becomes trustee from the date of this notice.

If the OR has decided not to call a meeting or hasn't yet decided, the creditors may request the OR to summon a meeting. If the request is backed by 25% by value of the creditors the OR must summon a meeting (s294). The meeting must be held within 35 days from request but subject to costs of the meeting being provided for (r6.87(2)).

Procedure on creditor's requisition (r6.83(1)):

- Creditors apply on Form 6.34 accompanied by:
    - List of concurring creditors and details of their claims.
    - Written confirmation of concurrence with each other.
    - Statement of purpose of the proposed meeting.
- The OR will fix a venue for the meeting and give creditors 21 days' notice.

If the OR decides to call a meeting he must fix a venue (not later than four months from the date of the bankruptcy order) for the first meeting of creditors.

He must:

- Notify the court 'as soon as reasonably practicable'.
- Give 21 days' notice to all creditors known to the OR or identified in the statement of affairs.
- Advertise the meeting (in the London Gazette and the notice may also be advertised in such other manner as the OR thinks fit).

The business at the first meeting is restricted by r6.80 as follows:

At the first meeting of creditors, no resolutions shall be taken other than the following:

- A resolution to appoint a named insolvency practitioner to be trustee in bankruptcy or two or more named insolvency practitioners as joint trustees.
- A resolution to establish a creditors' committee.
- (unless it has been resolved to establish a creditors' committee) a resolution specifying the terms on which the trustee is to be remunerated or to defer consideration of that matter.
- (if, and only if, two or more persons are appointed to act jointly as trustee) a resolution specifying whether acts are to be done by both or all of them, or by only one.
- (where the meeting has been requisitioned under s294) a resolution authorising payment out of the estate, as an expense of the bankruptcy, of the cost of summoning and holding the meeting.
- A resolution to adjourn the meeting for not more than three weeks.
- Any other resolution which the chairman thinks it right to allow for special reasons.

No resolution shall be proposed which has for its object the appointment of the OR as trustee (r6.80(2)).

The OR or a person nominated by him shall act as chairman of the meeting.

If the meeting fails to appoint a trustee the OR now has a duty to decide whether to refer the need for appointment to the Secretary of State.

If the OR decides not to refer he will become trustee (s295(4)) and must notify the court accordingly.

If he decides to refer, the Secretary of State will either:

- Decline to make an appointment (OR will become trustee and notify court accordingly), or
- Make an appointment (under s296) and give two copies of the certificate of appointment to the OR who sends one to the IP and one to the court.

If the meeting does appoint a trustee:

- Under r6.120 the potential trustee must provide the chairman with a written statement that he is a qualified IP and that he consents to act.
- The chairman of the meeting certifies the appointment.

POST BANKRUPTCY ORDER PROCEDURE

- The appointment takes effect from the date endorsed on the certificate of appointment.
- Copy certificates are sent to the OR who sends a copy to the trustee and the court.
- Trustee now advertises his appointment in 'such newspapers as he thinks most appropriate for ensuring that it comes to the notice of the bankrupt's creditors' (r6.124).
- The cost of advertising is borne by the trustee but he is entitled to reimbursement out of the estate.

Note. Where the trustee has been appointed by the Secretary of State the trustee gives notice to the creditors of his appointment or, if the court allows, advertises his appointment in accordance with the court's directions (s296(4)).

The meeting will appoint a trustee as follows:

- If only one nominee for appointment – he may be appointed by the meeting.
- If there is more than one nominee, a vote will be required:
  - If a nominee gets a simple majority of those attending and voting, he will be appointed.
  - If no nominee gets a simple majority – the nominee with the fewest votes drops out and the vote is taken again. The process is repeated until a clear winner emerges.

The chairman may put a resolution to the meeting at any time that joint nominees be appointed.

IP and connected persons may not exercise their votes/proxies' votes on matters in which they are interested.

5 Checklist of matters to be dealt with immediately by trustee upon appointment

Section overview

The trustee has to comply with a number of practical and regulatory matters on his appointment.

5.1 Checklist

A summary checklist is provided below. This list is not exhaustive, if you can think of other matters please add them to the end of the list.

5.1.1 Formalities and documentation

Trustee ensures he has office copy of document of appointment in his possession and obtains office copy of bankruptcy order.

Trustee must take steps to advertise his appointment. The notice of appointment must be Gazetted and may be advertised in such other manner as the trustee thinks fit (r6.124(1)).

Deal with OR's debit balance.

Open file, organise documentation – formal, case papers, working notes, correspondence, documents relating to assets and liabilities etc.

5.1.2 Professional

Inform insurers in respect of bordereau: general penalty bond of £250,000 and specific penalty bond of not less than the estimated value of the bankrupt's assets (minimum value £5,000 and maximum value £5,000,000).

Seek to recover premium out of first realisations.

Complete IP record (see 5.2 below).

Personal Insolvency

5.1.3 Assets – protection of the estate

Check that significant assets in the estate are insured, that the policies have not lapsed and cover is adequate and index linked

Notify any mortgagees (building society etc) of the trustee's interest.

If any property forming part of the estate is vacant, check physical security, instruct agents with a view to sale etc.

Notify any third parties holding assets of the bankrupt of the trustee's interest (eg banks, pension providers).

Consider disclaiming any onerous assets.

5.1.4 Legal

Notify solicitors.

Trustee has power to search Land Register.

Trustee may instruct solicitors to register cautions over land where appropriate.

5.1.5 Bankrupt

Arrange for bankrupt to attend at office a.s.a.p.

If no statement of affairs has been obtained, call for one.

Write to those owing money to the bankrupt requesting them to forward monies to the trustee direct.

5.1.6 Statutory duties triggered by appointment

Get in the estate (s305). It will be the trustee's duty in due course to realise for a proper price, distribute and account to the bankrupt for any surplus.

Pay cash receipts into the ISA once every 14 days or immediately if £5,000 or more.

Maintain receipts and payments accounts and IP Record.

Take possession of books, papers and other records (s311).

Call meeting of creditors if required to do so (on a 10% requisition).

Prepare and keep a separate financial record on each bankrupt. Such records must be retained for a period of six years following the trustee's vacation of office unless permission to destroy them is received from the OR.

Upon request of the Secretary of State, send to him an account of the trustee's receipts and payments.

5.2 IP Record

The trustee is required to maintain an IP case record. This should include details of the following matters (Schedule 3 IP Regs):

- Name of insolvency practitioner.
- Insolvency practitioner number.
- Principal business address of practitioner.
- Authorising body (including competent authority).
- Name of person in relation to whom the practitioner is acting.
- Nature of insolvency proceeding.
- Progress of the administration, administrative matters eg.
  - date of commencement of insolvency proceeding.
  - date of appointment as insolvency practitioner in insolvency proceeding.
- Distribution to creditors and others setting out amounts and dates paid.
- Record of filing of statutory returns.

6 General meetings of creditors

Section overview

Meetings of creditors may be convened by the Official Receiver (OR) or the trustee for the purposes of ascertaining the wishes of the creditors in any matter relating to the bankruptcy. Creditors may also requisition a meeting by making a request to the OR or trustee (r.6.83). The statutory provisions relating to creditors meetings are contained in r6.79 – r6.95.

6.1 Procedure for calling meetings

The convenor, in fixing a venue, date and time for the meeting must have regard to the convenience of the creditors.

Definition

Convenor: the person calling the meeting.

The meeting must commence between 10.00 – 16.00 hours on a business day.

21 days' notice must be given to all creditors appearing on the Statement of Affairs.

The notice must state:

- Purpose of the meeting.
- Date and time by which proxies and outstanding proofs must be lodged (minimum of four days pre meeting).
- Proxy forms must be included.

Notice of the meeting must be Gazetted. The trustee may also give notice by public advertisement if he thinks fit.

21 days' notice must be given to the bankrupt (r6.84) who may be required to attend the meeting.

6.2 Procedure at the meeting

6.2.1 Chairman

If the OR has convened the meeting, the OR or a person nominated by him will act as chair.

If the convenor is not the OR, the convenor or a person nominated by him, in writing, to act will be chair. Such a nominated person must be an IP, or an employee of the trustee or of his firm who is experienced in insolvency matters.

6.2.2 Attendance

The chairman has a wide discretion to admit the bankrupt or any other person who has given reasonable notice of his wish to be present.

6.2.3 Quorum

A quorum is at least one creditor entitled to vote, present in person or by proxy (r12.4A(2)).

If only one person is present who is entitled to attend and vote and the chairman is aware that there are others who would be so entitled, he must wait a further 15 minutes before commencing the meeting.

Personal Insolvency

6.2.4 Entitlement to vote

A creditor can vote if:

- He has lodged a proof of debt by the deadline in the notice calling the meeting, and
- The proof has been admitted in whole or in part under r6.94.
- Proxies have been filed before the deadline (if appropriate).

In exceptional circumstances the court may permit creditors (or a class of them) to vote without having proven their debts (Trustee can ask court to make consequential orders, eg allowing trustee to pay dividend to such unproven creditors).

Limitations on right to vote:

- Unliquidated or unascertained debts (except where the chairman agrees an estimated minimum value for the debt and admits the proof for purposes of voting).
- Secured creditors can only vote with any unsecured element of their debt.
- Debts on or secured on bills of exchange or promissory notes.

Proxies may be held by the chairman. If he holds a proxy requiring him to vote for a particular resolution and no other creditor proposes it the chairman has a choice:

- Propose the resolution, or
- If there is a good reason for not doing so, he need not propose it and should notify the principle forthwith after the meeting.

6.2.5 Questions

The chairman has the discretion to allow the creditors to ask the bankrupt questions.

6.2.6 Resolutions

Resolutions are passed by a majority in value of those present and voting in person or by proxy.

6.2.7 Adjournments

Meetings may be adjourned for a maximum of 21 days to such time and place as the chair thinks fit.

If no chairman present then:

- Some person entitled to attend and vote can, with the agreement of others present, adjourn in the same way as the chairman could have, or
- In default of agreement, the meeting is adjourned to the same time and place in the next following week

Chairman may adjourn, at his discretion, where:

- Bankrupt not present at the meeting and it is desired to put questions to him (this adjournment is with a view to obtaining his attendance).
- Meeting inquorate 30 minutes after time fixed for commencement.
- General power to adjourn under r6.91(1).

Chairman must adjourn where meeting so resolves.

Chairman may not adjourn where the purpose of the meeting is to remove the trustee and the trustee is himself chairman (unless a majority of creditors attending and voting, by value, vote in favour of adjournment).

6.2.8 Suspension of the meeting

R6.90 the chairman may, only once in the course of any meeting, declare the meeting suspended for any period up to one hour.

6.2.9 Minutes

The chairman, at any creditors' meeting, shall cause minutes of the proceedings at the meeting, signed by him, to be retained by him as part of the records of the bankruptcy (r6.95(1)).

He shall also cause to be made up and kept, a list of all the creditors who attended the meeting (r6.95(2)).

The minutes of the meeting shall include a record of every resolution passed and it is the chairman's duty to see to it that particulars of all such resolutions certified by him are filed in court not more than 21 days after the date of the meeting (r6.95(3)).

For best practice when recording meetings see SIP 12.

7 Final meetings of creditors

Section overview

Where it appears to the trustee that the administration of the bankrupt's estate is for practical purposes complete, he must convene a final meeting of creditors to receive the trustee's report and for the trustee to seek his release (s331).

The trustee will give 28 days' notice of the final meeting to all creditors of whom he is aware (not just those who have proved their debts) (r6.137). Notice must also be sent to the bankrupt.

The trustee will lay a report before the meeting under s331 which will include:

- A summary of his receipts and payments, and
- A statement that he has reconciled his account with the ISA.

At the final meeting the creditors may question the trustee with regard to any matter contained in his report and could resolve against him having his release.

The trustee gives notice to the court that the final meeting has been held, stating whether or not he received his release, together with a copy of his report. A copy of the notice is also sent by the trustee to the Secretary of State.

The trustee is released when the notice is filed in court, unless the creditors have resolved that the trustee shall not have his release, in which case he must obtain his release from the Secretary of State.

If there is no quorum present at the final meeting, the trustee shall report to the court that a final meeting was summoned in accordance with the Rules, but there was no quorum present, and the final meeting is then deemed to have been held and the creditors not to have resolved against the trustee having his release (r6.137(5)).

8 Creditors' committee

Section overview

A creditors' committee of between three and five members may be established at the first or subsequent meetings of creditors (s301). If no committee is appointed its functions vest in the Secretary of State.

8.1 Who may be appointed?

In order for a creditor to be eligible to sit on the committee they (r6.150):

- Must have proved a debt or have lodged a proof which has not been wholly refused for dividend or voting purposes.
- Debt must not be fully secured.

- Must consent to act on the committee.

Company creditors can only act through a representative. A person cannot appear as a representative for more than one committee member, or as a committee member and as a representative for another member. A person acting as a committee member's representative must hold a letter of authority entitling him to act.

No member may be represented by a body corporate, or by a person who is an undischarged bankrupt, or a disqualified director, or is subject to a bankruptcy restriction order, bankruptcy restriction undertaking or interim bankruptcy restriction order.

The acts of the committee are valid notwithstanding any defect in the appointment or qualification of any committee member's representative.

8.2 Formalities of establishment

The committee does not come into being, and accordingly cannot act, until the trustee has issued a certificate of its due constitution (r6.151(1)).

The trustee cannot issue the certificate until at least three persons elected to the committee have agreed to act. As and when other members (if any) agree, the trustee will issue an amended certificate.

The trustee shall file the certificate in court.

8.3 Vacation of office

A member will vacate office if he:

- Resigns by written notice to trustee.
- Becomes bankrupt (his trustee takes his place on the committee).
- Fails to attend, personally or through a representative, on three consecutive meetings (although committee can resolve that this rule is not to apply).
- Ceases to be, or is found never to have been, a creditor.

A member can be removed by a general meeting of creditors held on 14 days' notice.

Vacancies can be filled by the trustee, with the committee's agreement, or by a meeting of creditors. The creditor must consent to act in either case.

8.4 Creditors' committee meetings

Meetings of the committee shall be held when and where determined by the trustee (r6.153).

Notice: seven days' notice must be given.

8.4.1 First meeting

Must be held within three months of:

- Appointment of the trustee.
- Establishment of committee (if later).

Subsequent meetings may be held if:

- Called by trustee of own motion.
- Called by trustee within 21 days of any member's request.
- Committee so resolves.

8.4.2 Chair of meeting

Trustee or person nominated by trustee who must be:

- Qualified IP.
- Employee of trustee or his firm who is experienced in insolvency matters.

8.4.3 Quorum

A meeting of the committee will be quorate if notice of it has been given to all members and two members are present in person or by representative (r6.155).

8.4.4 Voting

Each member has one vote and resolutions are passed by simple majority. Members/representatives votes where they are interested in a transaction must be disallowed. Postal resolutions may be passed.

8.4.5 Minutes

Chairman must keep minutes of each meeting which are signed by him and retained as part of the records of the bankruptcy.

Every resolution passed must be recorded in writing, either separately or as part of the minutes, signed by the Chairman and kept with the records of the bankruptcy.

8.5 Functions of the creditors committee

To receive notice from the trustee of:

- Employment of a solicitor.
- Disposal of any assets to an associate of the bankrupt.

To fix the trustee's remuneration if the creditors' meeting has not reserved this matter to itself.

To receive reports on matters which the trustee considers are of concern to the committee, or which the committee have indicated are of concern to it. Trustee must report unless:

- The estate is without funds sufficient to enable him to comply.
- Costs of compliance would be too great having regard to the importance of the matter.
- The request is frivolous.

S314(2) – to consent to the trustee appointing the bankrupt to:

- Superintend the management of his estate.
- Carry on the business for the creditors' benefit.
- Assist in the administration of the estate.

Consent should be obtained at the outset, however the trustee may, without undue delay, seek later ratification in cases of urgency.

If committee is established more than 28 days after the trustee came to office – to receive a report from the trustee is summary form and to question the trustee.

To receive reasonable travelling expenses (directly incurred in attending meetings or on committee business) as an expense of the administration of the estate.

To receive six monthly reports from the trustee (or up to two monthly on committee's request) and to call for production of the trustee's accounts and records (and to consider whether to ask for an audit of trustee's records).

Review security for office given by trustee.

To give sanction for exercise of powers listed in Schedule 5 Part I IA.

To sanction, in its existing form, the division among the creditors of any property which cannot be readily sold (s326).

Personal Insolvency

Note that SIP 15 now provides guidance notes for members of creditors' committees in bankruptcy, insolvent liquidations, administration and administrative receivership.

Interactive question: Edward Jones

Prosper Pet Foods Ltd are owed £14,890 by Edward Jones who was declared bankrupt on 12 May 2009. They wish to sit on a creditors' committee and have approached you for some advice.

Requirement

Write a letter to the company advising them:

(a) How a company may act as a committee member.
(b) When committee meetings will be held.
(c) The functions of the creditors' committee.

See **Answer** at the end of this chapter.

Summary and Self-test

Summary

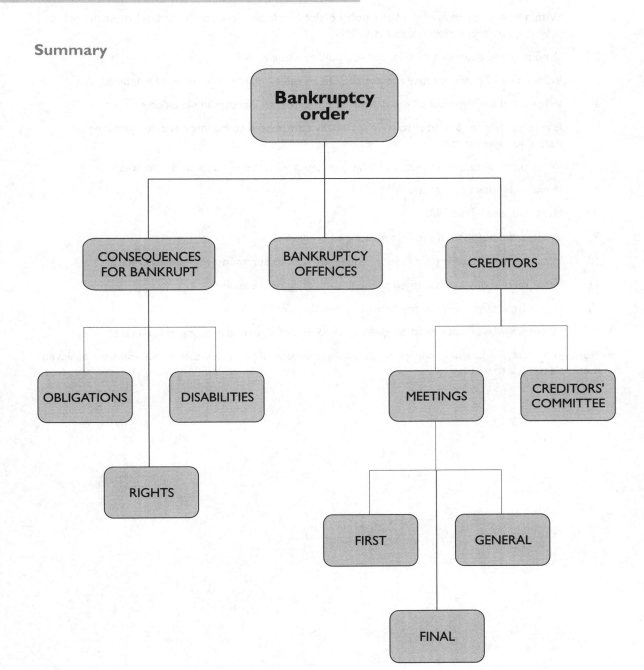

Self-test

Answer the following questions.

1. Within how many days of the bankruptcy order (made on a creditor's petition) must the debtor submit a statement of affairs to the OR?
2. Who may ask questions of a debtor at a public examination?
3. What value of creditors may require the OR to call a public examination of a debtor?
4. What are the obligations of the debtor if he receives an increase in his income?
5. Is it an offence for a debtor to have materially contributed to his insolvency by gambling or hazardous speculation?
6. What rights does a bankrupt have if he is unhappy with the conduct of the trustee?
7. What is the main role of the OR?
8. List the duties of the OR.
9. What is the purpose of the first meeting of creditors?
10. What percentage of creditors may request the OR to summon a meeting of creditors?
11. What resolutions may be taken at the first meeting of creditors?
12. How often must a trustee pay funds into the ISA a/c?
13. How many days notice must be given to creditors of a general meeting of creditors?

Now, go back to the Learning Objectives in the Introduction. If you are satisfied that you have achieved these, please tick them off.

Answers to Self-test

1. Within 21 days.

2. The OR, the trustee (if appointed), a special manager (if appointed), any creditor who has tendered a proof.

3. The OR must apply for a public examination if requisitioned by half or more of the creditors in value.

4. The debtor has 21 days in which to give notice to the trustee of his increase in income (s333).

5. Following changes introduced by EA 2002 it is no longer a criminal offence, however, it will be a consideration in whether a bankruptcy restriction order is made or not.

6. If he is dissatisfied by any act, omission or decision of the trustee he may apply to court.

    He may also complain to the relevant professional body of which the trustee is a member.

7. To protect the estate (s287).

8. To take all steps as he thinks fit for protecting the estate.

    To decide, in the period of 12 weeks from the date of the bankruptcy order, whether to call a meeting of creditors.

    To investigate the conduct and affairs of the bankrupt (unless he thinks an investigation is not necessary).

9. Appoint a trustee and establish a creditors' committee.

10. 25% of the creditors in value.

11. The business at the first meeting is restricted by r6.80 as follows:

    At the first meeting of creditors, no resolutions shall be taken other than the following:

    A resolution to appoint a named insolvency practitioner to be trustee in bankruptcy or two or more named insolvency practitioners as joint trustees.

    A resolution to establish a creditors' committee.

    (unless it has been resolved to establish a creditors' committee) a resolution specifying the terms on which the trustee is to be remunerated or to defer consideration of that matter.

    (if, and only if, two or more persons are appointed to act jointly as trustee) a resolution specifying whether acts are to be done by both or all of them, or by only one.

    (where the meeting has been requisitioned under s294) a resolution authorising payment out of the estate, as an expense of the bankruptcy, of the cost of summoning and holding the meeting.

    A resolution to adjourn the meeting for not more than three weeks.

    Any other resolution which the chairman thinks it right to allow for special reasons.

12. Once every 14 days or immediately if £5,000 or more.

13. 21 days.

Answer to Interactive Question

Interactive question: Edward Jones

(a) Company creditors can only act through a representative. A person cannot appear as a representative for more than one committee member, or as a committee member and as a representative for another member.

(b) Must be held within three months of:

    (i) Appointment of the trustee.
    (ii) Establishment of committee (if later).

Subsequent meetings may be held if:

    (i) called by trustee of own motion.
    (ii) called by trustee within 21 days of any member's request.
    (iii) committee so resolves.

(c) Functions of the committee:

To receive notice from the trustee of:

    (i) Employment of a solicitor.
    (ii) Disposal of any assets to an associate of the bankrupt.

To fix the trustee's remuneration if the creditors' meeting has not reserved this matter to itself.

To receive reports on matters which the trustee considers are of concern to the committee, or which the committee have indicated are of concern to it. Trustee must report unless:

    (i) No funds available in the estate to meet the costs of complying.
    (ii) Costs of compliance would be too great having regard to the importance of the matter.
    (iii) The request is frivolous.

S314(2) – to consent to the trustee appointing the bankrupt to:

- Superintend the management of his estate.
- Carry on the business for the creditors' benefit.
- Assist in the administration of the estate.

Consent should be obtained at the outset, however the trustee may, without undue delay, seek later ratification in cases of urgency.

If committee is established more than 28 days after the trustee came to office – to receive a report from the trustee and to question the trustee.

To receive reasonable travelling expenses (directly incurred in attending meetings or on committee business) as an expense of the administration of the estate.

To receive six monthly reports from the trustee (or up to two monthly on committee's request) and to call for production of the trustee's accounts and records (and to consider whether to ask for an audit of trustee's records).

Review security for office given by trustee.

To give sanction for exercise of powers listed in Schedule 5 Part 1 (see chapter 9, 1.1.6).

9

The trustee

Contents

Introduction
Examination context
Topic List
1 Duties of the trustee
2 Investigative powers of the trustee
3 Powers for getting in assets
4 Administrative powers of the trustee
5 Trustee's powers of realisation
6 Trustee's powers to make payments out
7 Remuneration of the trustee
8 Expenses and disbursements

Summary and Self-test
Answers to Self-test
Answer to Interactive Question

Introduction

Learning objectives

- Learn the powers which the trustee can exercise with and without sanction
- Identify the statutory provisions relating to the calculation and approval of trustee's fees
- Understand what information is to be provided to those responsible for the approval of fees
- Identify statutory provisions relating to the disclosure and drawing of disbursements

Working context

The trustee has a duty to get in and realise the bankrupt's estate. It is fundamental therefore that the trustee is aware of what powers he does have to aid him in his duty.

Stop and think

Why does the trustee require so many powers? Why should sanction be obtained before certain powers can be exercised? Who gives sanction? Why should the trustee seek approval of his fees from creditors? Why should he not be allowed to take whatever level of fees he deems necessary?

THE TRUSTEE

Examination context

The powers and duties of the trustee are regularly tested in the JIEB exam and should therefore be learnt thoroughly. Remuneration of the office holder may be tested in any of the three JIEB exam papers.

Exam requirements

Past questions to look at include:

2007	Question 3 (a)
2006	Question 1 (a) (b)
2004	Question 3 (i) (ii)
2000	Question 3 (a) (b)
1999	Question 1
1998	Question 2 (a) (b)
1995	Question 3 (a)
1994	Question 1 (a)
1992	Paper 1, Question 6 (a)

1 Duties of the trustee

Section overview

Sections 305 to 335 provide the statutory background for the function of the trustee which is to take possession of, realise and distribute the bankrupt's estate. The duties of the trustee come from both the principles of equity and statute. It is now a clearly established principle that the trustee should be treated as an officer of the court and as such the highest standard of conduct will be expected from the trustee in the discharge of his duties. This principle is derived from the case of *Ex. P James*, *Re Condon* and is often referred to as the rule in *Ex. P James*. The trustee must also ensure that he complies with the rules and code of conduct of his relevant professional body.

1.1 Officer of the court

1.1.1 To take possession of and realise the estate

The trustee has a duty to take possession of the estate including books, papers and records (s311). To realise the bankrupt's estate and distribute it in accordance with the IA 1986 (s305(2)). The trustee must be careful if he intends to enter into a transaction with an associate (as defined in s435) as unless the trustee has received prior court approval application may be made to the court to set the transaction aside. (Such an application is of course unlikely to be successful if the transaction was for value and the trustee was acting in good faith).

1.1.2 To provide information to the OR

Unless the trustee is also the OR, he is under a duty to comply with s305(3). This requires him to furnish the OR with such information, documentation and other assistance as he may reasonably require. This duty extends to the Secretary of State under Regulation 29 of Insolvency Regulations 1994.

1.1.3 To bank funds

The trustee has a duty to make payments into the Insolvency Services Account (ISA) of all monies received by him in the carrying out of his functions. Such payments must be made without deduction. The trustee must bank funds received once every 14 days or immediately if £5,000 or more has been received. (Detail of the mechanics of a payment in and out of the ISA can be found in Regulations 20 and 22 of the Insolvency Regulations 1994).

It should be remembered, however, that if the trustee intends to carry on the business of the bankrupt, he can make application to the Secretary of State to open a local bank account, ie a current account within the locality of the relevant insolvency court or locality of the business. (Detail in respect of the management of a local bank account is contained in Regulation 21 of the Insolvency Regulations 1994).

SIP 11 also gives guidance on the handling of funds.

1.1.4 To maintain records and accounts

The trustee has a duty to prepare and keep separate financial records in respect of each bankrupt, together with such supporting documentation as may be necessary. If the trustee is carrying on the bankrupt's business accounts must be kept in accordance with the Insolvency Regulations 1994.

The trustee is required to submit financial records to the creditors' committee on request and provide on 14 days notice a statement of his receipts and payments. Such statement can be requested by any creditor or the bankrupt.

All financial records and trading accounts shall be retained for a period of six years following his vacation from office, unless permission to destroy them is received from the OR (Insolvency Regulation 30).

SIP 7 also gives guidance on the maintenance of records and accounts.

1.1.5 To provide an account

Pursuant to Regulation 28 of the Insolvency Regulations 1994, the trustee must, at the request of the Secretary of State, send to him an account of his receipts and payments. This will cover whatever period the Secretary of State may direct and be certified by the trustee at the Secretary of State's request.

The trustee must provide the final meeting of creditors with a report including a summary of his receipts and payments and a statement that he has reconciled his accounts with that which is held by the Secretary of State in respect of the bankruptcy (r6.137(2). In addition, within 14 days of the holding of the final meeting of creditors, the trustee must send an account of his receipts and payments to the Secretary of State. This need only contain information not already provided in a previous account. (Regulation 28 Insolvency Regulations 1994)

1.1.6 To obtain sanction if required

Pursuant to s314 some of the trustee's powers require sanction of the creditor's committee (or Secretary of State) some do not. The main powers (found in Schedule 5) exercisable with sanction are:

- To carry on the bankrupt's business.
- Institute or defend legal proceedings.
- Refer to arbitration or compromise any claims, debts or liabilities incurred by other persons towards the bankrupt.

If the trustee does not obtain sanction he will lose his indemnity. The creditors' committee (or the court) can however ratify the actions of the trustee provided that it is satisfied that the trustee acted urgently and sought ratification without delay.

It should be noted that sanction is not required to appoint a solicitor but notice of the appointment should be given to the committee s314(6).

2 Investigative powers of the trustee

Section overview

The main source of the trustee's powers is s314 and Schedule 5. The powers of the trustee are both investigative, enabling him to ascertain and realise assets and administrative, to enable him to deal effectively with the bankruptcy.

The trustee has a number of powers to obtain information regarding the bankrupt's estate.

2.1 Public examination (s290)

OR may, at any time pre-discharge, apply to the court for public examination of bankrupt.

A simple majority of creditors by value may also requisition a public examination (s290(2)).

The trustee may attend and ask questions of the bankrupt, who will be examined as to 'his affairs, dealings and property and the causes of his failure'.

The following persons may also attend and ask questions:

- the OR.
- any person appointed as special manager.
- any creditor who has submitted a proof.

2.2 Private examination (s366)

The trustee/OR may apply to court for an order that any of the following be summoned before it:

- Bankrupt.
- Bankrupt's spouse or former spouse or civil partner or former civil partner.
- Any person known or believed to have any property comprised in the bankrupt's estate in his possession (who can be ordered by court to deliver it to the trustee or OR (s367(1)).
- Bankrupt's debtors (who may be ordered to pay all/part of debt to trustee or OR).
- Any person appearing to the court to be able to give information concerning the bankrupt or the bankrupt's dealings, affairs or property.

The court may require persons in possession of the bankrupt's property or relevant information, and the bankrupt's debtors to:

- Submit affidavits accounting for dealings with bankrupt.
- Produce any documents in their control/possession relating to the bankrupt or the bankrupt's dealings, affairs or property.

It should be remembered that the court has discretion as to whether or not to make an order under s366. If there are good grounds for failing to disclose information/property the court may take that into account when deciding whether or not to exercise that discretion (*Buchler v Al-Midani (No2) 2005*).

Where the person summonsed without reasonable excuse fails to appear, or has absconded or is about to abscond with a view to avoiding private examination, the court may issue a warrant for his arrest and seizure of any books, papers, records, money or goods in his persons possession (s366(3)).

The court will fix a venue for the examination (can be outside UK).

Persons summonsed may be examined on oath either orally or by written questions.

Note. Private examination is also available to interim receiver (s368).

2.3 Power to demand that HM Revenue and Customs produce document(s) (s369)

OR/trustee may apply to court for an order that for the purposes of public or private examination a Revenue official produce to court:

- Any return, account(s) submitted by the bankrupt (pre or post commencement of bankruptcy).
- Any assessment or determination made (pre or post commencement).
- Any correspondence (pre or post commencement).

The court can authorise disclosure of such documentation to OR/trustee/creditors.

If the document is not in the hands of the Revenue official to which the order is addressed, that official:

- Must take reasonable steps to secure possession.
- If fails to secure to report the reasons for failure to court.

Note. This power is not available to an interim receiver.

2.4 Power to seek redirection of mail (s371)

The OR/trustee may apply to court for order that the Post Office re-direct bankrupts mail to OR/trustee. Such an order may last for up to three months, however the OR/trustee may apply for subsequent orders.

2.5 Power to summon meetings of creditors (r6.81)

Such meetings can be requisitioned by creditors holding 25% or more in value of the bankruptcy debts.

The trustee must give the bankrupt 21 days' notice of the meeting (r6.84(1)), and *may* require him to attend (r6.84(3)).

If trustee doesn't require his attendance the bankrupt may still be admitted at the discretion of the chair whose decision will be final as to what (if any) intervention may be made by the bankrupt.

Where the bankrupt is present questions may be put to him by creditors, but again, this is at the chair's discretion (r6.84(6)).

2.6 Power to summon meetings of the creditors' committee (r6.153)

Members of the committee may seek explanation of any matter from the trustee. The trustee may in turn request information from the bankrupt.

2.7 Power of Arrest (s364)

The court has a general power to issue a warrant for the arrest of a debtor (against whom a bankruptcy petition has been issued) or a bankrupt and a general power to issue a warrant for the seizure of the books, papers, records, money, goods of such a person.

The power arises in five circumstances:

- He has absconded or is about to abscond.
- He is about to remove goods with a view to avoiding or delaying possession being taken by OR/ trustee.
- He has concealed or destroyed (or is about to conceal or destroy) any goods, books, papers or records which might be of use to creditors.
- He has (without leave of OR of trustee) removed any goods in his possession exceeding £100 in value.
- He has failed to attend any examination ordered by the court (without reasonable excuse).

Note. This is really a power of court rather than trustee.

2.8 Power of seizure (s365)

The trustee/OR may apply to court to issue a warrant for the seizure of:

- Any property comprised in bankrupt's estate.
- Any books, papers or records relating to the bankrupt's affairs or property.

S365(2) makes it clear that a person executing a warrant may break into premises and any 'receptacle of the bankrupt'.

The court has the power to issue warrants to enter the premises of third parties but only where satisfied bankrupt's property is concealed there.

2.9 Obtaining copies of entries in Land Registry

The trustee can apply for and obtain these and copy documents kept by the registrar.

The trustee provides a certificate that:

- He has reasons to believe the register may contain information.
- Which will assist in the discharge of the trustee's functions, and
- That the enquiries relate to the land described in the trustee's certificate.

Personal Insolvency

3 Powers for getting in assets

Section overview

The trustee has a number of powers for getting in assets in the bankrupt's estate.

3.1 General power of trustee (s311)

The trustee has a general power under s311/s312 to demand delivery of estate assets, books, papers and records. He is in the same position as if he were a receiver of property appointed by the High Court.

The bankrupt has a duty to deliver these to the OR or trustee. The OR in turn has a duty to deliver to the trustee. The duty also extends to supervisors of an IVA and third parties such as agents, bankers, solicitors and other advisors.

S349 makes it clear that liens (or other rights of retention) over books/papers or records of a bankrupt are unenforceable to the extent that enforcement would deny the OR or trustee possession.

The rule does not extend to documents of title held as such.

3.2 Private examination (s366)

Following a private examination under s366 the court has the power to make an order for delivery up of any property held by the bankrupt or third parties. The bankrupt's debtors can also be compelled to make payment to the trustee.

3.3 Power of arrest (s364)

The court has a general power under s364 to issue a warrant for the arrest of a debtor (against whom a bankruptcy petition has been presented) and the power to issue a warrant for the seizure of books, papers, records, money or goods of such a person.

3.4 Seizure of bankrupt's property (s365)

The trustee/OR may apply to court to issue a warrant for seizure of any property comprised in the bankrupt's estate.

3.5 Power to redeem assets subject to security (r6.117)

The trustee can redeem at the value given in the secured creditor's proof (costs of transfer will be born by estate).

The trustee must give the secured creditors 28 days' notice and creditors then have 21 days in which to revalue the security. If the creditor does revalue, trustee can only redeem at the new value. The creditor can also, by written notice, force the trustee to decide whether to redeem.

3.6 Power to redeem pledged goods (s311(5))

The trustee can serve notice on any third party holding estate goods by way of pledge, pawn or other security.

The effect of this is:

- Trustee can inspect goods (unless OR has already done so under the parallel provisions in s285(5)).
- Third party may not realise security until trustee has had reasonable opportunity to inspect.
- Trustee can exercise bankrupt's right of redemption.

4 Administrative powers of the trustee

Section overview

The trustee has a number of administrative powers.

4.1 Powers in Schedule 5 (ancillary)

Part III of the Schedule provides that for the purposes of any of his powers under Parts VIII to XI of the Act the trustee may, by his official name:

- Hold property of every description.
- Make contracts.
- Sue and be sued.
- Enter into any engagements binding on himself, and in respect of the bankrupt's estate, on his successors in office.
- Employ an agent.
- Execute any power of attorney, deed or other instrument.

He may do any other act which is necessary or expedient for the purposes of or in connection with the exercise of those powers.

4.2 Powers in Schedule 5 exercisable with sanction

(Sanction is given by the creditors' committee or the Secretary of State. Sanction can be given retrospectively and should not be unreasonably refused. If a trustee acts without sanction he will risk losing his indemnity.)

- Power, where any right, option, or other power forms part of the bankrupt's estate, to make payments or incur liabilities with a view to obtaining for the benefit of the creditors, any property which is the subject of the right or option or power.
- Carry on the bankrupt's business (so far as lawful under any enactment) with a view to beneficial winding-up.
- Institute or defend legal actions relating to property forming part of the bankrupt's estate.
- Refer to arbitration or compromise any claims, debts or liabilities incurred by other persons towards the bankrupt.

4.3 Powers in Schedule 5 exercisable without sanction

Power to deal with entails to same extent as bankrupt.

Power to prove, rank, claim and draw a dividend in respect of debts due to the bankrupt.

To give receipts for any money received by him, being receipts which eventually discharge the person paying the money from all responsibility in respect of its application.

4.4 Power to appoint a special manager (s370)

Application is by the OR or trustee on the ground that it appears that the nature of the estate, property or business, or the interests of creditors generally require the appointment of another person to manage the estate, property or business.

Personal Insolvency

Procedure

- The application must be accompanied by a report setting out:
    - Reasons for the application.
    - The estimated value of property which special manager is to manage.
- The court will make an order specifying the duration of the appointment (fixed or until court makes further order).
- Security (special or general) must be given by the appointee to the appointor up to at least the estimate of asset value given in the report. Appointor files a certificate of adequacy of security in court.
- Remuneration will be fixed by the court.
- Expenses of providing security are paid in the first instance by the special manager who is then entitled to be reimbursed out of the estate.

Powers are set out in court order (may include any of the powers exercisable by trustee).

Duties are production of three-monthly accounts containing details of receipts and payments, for the approval of the trustee and provision of such security as may be prescribed.

Termination of appointment is at end of fixed period or by the court on application of trustee (such an application may be requisitioned by a simple majority of creditors).

Note. OR has the same right to apply for appointment of special manager. OR might do this where:

- He has been appointed interim receiver (under s286) after presentation of petition but before bankruptcy order, or
- Becomes receiver of bankrupt's estate on making of bankruptcy order.

4.5 Powers in relation to public utilities (s372)

The trustee can demand supplies of gas from a gas supplier; electricity from an electricity supplier; water from a statutory water undertaking; and telecommunication services from a public telecommunications operator.

The supplier may make it a condition of the giving of the supply that the trustee personally guarantees the payment of charges but may NOT make it a condition that any outstanding charges for pre-commencement supplies are paid.

4.6 Power to appoint bankrupt (s314)

Under s314(2) the trustee may appoint the bankrupt to:

- Superintend the management of the whole or part of the estate.
- Carry on the business for the creditors benefit, or
- Assist in the administration of the estate.

Either the creditors' committee or the court must give permission. The permission must be specific not general and must be obtained by the trustee in advance of the exercise of the power. If it isn't the committee or court may ratify (for the purpose of enabling the trustee to meet his expenses out of the bankrupt's estate), but only if satisfied that trustee acted in a case of urgency and has sought ratification without undue delay.

Persons dealing with the trustee in good faith and for value do not have to enquire whether permission given.

4.7 Power to transfer shares (s311(3))

The trustee has the same right to transfer:

- Stock or shares in a company.
- Shares in a ship, or
- Any other property transferable in the books of a company, office or person, as the bankrupt would have had but for the bankruptcy.

4.8 Power to apply to court for directions (s303)

A trustee is entitled to use his own discretion in administering the estate.

A trustee cannot transfer the exercise of that discretion to the court by applying for directions. However, he may apply to court for directions in relation to any particular matter arising under the bankruptcy.

Directions should only be applied for in cases of genuine difficulty. The court has power to direct the bankrupt to do anything for the purposes of the bankruptcy (s363(3)). Non-compliance is a contempt of court.

4.9 Power to appoint a solicitor

The trustee must give notice of any appointment of a solicitor to the creditors' committee.

5 Trustee's powers of realisation

Section overview

The trustee has a number of powers to assist him in realising the bankrupt's estate.

5.1 Powers in Schedule 5 exercisable without sanction

Power to sell any part of the estate including book debts and goodwill.

Power to prove rank, claim and draw a dividend in respect of debts due to the bankrupt.

5.2 Powers in Schedule 5 exercisable with sanction

Power to accept as consideration for the sale of any part of the estate a sum of money payable at a future time, subject to such stipulations as to security or otherwise as the committee or court thinks fit.

5.3 Power to dispose of property to the bankrupt's associates (s314(6))

The permission of the committee is not required but the committee must be notified.

Associates of the bankrupt are defined in s435:

- Spouse or civil partner.
- Relatives of the bankrupt and spouse or civil partner.
- The spouses of those relatives.
- Partners (and their families).
- Employers/employees of bankrupt.
- Trustees.
- Companies controlled by the bankrupt and/or his associates.

Personal Insolvency

6 Trustee's powers to make payments out

Section overview

The trustee has a number or powers.

6.1 Powers in Schedule 5 exercisable with sanction

Compromise or make arrangements with creditors in respect of their bankruptcy debts.

Mortgage or pledge assets to raise money for the payment of debts.

Enter into any compromise or arrangement in respect of claims against the estate.

6.2 Estimate the value of any debt (s322(3))

If a debt which, by reason of it being subject to any contingency or contingencies or for any other reason, does not bear a certain value then the trustee can estimate its value.

If the value of a debt is estimated by the trustee the amount provable in the bankruptcy is the amount of the estimate.

6.3 Refund premiums

The trustee can refund articled clerks or apprentices' premiums as may be appropriate having regard to the unexpired portion of the contract (which can also be transferred).

6.4 Distribute property in specie under s326(1)

The trustee may, with the permission of the creditors' committee, divide in its existing form amongst the bankrupt's creditors, according to its estimated value, any property which from its peculiar nature or other special circumstances, cannot be readily or advantageously sold.

Permission of the committee must be sought. Terms are the same as for s314.

7 Remuneration of the trustee

Section overview

Office holders obtain payment of their fees out of assets which would otherwise be available to creditors. It is important therefore that those with a direct financial interest in the level of the office holder's fees feel confident that the rules relating to the charging of remuneration have been properly complied with.

The statutory provisions relating to remuneration in bankruptcy is set out in r6.138 to r6.142 and SIP 9 ensures that office holders are familiar with the statutory provisions relating to the calculation, disclosure and drawing of remuneration.

7.1 Basis of calculation

The trustee is entitled to receive remuneration for his services decided either as a percentage of the value of the bankrupt's estate which is realised or distributed, or by reference to time spent on the bankruptcy.

Unless the trustee is the OR, the creditors will fix the trustee's remuneration either through the creditors' committee or if there is no committee by resolution of a creditors' meeting. The creditors will decide whether the trustee is to be remunerated on a percentage or time basis and to determine the relevant percentage.

If the creditors do not fix the trustee's remuneration, the trustee will automatically receive remuneration laid down in the Schedule 6 scale. The scale may be found in the Insolvency Regulations 1994. The tables showing the remuneration are set out in Schedule 6 to those regulations (r6.138A).

If the trustee is dissatisfied with the amount of remuneration set by the creditors' committee he may request it be increased by resolution of the creditors or by the court (the court may also intervene where remuneration has been set by the creditors on the Schedule 6 scale).

The procedure for such court application is contained in r6.141.

The trustee must give at least 14 days' notice of his intention to apply to court to the creditors' committee who may appoint one or more members to appear, and to be heard, on the application.

If there is no creditors' committee the trustee should give notice of his application to one or more of the bankrupt's creditors as directed by the court. The notified creditors may appear or be represented at the hearing. The court may, if it appears to be a proper case, order the costs of the trustee's application to be paid out of the estate.

7.2 Criteria

The following criteria should be used to judge the reasonableness of the fees being requested (r6.138(4)):

- The complexity or otherwise of the case.
- Any responsibility of an exceptional kind or degree which falls on the office holder.
- The effectiveness with which the trustee is or has carried out his duties.
- The value and nature of the assets in the estate.

7.3 Creditor dissatisfaction (r6.142)

Any creditor with the support of at least 25% in value of the creditors may apply to court for an order that the trustee's remuneration be reduced. The 25% includes the dissatisfied creditor. The ground for the application is that the remuneration is excessive (r6.142).

The court may, if it thinks that no sufficient cause is shown for the application, dismiss it, but it shall not do so unless the applicant has had an opportunity to attend the court for an ex parte hearing, of which he has been given at least seven days' notice.

If a venue for the hearing is set, the applicant must give 14 days' notice to the trustee, accompanied by a copy of the application and any evidence which the applicant intends to provide in support of it. The court may make an order fixing the remuneration at a reduced rate.

Unless the court orders otherwise, the costs of the application shall be paid by the applicant and do not fall on the estate.

7.4 Realisation of secured assets

Pursuant to r6.139, where the trustee sells assets on behalf of a secured creditor, he is entitled to remuneration out of the proceeds of sale. The amount of the remuneration will be equivalent to the amount that could be charged by applying the Schedule 6 scale.

7.5 Schedule 6 scale

The scale acts as a fall back position for trustees where neither the creditors' committee nor a general meeting of creditors has determined the basis of fees. Until 1 April 2004 this scale was referred to as the 'OR's scale', although the ORs are now entitled to flat rate administration fees.

Personal Insolvency

The Schedule 6 scale is as follows:

Band		Realisation scale %	Distribution scale %
First	£5,000	20	10.0
Next	£5,000	15	7.5
Next	£90,000	10	5.0
All further sums		5	2.5

7.6 Official receiver (OR)

Where the OR is the trustee and the order was made after 1 April 2004 the OR scale will no longer apply. Instead the OR will be entitled to a flat rate administration fee of £1,715.

In addition, the OR is entitled to revised hourly rates for work on the case, such as:

- the appointment of agents re realising assets.
- the making of a distribution to creditors.
- the realisation of assets on behalf of holders of fixed and floating charges.
- the supervision of a special manager.

7.7 Secretary of State administration fees

In bankruptcy Secretary of State administration fees must be paid on amounts paid into the Insolvency Service Account.

The relevant fee is 17% of chargeable receipts over £2,000 up to a maximum of £80,000. Chargeable receipts mean sums paid into the Insolvency Service Account after deduction of sums paid to secured creditors and sums spent in carrying on the business of the bankrupt.

Secretary of State administration fees will not be chargeable where monies are paid into the ISA just to meet the OR's debit balance on a case.

7.8 SIP 9

SIP 9 sets out provisions regarding the remuneration of all office holders, liquidators, administrators, administrative receivers, trustees in bankruptcy and supervisors of individual and company arrangements.

SIP 9 ensures that office holders are familiar with the statutory provisions regarding remuneration and covers, amongst others:

- On what basis remuneration is to be calculated.
- What criteria should be used to judge the reasonableness of fees.
- Who should authorise the drawing of fees.
- What an office holder can do if he is dissatisfied with the level of fees.

The SIP also includes a series of pro-forma guidance notes which can be made available to creditors and which summarise their rights under insolvency legislation.

7.9 Provision of information

SIP 9 sets out best practice with regards to the provision of information to those responsible for the approval of fees.

The office holder must ensure that those charged with approving his fees have access to sufficient information about the basis of fees to be able to make an informed judgement as to the reasonableness of the proposed fees when:

- Seeking approval to the terms of remuneration.
- Seeking approval to fees to be taken.

The guidance given in SIP 9 relates to all insolvency appointments not just bankruptcies.

7.10 Seeking agreement to the terms of remuneration

When agreement is sought as to the terms on which the office holder is to be remunerated, he should provide the meeting with details of the charge out rates of all grades of staff which are likely to be involved in the case.

Before any resolution is passed to fix the remuneration, the office holder should send to the creditors the appropriate SIP 9 Appendix C explanatory note or provide the equivalent information in some other suitable format (see 7.13 for details).

When agreement to fees is sought the office holder should provide an up to date receipts and payments account.

Where fees are based on a time cost basis, the office holder should disclose details of time spent and charge out values and such additional information as may reasonably be required having regard to the size and complexity of the case. This would include an analysis of time spent on the case by activity and grade of staff.

Appendix D of SIP 9 sets out a suggested format for producing the information required. This suggested format classifies work functions as follows:

- Administration and planning.
- Investigations.
- Realisation of assets.
- Trading.
- Creditors.
- Case specific matters.

The table classifies the hours spent on those functions by grade of staff as follows:

- Partner.
- Manager.
- Other senior professional.
- Assistants and support staff.

The degree of analysis should be proportionate to the size and complexity of the case.

7.11 Sub contracted work

Where fees are based on a % basis, the office holder must provide details of any work which has or is to be sub-contracted out which would normally be carried out by the office holder.

7.12 Requests for information

Where an office holder is appointed on or after 1 April 2005, under Regulation 36A they are required to provide certain information about the time spent on a case, free of charge, upon request. The persons who are entitled to ask for this information are:

- Any creditor in the case.
- Where the case relates to a company, any director or contributory, of that company.
- Where the case relates to an individual, that individual.

The information to be provided is:

- The total number of hours spent on the case by the office holder or staff assigned to the case.
- For each grade of staff, the average hourly rate at which they are charged out at.
- The number of hours spent by each grade of staff in the relevant period.

The information must be provided within 28 days of receipt of the request by the office holder.

Personal Insolvency

7.13 SIP 9 Appendix C – creditor's guidance note

The SIP 9 Appendix C guidance note contains the following information:

- Explanation that costs are payable out of assets, therefore creditors have a direct interest in cost/remuneration levels. Consequently, legislation provides a mechanism for creditors to fix fees.
- Brief description of the nature of the insolvency appointment.
- Brief description of the constitution and function of the committee (not VAs).
- Explanation of:
    - Basis of fees.
    - Criteria to be applied.
    - Who is responsible for deciding on the basis and amount of remuneration.
- Information which should be provided by the office holder.
- Rights of creditors if dissatisfied.
- Rights of office holder if dissatisfied.

Interactive question: Kay Baldwin

You are trustee in bankruptcy of Kay Baldwin and have realised all assets and paid all costs and expenses and made an initial dividend payment to creditors. You have just received a letter from Kay claiming that your remuneration is excessive by at least £5,000. Your remuneration was fixed by the creditors' committee, however, Peter Smith, the bankrupt's brother (who is not on the committee despite being a major creditor) agrees.

Requirement

How would you deal with the complaint from Kay?

See **Answer** at the end of this chapter.

8 Expenses and disbursements

Section overview

SIP 9 sets out best practice with regard to the drawing and disclosure of expenses and disbursements:

- All disbursements should be disclosed.
- Category 1 disbursements do not require approval.
- Category 2 disbursements require approval.

8.1 Disclosure

Office holders should disclose and explain how charges are made up and the basis upon which they have been calculated. They should be disclosed to those responsible for approving remuneration, that is, the creditors' committee or the general body of creditors.

8.2 Category 1 disbursements

Approval is not required for the drawing of category 1 disbursements. These comprise specific expenditure which relates to the administration of the insolvency case and which are paid to an independent third party.

Examples include telephone calls, postage and case advertising. It will also include case specific services which cannot be provided internally such as printing, room hire and document storage.

8.3 Category 2 disbursements

Category 2 disbursements require approval. They represent costs which, whilst being in the nature of expenses or disbursements, include elements of shared or allocated costs. Examples include room hire or document storage in the office holder's own offices, copying and printing. Such disbursements must be specific to the case and are normally expected to be in line with the cost of external provision.

Solicitor liquidators, trustees and administrators must ensure that they seek authorisation for payment of profit costs to their own firm (for any legal work done on behalf of the company/individual).

Summary and Self-test

Summary

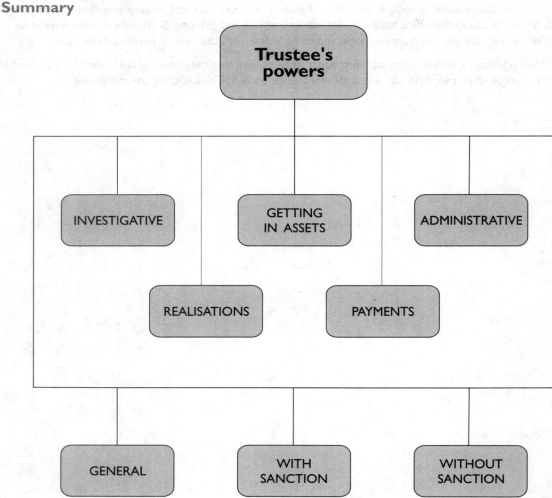

Self-test

Answer the following questions.

1. What are the general duties of the trustee?
2. What value of creditors may requisition a public examination of a bankrupt?
3. Who may be summoned by the trustee/OR for a private examination?
4. The court has a general power to issue a warrant for the arrest of a bankrupt. In what circumstances will such a power arise?
5. Under s314(2) the trustee may appoint the bankrupt to do what?
6. Which of the following powers are exercisable without sanction?
   - Carry on the bankrupt's business.
   - Institute or defend legal actions relating to property forming part of the bankrupt's estate.
   - Power to prove, rank, claim and draw a dividend in respect of debts due to the bankrupt.
   - Compromise or make arrangements with creditors in respect of their bankruptcy debts.
   - Power to sell any part of the estate including book debts and goodwill.
7. On what basis may a trustee be remunerated?
8. Who will fix the basis of the trustee's remuneration?
9. If a creditor is dissatisfied with the level of the trustee's remuneration what may he do?
10. You have been appointed trustee in bankruptcy of Sarah Harding. To date assets have been realised in the sum of £128,000 and a dividend to unsecured creditors has been paid totalling £76,000. Calculate your remuneration using the Schedule 6 Scale.

Now, go back to the Learning Objectives in the Introduction. If you are satisfied that you have achieved these, please tick them off.

Answers to Self-test

1. To take possession of and realise the estate.

   To distribute the estate.

   Furnish the OR with such information, documentation and other assistance as he may reasonably require.

   Bank funds in ISA every 14 days or immediately if over £5,000.

   Prepare and keep separate financial records in respect of each bankruptcy.

   Send an account of receipts and payments to the Secretary of State upon request and within 14 days of the final meeting.

   Obtain sanction if required.

2. A simple majority of creditors by value (s290(2)).

3. Bankrupt.

   Bankrupt's spouse or former spouse, or civil partner or former civil partner.

   Any person known or believed to have any property comprised in the bankrupt's estate in his possession.

   Bankrupt's debtors.

   Any person appearing to the court to be able to give information concerning the bankrupt or the bankrupt's dealings, affairs or property.

4. He has absconded or is about to abscond.

   He is about to remove goods with a view to avoiding or delaying possession being taken by OR/ trustee.

   He has concealed or destroyed (or is about to conceal or destroy) any goods, books, papers or records which might be of use to creditors.

   He has, without leave of OR or trustee, removed any goods in his possession exceeding £1,000 in value.

   He has failed to attend any examination ordered by the court (without reasonable excuse).

5. (a) Superintend the management of the whole or part of the estate.
   (b) Carry on the business for the creditor's benefit.
   (c) Assist in the administration of the estate.

6. Power to prove, rank, claim and draw a dividend in respect of debts due to the bankrupt.

   Power to sell any part of the estate including book debts and goodwill.

7. (a) As a % of the value of the bankrupt's estate which is realised or distributed, or
   (b) By reference to time spent on the bankruptcy.

8. The creditors, either through a creditors' committee or if there is no committee, by resolution of a creditors' meeting.

9. Any creditor with the support of at least 25% in value of the creditors may apply to court for an order that the trustee's remuneration be reduced on the grounds that it is excessive.

10 Realisations:

		£
5,000 @ 20%		1,000
5,000 @ 15%		750
90,000 @ 10%		9,000
28,000 @ 5%		1,400
128,000		12,150

Distributions:

		£
5,000 @ 10%		500
5,000 @ 7.5%		375
66,000 @ 5%		3,300
76,000		4,175

Total remuneration £12,150 + £4,175 = £16,325.

Answer to Interactive Question

Interactive question: Kay Baldwin

Write to Kay explaining:

- Trustee has a right to remuneration for services.

- Calculated either (r6.138):
    - As a % of assets realised and distributed, or both.
    - By reference to the time properly given by the trustee and his staff.

- Where the trustee is other than the OR it is for the creditors' committee to determine the basis upon which the fees are drawn.

- In arriving at the determination the committee must have regard to the following matters:
    - Complexity or otherwise of the case.
    - Any exceptional responsibility involved.
    - Effectiveness with which carried out duties.
    - Value and nature of assets within the estate.

- If there is no creditors' committee, or committee doesn't fix, the trustee's remuneration may be fixed by a resolution of the creditors in general meeting.

- Ensure requirements of SIP 9 met regarding disclosure of information re hours spent/charge out rates etc.

- Ensure appropriate approval obtained prior to drawing fees.

- Advise Kay that if a creditor is unhappy with the level of fees then under r6.142 they can, with the concurrence of 25% in value of the creditors, apply to court for an order that the remuneration be reduced on the grounds that it is, in all the circumstances, excessive.

- The court may dismiss the application if thinks no cause shown (applicant has opportunity to attend an ex parte hearing on seven days' notice).

- If the application is not dismissed the court will fix a hearing. 14 days' notice must be given to the trustee, accompanied by a copy of the application and any evidence.

- If court considers application to be well founded it will order remuneration to be reduced.

Note. the bankrupt herself cannot apply to court for the remuneration to be reduced, but her brother, Peter Smith, could as a creditor.

10

Bankruptcy estate

Contents

Introduction
Examination context
Topic List
1 The estate
2 Powers of the trustee to augment the estate
3 Antecedent transactions
4 The matrimonial home
5 Realising the equity
6 Steps if equity cannot be realised
Appendix 1 Insolvency Guidance Paper – Bankruptcy – family homes

Summary and Self-test
Answers to Self-test
Answers to Interactive Questions

Personal Insolvency

Introduction

Learning objectives

Tick off

- Identify those assets which form part of the bankruptcy estate and those that don't ☐
- State the powers of the trustee to augment the estate ☐
- Identify antecedent transactions and the powers of the trustee to challenge such transactions ☐
- Understand the steps the trustee will take to ascertain, protect and realise a bankrupt's share of the matrimonial home ☐
- Equitable accounting- know when it is used and be able to make a simple calculation of the bankrupt's interest ☐
- Understand the steps the trustee can take when he is unable to realise the bankrupt's share of the equity in the matrimonial home ☐

Working context

A trustee's main duty is to realise the assets of the debtor for the benefit of the bankruptcy creditors. In order to do this the trustee must know what assets form part of the bankruptcy estate and what powers he has to realise those assets. A share in a matrimonial home is often the bankrupt's most significant asset. It is therefore important to understand the legislation regarding the realisation of this asset and the practical difficulties faced by a trustee when seeking to realise this asset.

Stop and think

Why are some assets excluded from the bankruptcy estate? Why is it sometimes difficult for a trustee to realise a share in a matrimonial home? Why aren't properties always owned 50:50?

BANKRUPTCY ESTATE 10

Examination context

The bankruptcy estate is a very popular topic for the JIEB exam, in particular, how the trustee may augment the estate and the matrimonial home.

Exam requirements

Past questions to look at include:

2008	Question 2 (b)
2007	Question 3 (b)
2007	Question 4 (a)
2004	Question 1
2004	Question 3 (i) (ii)
2003	Question 4 (i)
2003	Question 5 (i)
2002	Question 2
2002	Question 3
2001	Question 1
2000	Question 2
1999	Question 4
1998	Question 1
1997	Question 2
1996	Question 2 (i)
1996	Question 3
1996	Question 5
1995	Question 1
1995	Question 5 (b)
1994	Question 4
1994	Question 5
1993	Question 4
1992	Paper II, Question 6
1990	Paper I, Question 5 (a)

Personal Insolvency

1 The estate

Section overview

A bankrupt's estate comprises all property belonging to or vested in the bankrupt at the commencement of bankruptcy (s283(1)). The bankruptcy legislation seeks to both protect the bankrupt's estate and ensure that the OR (and trustee in bankruptcy) receives all relevant information concerning the bankrupt and his estate.

Definition

Property: includes money, goods, things in action, land and every description of property wherever situated and also obligations and every description of interest, whether present or future, vested or contingent, arising out of or incidental to property (s436).

Commencement: a bankruptcy is deemed to commence on the date of the bankruptcy order.

1.1 Vesting of the estate

The bankrupt's estate vests in the trustee immediately on his appointment taking effect, or in the case of the OR, on his becoming trustee (s306(1)).

When the appointment takes effect depends upon the manner of the trustee's appointment:

- Trustee appointed by a creditors' meeting – appointment takes effect as of the date of the chairman's certificate.
- Trustee appointed by the court, this happens in two situations:
  - On a debtor's petition when the court orders the practitioner to 'inquire and report': If the outcome is that no voluntary arrangement is entered into the court may appoint the practitioner as trustee.
  - Where bankrupt was previously subject to a voluntary arrangement the court can appoint the supervisor as trustee.

  The appointment takes effect at the time specified in the court order.
- Trustee appointed by the Secretary of State – the appointment takes effect at the time specified in the Secretary of State's certificate (r6.122(2)).

The estate vests in the trustee by operation of law, there is no need for any conveyance, assignment or transfer (s306(2)).

1.2 Assets excluded from the estate

The following assets do not form part of the bankrupt's estate:

- Such tools, books, vehicles and other items of equipment as are necessary to the bankrupt for use personally by him in his employment, business or vocation.
- Such clothing, bedding, furniture, household equipment and provisions as are necessary for satisfying the basic domestic needs of the bankrupt and his family.
- Property held by the bankrupt on trust for any other person.
- Income for reasonable domestic needs.
- After acquired property.

- Assets subject to forfeiture clauses (for example, a commercial lease usually provides for forfeiture and re-entry on non-payment of rent or on bankruptcy).
- Peerages and titles of honour.
- Liens on books, papers or records of the bankrupt are unenforceable to the extent they would deny possession to the trustee – s349.
- Rights under an approved pension scheme for petitions presented after 29 May 2000.
- Student loans are specifically excluded from the estate (Higher Education Act 2004).

1.3 Trust property

Where the bankrupt is trustee s283(3) provides that property held by the bankrupt on trust for any other person is excluded from the estate. Examples include:

- Money held by the bankrupt on resulting trust
    - *Re Kayford* – trust of monies paid by customers for mail order goods
    - *Barclays Bank Ltd v Quistclose Investments.*
- Bankrupt is an executor of a deceased's estate.
- Bankrupt is a trustee of an express trust.
- Bankrupt is a solicitor holding client account money, *Re A Solicitor 1951*.
- Building contracts on terms which specify that the contractor (the bankrupt) holds monies paid by the client on trust for sub-contractors.
- Property held by the bankrupt on constructive trust, eg where a director or trustee is in breach of equitable, fiduciary duties, eg by making a secret profit (*IDC v Cooley*). The company or trust claiming the property from the bankrupt must be able to trace it for the constructive trust to apply. If it cannot be traced the company or trust are only creditors of the bankrupt.

If the bankrupt is a beneficiary – the trustee will claim the beneficial interest. If it is vested in the bankrupt pre-commencement it will automatically vest in the trustee. If it vests in the bankrupt post commencement the trustee will have to claim under the windfall provisions (see post).

There is an exception – 'Protective Trusts' under s33 Trustee Act 1925. In such a trust a (usually) improvident beneficiary is made a life tenant. His interest terminates if he becomes bankrupt or seeks to alienate his interest. A discretionary trust then arises in favour of the bankrupt and his family.

If the bankrupt is a settlor the trustee may challenge the settlement under s339 or s423 (transactions at an undervalue).

2 Powers of the trustee to augment the estate

Section overview
The trustee has a number of powers which enable him to bring assets into the estate which would otherwise be excluded.

2.1 Items of excess value

The general provision is that household effects are excluded from the bankruptcy estate (s283(2)). However, s308 allows the trustee to claw back such items where realisation would benefit the creditors.

Where it appears to the trustee that the realisable value of the whole or any part of that property exceeds the cost of a reasonable replacement for that property or that part of it the trustee may give written notice claiming the property.

Personal Insolvency

By s309 the trustee must serve the notice within 42 days from the date on which the property in question first came to his 'knowledge':

- Successor trustees are deemed to have the knowledge of their predecessors in title but
- Pre-appointment knowledge of a trustee is not deemed to come to his knowledge until appointment.

The effect of serving of notice is that the:

- Property vests in trustee and is now part of the bankrupt's estate.
- Trustee's title relates back to commencement (subject to the rights of any bona fide purchaser for value without notice).
- Trustee now has a duty to apply estate funds to the purchase by or on behalf of the bankrupt of a reasonable replacement for the property clawed-back. (s308(3)) (obviously only applies once there are sufficient funds to buy the replacement).

Note. This duty to replace has priority over the obligation of the trustee to distribute the estate.

Definition

Reasonable: 'Reasonably adequate for meeting the needs met by the other property' (s308(4)).

A dissatisfied bankrupt may apply to the court under s303. The court can do as it thinks fit. It will probably think fit to dismiss the application.

Procedure under s308:

- The replacement item can be purchased before or after the realisation of the property it replaces.
- A third party can buy-off the trustee by paying a sum of money sufficient to leave the bankrupt in possession of the item(s) being clawed back.

2.2 Income

Income generally does not form part of the bankrupt's estate, however, s310(1) allows the trustee to apply to the court for an order that part of the bankrupt's income be paid over. Such income now becomes part of the estate.

In practice the trustee will only apply if he is unable to negotiate a figure with the bankrupt. (The trustee can apply to court for an income payments order (IPO) or following EA 2002 the bankrupt can consent to an income payments agreement (IPA)).

An application for an IPO/IPA must be made before the discharge of the bankrupt.

The procedure for the trustee to follow to claim the income is as follows:

2.2.1 Procedure (r6.189)

The trustee applies to the court and a venue is fixed. (The application must be made pre-discharge of the bankrupt.)

The trustee gives the bankrupt 28 days' notice of the hearing together with a copy of the application and a short statement of the grounds of the application.

The bankrupt can now:

- Consent in writing to the application (to court and trustee) at least seven days before the hearing, or
- Attend the hearing (this will be mandatory) and show cause why the order should be other than that applied for.

The order must leave the bankrupt with sufficient income for meeting the reasonable domestic needs of the bankrupt and his family (s310(2)).

BANKRUPTCY ESTATE 10

An IPO must specify the period during which it is to have effect. The IPO may end after the discharge of the bankrupt but may not end after the period of three years beginning with the date on which the order is made (s310(6)).

At the hearing two types of order can be made (s310(3)):

- Bankrupt to pay trustee, or
- person who pays bankrupt to pay trustee direct (instead of via bankrupt).

(1) Bankrupt to pay trustee:

Bankrupt will be sent copy of court order by trustee (r6.190(1)).

If the bankrupt fails to comply trustee can apply to court to vary the terms of the order so that payor pays trustee direct.

(2) Person who pays the bankrupt to pay trustee direct:

Payor will be sent copy of court order by trustee (bankrupt also gets copy).

Payor must now 'make arrangements requisite for immediate compliance with the order' (r6.192(1)). Payor may deduct clerical and administrative costs from the amount to be paid and must give the bankrupt a written statement of those deductions.

Payor notifies trustee if no longer liable to make payments.

Where court makes an income payments order it may vary or discharge any attachment of earnings order currently in force (s310(4)).

Court may always vary or discharge the order.

- Trustee or bankrupt may apply.
- If the trustee applies the procedure is the same as when a trustee applies for an order in the first place (r6.193(2)).
- If the bankrupt applies he must provide a short statement of the grounds of the application.
- Applicant must be given the chance to be heard by the court (attendance on seven days notice) before court dismisses application. If court does not dismiss it will then set a venue.
- Trustee may appear at hearing. Alternatively can file written report of any matters which he thinks should be drawn to the courts attention.

2.2.2 Income Payment Agreements

S310A introduces a new Income Payment Agreement (IPA) procedure to remove the need for court involvement in non-contentious cases. The procedure is contained in r6.193A–C.

An IPA is a written agreement made between the bankrupt and his trustee by which the bankrupt voluntarily agrees to pay a specified sum to his estate for a specified period of time. It comes into force on the date on which the OR, or the trustee, dates it.

As with an IPO an IPA must be entered into prior to discharge. An IPA can be enforced in the same way as an IPO.

The bankrupt, or the trustee, can vary an IPO/IPA on application to the court. The application can be made before or after discharge. The procedure is contained in r6.193.

Prior to EA 2002 IPO's generally ceased upon the discharge of the bankrupt. Given the reduced period of automatic discharge to 12 months, the period of the IPO is now a maximum period of three years from the making of the order (or agreement) s310. This means therefore that the bankrupt may have to continue to pay into the estate notwithstanding the discharge from bankruptcy.

2.3 After acquired property

The trustee can, by written notice, claim for the bankrupt's estate any property which has been acquired by or devolves upon the bankrupt since commencement of the bankruptcy (s307(1)). Excluded property cannot be claimed (s307(2)). By s309(1) the trustee must serve notice on the bankrupt within 42 days of when it first came to the knowledge of the trustee that the property had been acquired. Again a new trustee is deemed to have the knowledge of the old and a trustee who has 'knowledge' pre-appointment is only deemed to know from appointment. The court will not extend time limits unless the trustee makes out a substantial case for it being just and proper for the court to exercise its statutory discretion to extend time.

S307(4) provides protection for:

- Bona fide purchasers for value without notice.
- A banker entering into a transaction in good faith and without notice.

The effect of giving notice under s307 is that the property vests in the trustee as part of the bankrupt's estate and the trustee's title relates back to the moment of acquisition.

2.4 Pensions

It is important to understand the various different types of pensions referred to in the legislation.

A personal pension policy is a contractual agreement with a pension provider (eg Equitable Life), which is, essentially, a form of investment agreement.

An occupational scheme is a pension trust set up by an individual's employer. The employer will usually be 'principal employer' under the scheme and trustees will be appointed to administer it. The employer will make contributions to the scheme as well as the employee.

An approved pension scheme is defined in s11 Welfare Reform and Pensions Act 1999 (WRPA) and includes personal pension policies and occupational pension schemes approved by HM Revenue and Customs. HM Revenue and Customs sets limits with regard to the amount that individuals are allowed to contribute into both types of pension arrangements.

With both a personal pension and an occupational pension scheme an employee may 'contract out' of the State Second Pension (SP2). This element is known as a 'guaranteed minimum pension' (GMP) or 'protected rights', depending on the type of pension and the time the pension was taken out.

The protected rights or GMP element are protected from an individual's insolvency by virtue of the s159(5) Pension Schemes Act 1993 ie. They do not vest in the trustee. Consequently, it is the other constituents of the fund that a trustee may be interested in.

S11 WRPA provides that where a bankruptcy order is made against a petition presented after 29 May 2000, any rights under an approved pension arrangement are excluded from the estate. Both personal and occupational approved pension arrangements are protected.

However, a trustee will be able to apply for an income payments order in respect of any pension payments made to the bankrupt. This is because the WRPA inserts the words 'despite anything in s11 or s12 of WRPA 1999' into s310(7).

Further powers have been given to the trustee by s15 WRPA, which came into force on 29th May 2000. S15 inserts new sections 342A into the IA. These sections provide that a trustee can apply to court for an order that excessive contributions previously made by a bankrupt into his pension, that have unfairly prejudiced his creditors, be paid back to the estate. The trustee can attack contributions made by the bankrupt, or on his behalf by someone else, made at any time ie. There is no set relevant time limit.

The court will consider:

- Whether any of the contributions were made for the purpose of putting assets beyond the reach of creditors, and
- Whether the total amount of any contributions made are excessive in view of the individual's circumstances when those contributions were made.

The court may make such order as it thinks fit for restoring the position to what it would have been had the excessive contributions not been made. This might include:

- Requiring the person responsible for the pension arrangement to pay an amount to the individual's trustee in bankruptcy.
- Adjusting the liabilities of the arrangement in respect of the bankrupt or any other beneficiary, and
- Payment of the costs of the person responsible complying with the court order.

Unapproved pension schemes are not excluded and will vest in the trustee. However, S12 WRPA, which came into force in April 2002, provides that the court may exclude pension rights in unapproved arrangements from a bankrupt's estate. The court will take into consideration the future likely needs of the bankrupt and his family and whether any benefits under the pension appear likely to be adequate for meeting those needs.

S14 refers to personal pensions only and will provide that a bankrupt's rights cannot be forfeited.

2.5 Disclaimed property

The trustee can disclaim onerous property.

Definition

Onerous property: Any unprofitable contract, or any other property comprised in the debtor's estate which is unsaleable, or not readily saleable, or such that it may give rise to a liability to pay money or perform any onerous act (s315).

The trustee can disclaim property even if he has:
- Taken possession of the property.
- Endeavoured to sell the property.
- Exercised rights of ownership in relation to it.

However, the trustee cannot disclaim, except with leave of court, property which has been claimed by the trustee as:
- After acquired property, or
- Household effects exceeding reasonable replacement value.

2.5.1 Effect of disclaimer

S315(3):
- A disclaimer determines, from date of disclaimer, the rights, interests and liabilities of the bankrupt and his estate in respect of the disclaimed property, and
- Discharges the trustee from all personal liability in respect of the property disclaimed as from appointment as trustee.

2.5.2 Rights of Third Parties

Disclaimers only affect third parties to the extent necessary to release the bankrupt and trustee from their obligations.

A third party suffering loss as a result of disclaimer can claim in the bankruptcy.

S316 allows any person interested in property to apply, in writing, to the trustee requiring trustee to decide whether or not to disclaim:
- Application is in Form 6.62 (notice to elect) or a substantially similar form (r6.183(2)(b)).
- Person interested delivers the application to the trustee personally or by registered post.
- Trustee now has 28 days in which to disclaim the property.

Personal Insolvency

- If he fails to disclaim he can now no longer do so (s316(1)) and is deemed to have adopted any contracts (s316(2)).

S320 allows interested parties to apply to the court for an order vesting the disclaimed property in them.

2.5.3 Court orders vesting disclaimed property (s320)

The following people may make an application to the court for a vesting order:

- Any person who claims an interest in the disclaimed property.
- Any person under a liability in respect of the disclaimed property (unless the disclaimer will discharge it).
- Where the disclaimed property is property in a dwelling house any person in occupation or entitled to occupy at date of petition.

The application must be made within three months of either the applicant becoming aware of the disclaimer *or* service of notice of disclaimer, whichever is earlier.

The application is by way of an affidavit detailing:

- Category of applicant under s320(2).
- Date applicant became aware/received notice of the disclaimer.
- Grounds of application for a vesting order.
- Order applicant desires court to make.

The court fixes a venue. The applicant gives seven days' notice and a copy of the affidavit to the trustee (r6.179).

On hearing the application the court can make an order on such terms as it thinks fit vesting or delivering disclaimed property to any person within the three categories of potential applicant (s320(3)).

It can only do this where 'it would be just to do so for the purpose of compensating' that person (s320(4)).

Formalities (s320(6)) – None are needed, ie no conveyance, assignment or transfer.

The court can only make vesting orders of leasehold property conditional on the new owner taking on the liabilities and obligations of the bankrupt at date of commencement. If the applicant is not willing to take the property on under these conditions they will be excluded from all interest in the property and:

- Court may vest the property in any person who is liable (whether personally or in a representative capacity and whether alone or jointly) with the bankrupt to perform the lessee's covenants in the lease.
- Court may vest the property in this way discharged from all estates, encumbrances and interests created by the bankrupt (s321).

2.5.4 Procedure on disclaimer

Trustee files signed notice of disclaimer with the court (+ copy).

Court seals and endorses notice and returns copy to trustee.

Within seven days of return trustee must send a copy to:

- (Where the property is leasehold) – every person who to his knowledge claims under the bankrupt as underlessee or mortgagee.
- Where the property is a dwelling – every person who to his knowledge is in occupation or claims a right to occupy (but minors validly served by service on parent or guardian).
- Anyone who claims an interest in the property.
- Anyone who is under any liability in respect of the property (unless it will be discharged by the disclaimer).
- Where the property is an unprofitable contract – all parties to the contract or all those who have interests under it.

If the trustee subsequently discovers anyone who should have received notice he must now serve notice on them unless:

- He is satisfied that the person is already aware of the disclaimer (and its date), or
- The court so orders on the trustee's application.

Trustee may also serve disclaimer on anyone else if in public interest or otherwise.

Trustee must notify the court of the names, addresses and interests of all those served under above rules.

If Trustee is unsure whether a person is interested in the property to be disclaimed, he can serve a notice on him under r6.184 requiring him to declare within 14 days whether he claims an interest and if so its nature and extent.

If the person fails to respond the trustee can treat him as having no interest.

In relation to leaseholds s317(2) allows the court to make orders in regard to fixtures, tenants improvements and other matters arising out of the lease.

2.6 Assets subject to forfeiture clauses

Forfeiture clauses may result in the trustee being deprived of assets. Examples include the following:

- A commercial lease usually provides for forfeiture and re-entry on non-payment of rent or on bankruptcy.
- Forfeiture clause in a partnership deed in which the partners share vests in the remaining partners on bankruptcy is void as a fraud on bankruptcy law (*Whitmore v Mason (1861)*).
- In building contracts a clause may provide for the forfeiture of the materials on site in the event of the builder not completing the work (for any reason including bankruptcy – *Re Keen and Keen 1902*).

2.7 Titles and offices

Peerages and titles of honour constitute property but do not vest in the trustee.

Right of nomination to a vacant ecclesiastical benefice does not pass to the trustee (s283(3)(b)).

2.8 Rights to sue/damages

If the bankrupt has a cause of action against another person this will vest in the trustee pursuant to s306. The bankrupt therefore loses all legal standing to commence or continue with litigation. The fact that the Legal Services Commission grants legal aid to a bankrupt cannot give the bankrupt a legal standing that he does not have (*James v Rutherford Hodge & Others 2005*). However personal actions such as defamation will not vest.

The damages arising from causes in action that vest, fall into the estate.

Claims are sometimes referred to as 'hybrid claims'. Although there is one cause of action there may be two heads of damage. For example a claim for financial losses following a road traffic accident may be coupled with a personal claim for damages for pain and suffering.

In such hybrid claims the cause of action vests in the trustee but damages relating to personal claims are held on constructive trust for the bankrupt, *Ord v Upton 1999*.

If a bankrupt is unhappy with any decision of the trustee in respect of any legal proceedings his remedy is to apply to the court under s303(1) to seek a review of the trustee's decision.

Personal Insolvency

2.9 Avoidance of general assignment of book debts

By s344 any general assignment (whether absolute or by way of security) of existing or future book debts or any class of them executed by a person subsequently adjudged bankrupt is void against the trustee in bankruptcy unless the:

- Assignment was registered with the Registrar of Bills of Sale under the Bills of Sale Act 1878 as though it were not a security bill.
- Assignment relates to debts due from specified debts or becoming due under specified contracts.
- Debts were paid before presentation of a petition (s344(2)).
- Debts were assigned as part of a bona fide transfer of a business, or
- Assignment is for the benefit of creditors generally.

Interactive question 1: James Bolton

James Bolton, a bankrupt, has recently won £19,000 in a competition and is also in receipt of a regular salary from his new employment.

Requirement

Explain to the trustee in bankruptcy the circumstances in which he may claim all or part of these monies for the bankrupt's estate and outline the procedures that must be followed in each case.

See **Answer** at the end of this chapter.

3 Antecedent transactions

Section overview

The trustee has the power to take action to recover assets for the estate in respect of:

- Transactions at an undervalue s339
- Preferences s340
- Extortionate credit transactions s343
- Transaction defrauding creditors s423
- Excessive pension contributions s342A

3.1 Transaction at an undervalue s339

An individual enters into a transaction with a person at an undervalue if he:

- Makes a gift to that person or he otherwise enters into a transaction with that person on terms that provide for him to receive no consideration.
- Enters into a transaction with that person in consideration of marriage, or the formation of a civil partnership.
- Enters into a transaction with that person for a consideration the value of which, in money or money's worth, is significantly less than the value, in money or money's worth, of the consideration provided by the individual.

The trustee can only apply to the court if the transaction was made at a 'relevant time:

- S341(1)(a) '... at a time in the period of five years ending with the day of the presentation of the bankruptcy petition on which the individual is adjudged bankrupt.'

186

- S341(2) goes on to say that from five to two years pre-commencement will not qualify as a relevant time unless the individual is:
  - Insolvent at that time, or
  - Becomes insolvent in consequence of the transaction (or preference).

  Insolvency will be presumed if the other party to the transaction was an associate (but not by reason only of being an employee).

- From two years to commencement will be a 'relevant time' and there is no need to prove insolvency.

- S341(3) defines insolvent as:
  - unable to pay debts as they fall due, or
  - value of assets less than liabilities (including contingent and prospective liabilities).

The court shall, on such an application, make such order as it thinks fit for restoring the position to what it would have been if that individual had not entered into that transaction (s339(2)).

The court may:
- Require any property transferred to be vested in the trustee.
- Require proceeds of sale of property to be vested in the trustee.
- Release or discharge (in whole or in part) any security given by the individual.
- Require any person to pay such sums to the trustee as the court may direct.
- Vary the right of any surety or guarantor.
- Order provision of security.
- Allow any recipient of the transaction to prove in the bankruptcy.

Orders may be made against persons whether or not they were the direct recipients of the transaction. Such an order:

- Shall not prejudice any interest in property which was acquired from a person other than that individual and was acquired in good faith, for value and without notice of the relevant circumstances, or prejudice any interest deriving from such an interest.

- Shall not require a person who received a benefit from the transaction or preference in good faith, for value and without notice of the relevant circumstances to pay a sum to the trustee of the bankrupt's estate, except where he was a party to the transaction or the payment is to be in respect of a preference given to that person at a time when he was a creditor of that individual.

3.2 Preferences s340

An individual gives a preference to a person if:

- That person is one of the individual's creditors or a surety or guarantor for any of his debts or other liabilities.
- The individual does anything or suffers anything to be done which (in either case) has the effect of putting that person into a position which, in the event of the individual's bankruptcy, will be better than the position he would have been in if that thing had not been done.

Examples could include paying off a creditor early or granting them security over the debtor's assets.

S340(4) The court shall not make an order under this section in respect of a preference given to any person unless the individual who gave the preference was influenced in deciding to give it by a desire to produce in relation to that person the effect mentioned above.

S340(5) An individual who has given a preference to a person who, at the time the preference was given, was an associate of his (otherwise than by reason only of being his employee) is presumed, unless the contrary is shown, to have been influenced in deciding to give it by such a desire as is mentioned.

S340(6) The fact that something has been done in pursuance of the order of a court does not, without more, prevent the doing or suffering of that thing from constituting the giving of a preference.

Personal Insolvency

The relevant time for a preference is six months in the case of independent creditors and two years in the case of associates.

The debtor must have been insolvent at the time of the transaction. Whilst desire to prefer is assumed in the case of an associate, insolvency is never presumed.

The court may make such order as it thinks fit for restoring the position to what it would have been if that individual had not given the preference (s340(2)).

3.3 Extortionate credit transactions s343

S343(1) applies where a person is adjudged bankrupt who is or has been a party to a transaction for, or involving, the provision to him of credit.

The court may, on the application of the trustee of the bankrupt's estate, make an order with respect to the transaction if the transaction is or was extortionate and was not entered into more than three years before the commencement of the bankruptcy.

A transaction is extortionate if, having regard to the risk accepted by the person providing the credit:

- The terms of it are or were such as to require grossly exorbitant payments to be made (whether unconditionally or in certain contingencies) in respect of the provision of the credit.
- It otherwise grossly contravened ordinary principles of fair dealing.

It shall be presumed, unless the contrary is proved, that a transaction with respect to which an application is made under this section is or, as the case may be, was extortionate.

An order under this section with respect to any transaction may contain such one or more of the following as the court thinks fit. That is to say, provisions:

- Setting aside the whole or part of any obligation created by the transaction.
- Otherwise varying the terms of the transaction or varying the terms on which any security for the purposes of the transaction is held.
- Requiring any person who is or was party to the transaction to pay to the trustee any sums paid to that person, by virtue of the transaction, by the bankrupt.
- Requiring any person to surrender to the trustee any property held by him as security for the purposes of the transaction.
- Directing accounts to be taken between any persons.

3.4 Transaction defrauding creditors s423

S423(1) states that the section applies to transactions at an undervalue and defines these as in s339.

Where a person has entered into such a transaction, the court may make such order as it thinks fit for:

- Restoring the position to what it would have been if the transaction had not been entered into.
- Protecting the interests of persons who are victims of the transaction.

In the case of a person entering into such a transaction, an order shall only be made if the court is satisfied that it was entered into by him for the purpose of:

- Putting assets beyond the reach of a person who is making, or may at some time make, a claim against him.
- Otherwise prejudicing the interests of such a person in relation to the claim which he is making or may make.

An order under s423 may be applied for by:

- OR.
- Trustee.
- Victim, ie person who is capable of being prejudiced by the transaction. (with courts consent).
- Supervisor of voluntary arrangement (if in force).

There is no relevant time, the trustee can go back indefinitely.

3.5 Excessive pension contributions s342A

The trustee can apply to court for an order that excessive pension contributions previously made by a bankrupt into his pension (that have unfairly prejudiced his creditors) be paid back to the estate. The trustee can attack contributions made at any time.

The court will consider:

- Whether any of the contributions were made for the purpose of putting assets beyond the reach of creditors, and
- Whether the total amount of any contributions are excessive in view of the individual's circumstances when those contributions were made.

The court may make such order as it thinks fit for restoring the position to what it would have been had the excessive contributions not been made.

4 The matrimonial home

Section overview

In most cases the most significant asset is likely to be the bankrupt's home. In dealing with the matrimonial home the trustee will need to consider the following points:

- What equity is available and how much of that equity vests in the trustee.
- Whether the share of the equity has been affected by equitable accounting/exoneration.
- How the trustee can realise the equity.
- What steps should be taken if the equity cannot be realised.

4.1 Available equity

The trustee will have to make all due enquiries to determine whether any equity is available in the property. This will involve obtaining an up to date valuation and mortgage redemption statement. What vests in the trustee will essentially depend upon whether the property is held in joint names or the sole name of the bankrupt or spouse.

4.1.1 House in joint names

In practice lenders will normally require that couples (married or otherwise) hold the property as joint tenants.

The effect of this is that the right of survivorship will apply, ie should either die the other will automatically acquire the deceased's share of the beneficial interest. The mortgage will state that the couple are jointly and severally liable for monies owed to the lender. The appointment of a trustee in bankruptcy will have the effect of severing the joint tenancy, converting it into a tenancy in commons.

The trustee will need to ascertain how much of the equity vests when valuing the bankrupt's share. Two situations may arise:

1   The couple may have expressly declared in what shares they will hold the equitable interest. 50:50 shares would be likely. These declared shares are usually decisive *(Godwin v Bedwell 1982)*. However the trustee may be able to attack the declaration as a transaction at an undervalue if it provides for non-bankrupt spouse to receive an 'over generous' share. S53(1)(b) LPA 1925 provides that such a declaration must be evidenced in writing, though the court will be able to enforce an oral declaration as a constructive trust, (no formalities will be required – s53(2) LPA 1925). (Where there is an express declaration by the parties (written or oral) as to the proportion in which equity will be shared there is no need for the courts to look for evidence of what was intended. The declaration is decisive.)

Personal Insolvency

Shares are ascertained at date of declaration (but valued at date of sale).

2   There may have been no express declaration of trust as to the proportion in which the equity is shared (written or oral). In this case the court will presume that the equity is held 50:50.

Pettitt v Pettitt

Where there is no express declaration of trust the court will require evidence of an actual agreement as to equity between the couple.

Should one party claim a higher than 50% share of the property, the burden will be on that party to prove an intention to split the equity in unequal shares (*Stack v Dowden 2007*).

4.1.2 House in sole name of bankrupt

Prima facie all of the equity will vest in the trustee. However, non-owning spouse may be able to claim a share through the mechanism of resulting or constructive trusts, ie the creation by the court of a trust to enforce equitable principles.

Gissing v Gissing – where no express declaration of trust in favour of the non-owning spouse the court will need to see evidence of:

- Intention – couples rarely express such intention in clear words and an intention will normally have to be inferred or presumed by the court.

- Detriment to non-owning spouse – detriment must be shown by contributions to:
    - deposit/purchase price.
    - mortgage instalments.
    - some other substantial contributions referable to the acquisition of the property.

The courts are looking for both intention to give a beneficial interest in the property and detriment suffered by the non-owning spouse. The detriment is important. Providing the non-owning spouse has relied upon the intention to give a beneficial interest it becomes inequitable for the owning spouse to go back on the promise/intention. Case law is very narrow in what it accepts as proper detriment. Some key illustrative cases in this area are:

Cook v Head 1972

Head paid for a plot of land for development and paid a builder to build a new house. Cook did not contribute financially but operated a cement mixer, used a sledgehammer and a wheel-barrow. Cook claimed a share of the equity. The court held that her physical work constituted 'other substantial contribution'. Cook was awarded 30% of the equity. Lord Denning's decision and equity share for Cook looks generous in the light of more recent case law.

Lloyds Bank v Rossett 1991

No equity for wife of sole owner where wife had arranged for extensive renovations and carried out some redecoration. The court held that where there is no agreement, arrangement or understanding based on evidence of express discussions then the court must rely on the conduct of the parties. Direct contributions to the purchase price would 'readily justify an inference' of an agreement to share equity in given proportions. 'It is extremely doubtful anything else will do'. *Lord Walker in Stack v Dowden* expressly disapproves of this decision saying that the law had 'moved on'.

Stack v Dowden 2007

An important House of Lords decision which reviews the law in this area. Following the case the correct approach to take in the exam is as follows:

- Is there a Deed of Trust setting out how the parties intend to split the equity?
- If not, was there an actual agreement between the couple as to how the equity should be split?
- If not, assume 50:50.
- The burden will be on the party claiming more than 50% to prove that the beneficial shares are different from the legal interests.

Factors to be taken into account in ascertaining equity shares where the court does depart from the normal assumption that joint owners intended to hold the equity 50:50:

- Advice or discussions at the date of transfer.
- Purpose for which the home was acquired.
- Nature of the parties' relationship.
- Whether they had any children for whom they both had a responsibility to provide a home.
- How the purchase was originally funded and subsequently.
- How the parties arranged their finances, separately or together.
- Parties individual characters and personalities.

At the end of the day, having taken all this into consideration, cases where beneficial interests are different from the legal interests will be very unusual.

Midland Bank v Dobson 1986

No 'detriment' suffered by a non-owning spouse who had decorated house and bought domestic appliances.

4.1.3 House in sole name of non-bankrupt spouse

Prima facie none of the equity will vest in the trustee. However the trustee may be able to claim a share through the same process detailed above.

The trustee should also consider whether the spouse acquired the property for value for 'transaction at an undervalue' purposes.

4.2 Equitable accounting

This is necessary where the couple have separated and only the spouse in occupation is now responsible for mortgage payments and outgoings.

It is necessary both where the property is held as joint tenants (with or without declaration of trusts) and where it is held as tenants in common.

The following pro-forma should be used to calculate the adjusted equity split.

EQUITABLE ACCOUNTING PRO-FORMA (non bankrupt spouse in occupation)

		Bankrupt		Non-bankrupt	
		£	£	£	£
Proceeds of sale		X			
Less required to redeem mortgage		(X)			
Equity		X			
(1)	Apportion		X		X
(2)	Credit improvements of non-bankrupt spouse		(X)		X
(3)	Credit capital element of non-bankrupt spouse's mortgage payments		(X)		X
(4)	Debit an 'occupation rent' to non-bankrupt spouse	X		(X)	
(5)	...but net of non-bankrupt spouse's interest payments under the mortgage	X		X	
(6)	Net occupation rent		X		(X)
(7)	Totals		X		X

Notes to equitable accounting pro-forma

(1) Apportion according to the spouses respective shares of the beneficial interest in the property (probably 50:50). **Accordingly all adjustments should then be split in the same shares**.

(2) In practice should only credit the non-bankrupt spouse with the lower of the:
- Cost of the improvements
- Increase in the value of the home resulting from those improvements.

(3) Likewise in practice the non-bankrupt spouse would only be credited with the lower of the capital payments or the increase in value of the house.

(4) 'Occupation rent' should be debited to the non-bankrupt spouse. This is based on the idea that now only the non-bankrupt spouse is residing in the property alone, only they have the benefit of the former family home and therefore should 'pay' the bankrupt a rent. Occupation rent should only be charged from the date that the bankrupt is **excluded** from the property. (*Re Pavlou*) NOT from the date of **separation**. Exclusion might be:

- Where the bankrupt has been excluded by court order (eg an injunction in matrimonial proceedings).
- Where the non-bankrupt spouse has presented a petition for divorce (*Re Pavlou*).
- Other evidence that the bankrupt is 'no longer welcome' (*Re Pavlou* again).

(5) Mortgage interest paid by the non-bankrupt spouse since separation can be netted off against occupation rent. Obviously this can only go to reduce occupation rent to zero and not to provide the non-bankrupt spouse with a further credit.

Re Pavlou 1993

The case dealt with the situation where the couple were separated with the party in occupation paying all outgoings. From the date of separation the party in occupation should be credited with 50% of:

- The lower of the cost of any capital improvements made to the property and the equity uplift, and
- Capital payments under the mortgage.

As the spouse in occupation had the sole enjoyment of the property she should be debited with an occupation rent being 50% of the rental value of the property. This should be payable from where the husband was 'no longer welcome'. The decree nisi was taken as the date from which it could be assumed the husband was no longer welcome in this case. The spouse in occupation is entitled to net off 50% of the interest payments she has made under the mortgage. The effect of the net off can only be to reduce occupation rent to zero and not to produce a further credit to the spouse in occupation.

French v Barcham (2008).

This case looked at the question of occupational rent when one party is not in occupation. Mr Barcham was bankrupt and his beneficial share in the home had vested in his trustee in bankruptcy. His trustee in bankruptcy was claiming an occupation rent from Mrs Barcham who had remained in the house.

The court held that the trustee was entitled to occupation rent because he was unable to realise the property due to Mrs Barcham being in occupation. This was despite the fact that the trustee had no statutory right of occupation of the property. The judge held that it was not reasonable to expect the trustee in bankruptcy to take up actual occupation of the property given the basis on which the bankrupt's share in the property vested in him.

Mrs Barcham's half share of the sale proceeds was reduced by a sum equal to one half of the property's letting value since Mr Barcham's bankruptcy.

4.3 Equitable exoneration

This only applies where one party has charged their share of the matrimonial home for the benefit of the other spouse. As the charge has to be for the benefit of the other spouse the court will be concerned to ascertain what the monies provided were used for.

For example, in *Re Pittortou 1985*, a second mortgage was taken over the matrimonial home. The monies raised were used for a number of purposes including funding the husband's business and the husband setting up home with another woman. The wife argued that she did not benefit from either of these expenditures. Her husband's business was loss making, she did not participate in it and she had her own independent source of income. The effect of exoneration is that the wife's position becomes that of a surety. In other words, recourse will only be had from the wife's share to the extent that her husband's share is insufficient to repay the mortgage in full.

BANKRUPTCY ESTATE 10

Interactive question 2: Fred Band

Fred Band was declared bankrupt nine months ago in August 2009. His trustee has realised all of the bankruptcy assets except for his share in the matrimonial home, details of which are as follows:

(1) The property is a five bed roomed, detached house with a double garage. It has recently been professionally valued in the sum of £385,000.

(2) The property is subject to a mortgage owed to Barwest Bank PLC in the sum of £184,000.

(3) Fred owns the property jointly with his wife. He lived there with her and their three children until 19 months ago when they separated. Fred moved out of the property and his wife continued to pay the mortgage and interest payments as they fell due as follows:

	Nov 08 to Aug 09 £	Sept 09 to May 10 £
Mortgage capital - per month	600	600
Interest - per month	400	400

(4) Six months ago Mrs Band added a conservatory to the house at a cost of £25,000.

(5) The property would command a rent of £6,000 per annum.

(6) Fred obtained a business loan shortly after the property was purchased, in the sum of £30,000 secured against the equity in the property. Despite her name appearing on the loan documents, Mrs Band denies any knowledge of agreeing to such a loan being secured against the property.

Requirement

Prepare a schedule showing the equitable accounting in the property for both Mr and Mrs Band as at May 10. Support your calculations with any relevant narrative.

See **Answer** at the end of this chapter.

5 Realising the equity

Section overview

The trustee has a number of options to realise the equity available.

5.1 Without court proceedings

The trustee should approach the non-bankrupt spouse with a view to buying out the bankrupt's share of the equity. A lower value would probably be acceptable since the costs of sale or proceedings are being avoided.

The non-bankrupt spouse could agree to put the property up for sale on the open market. Following a sale the trustee would receive the bankrupt's share of the equity in the property.

The trustee could come to an agreement with the debtor whereby the debtor will make payments into the estate in respect of his interest in the property in return for the property re-vesting in him. The legislation is quite vague on this area and no length for the agreement is specified neither is any interest rate. Trustees will need to be cautious if choosing this course of action to prevent any agreements being caught under the Consumer Credit Act 1974.

5.2 Order for possession and sale

If the non-bankrupt spouse cannot or will not co-operate the trustee will apply to the court for an order of sale under:

- S14 Trust of Land and Appointment of Trustees Act 1996 (TLATA) (where property held as joint tenants). This will be an order to enforce the trust for sale.
- S1 MHA 1983 as amended by the Family Law Act 1996 (FLA 1996) (where property in sole name of bankrupt but non-bankrupt spouse is in occupation).

In either case the application should be made to the bankruptcy court (s336(2)(b).

By s336(4) on such an application court shall make such order as it thinks just and reasonable having regard to:

- Interests of bankrupt's creditors.
- Conduct of spouse/former spouse as contributing to the bankruptcy and needs and resources of spouse/former spouse.
- Needs of any children.
- All circumstances of case (but not bankrupt's interest).

Note that under Schedule 5 Part I of the Act the power to institute legal proceedings relating to property comprised in the bankrupts estate requires sanction.

- By s314(1) the trustee may obtain sanction from the committee.
- By s302(1) where there is no committee its functions are vested in the Secretary of State.
- By r6.166(2) these functions may be exercised by the OR.

5.3 Rights of occupation

In two situations there will be rights of occupation which may delay the trustee in obtaining the order of possession. Under s1 MHA 1983 the non-bankrupt spouse has a right of occupation (irrespective of whether she has a share in the property) and under s337 the bankrupt has a right of occupation where he:

- Has a beneficial interest in the property.
- Any person under 18 has their home (at the time of presentation of petition) with the bankrupt.

By s336(5) and s337(6) where either (or both) of these two situations apply, after a period of one year from date of appointment of trustee:

- The court shall assume that the interests of the bankrupt's creditors outweigh all other considerations.
- Unless the circumstances of the case are exceptional.

Case law helps to give guidance as to what may be considered exceptional:

- *Re Citro 1991*

    Hardship to wives and young children is not exceptional (also *Re Lowrie 1981*).

    The non-bankrupt spouse (the wife) argued that if the house were sold she would not have enough equity to buy a house in the same area and therefore she would have to buy a house in a cheaper area and would have to move the children out of their present schools where they were settled. The court said that this was the normal and 'melancholy effect of debt and improvidence' and was not exceptional.

- *Re Holliday 1981*

    The court held the fact that the bankruptcy case was exceptional. Essentially Holliday would eventually be able to pay his creditors 100p in the £ plus statutory interest and therefore the court felt able to postpone a sale of the house despite the fact that this would result in the creditors having to wait to receive their money.

- *Judd v Brown 1997* A sudden grave and unforeseen illness of the bankrupt's wife was held to be exceptional.

- *Jones v Ravel 1998* paranoid schizophrenia would be exceptional.

- *Re Mott 1987*

    Exceptional circumstances were found where the bankrupt's unwell and elderly mother was living with him. The sale was postponed until after the mother's death.

If the trustee makes an application for either of these orders and the application is dismissed by the court then the property will also vest back in the bankrupt unless the court orders otherwise. Therefore if the court ordered that possession be refused because of an 'exceptional circumstance' eg. Grave and unforeseen illness, it will be important to ensure that the proceedings are merely adjourned NOT dismissed.

6 Steps if equity cannot be realised

Section overview

If the property cannot be realised the trustee has the option of applying for a s313 charging order.

6.1 Purpose of charging orders

The trustee has the power to apply to court under s313 for the imposition of a charge where:

- He is unable to realise (for any reason)
- An interest in a dwelling house
- Occupied by the bankrupt, spouse or former spouse.

A trustee cannot call a final meeting to obtain his release if he has been unable to realise an interest in a dwelling, unless he has applied for a charge (whether or not the court makes a charging order) s332(1).

If a s313 charging order is an unsuitable option, the trustee may apply to the Secretary of State for certification that it is inappropriate or inexpedient to apply for a charge. It may be inappropriate where there are no funds in the estate to make a s313 application and the creditors are unwilling to fund further litigation.

The effects of a s313 charging order are:

- The benefit of the charge is comprised in the bankrupt's estate (ie vested in trustee).
- The property ceases to be comprised in the estate and re-vests in the bankrupt. The practical effect is that the trustee loses control of how and when the property is sold

The value of the charge will be limited to the value of the bankrupt's interest in the property as at the date of the s313 charge together with interest under the Judgments Act 1838. Consequently any rise in property prices will result in the benefit being passed to the bankrupt in full rather than being taken by the estate.

When determining the bankrupt's interest the amended r6.237D(10) provides that there shall be excluded from the value of the property any amounts owing in respect of any:

- Loan secured by a mortgage, or other charge against the property.
- Third party interest.
- Reasonable costs of sale.

6.2 Procedure for obtaining a charge r6.237

The trustee must:

- Make non-bankrupt spouse or civil partner a respondent to the action.
- Seek to agree the terms of the charge (ie how much it is for) with the bankrupt and co-owner (if this can't be agreed the court will settle terms).

Personal Insolvency

- File a report on the:
    - Extent of the bankrupt's interest in the property.
    - Amount remaining owing to unsecured creditors.
    - An estimate of the cost of realising the asset.

If the court makes a charging order this will detail the following:

- Description of property.
- If registered the title number.
- The extent of the bankrupt's interest.
- How the amount of the charge is to be ascertained (this will be by reference to amount payable out of the estate plus interest).
- Identify the date any property charged under s313 shall cease to be comprised in the bankrupt's estate and shall vest in the bankrupt.

6.3 Low value homes

If the trustee makes an application for an order for sale, possession or for a charging order and the level of the bankrupt's interest is below the prescribed amount then the court will dismiss the application.

The prescribed amount has been set at £1,000 pursuant to Insolvency Proceedings (Monetary Limits) (Amendment) Order 2004.

6.4 The three year rule

The position in relation to the matrimonial home has been amended by EA 2002. The bankrupt's interest in the matrimonial home will still vest in the trustee however s283A compels the trustee to deal with the interest in the matrimonial home within a three year period.

This period runs from the date of the bankruptcy order provided that the OR or trustee was informed of the bankrupt's interest within three months of the commencement of the bankruptcy. If there was no such disclosure the time period runs from the date that the trustee became aware of the existence of such an interest (s283A(5)).

'Matrimonial home' for the purpose of the legislation is any property resided in by the bankrupt, his spouse or former spouse or civil partner or former civil partner as his sole or principal residence, in which the bankrupt has an interest. It is possible therefore that the trustee will have more than one property with which to deal.

Although the bankrupt's interest will vest in the estate it will cease to be part of the estate and re-vest in the bankrupt at the end of the said three year period. If there is more than one property that has not been dealt with all properties will re-vest in the estate.

The three year period can be extended in exceptional circumstances but this would not include delay on the part of the trustee.

If the trustee forms the view that the property is subject to the provisions of S283A he is obliged to serve a notice to all interested parties pursuant to r6.237. The latest date for such issue will be 14 days prior to the expiry of the three year period.

If re-vesting in the bankrupt occurs then the trustee must notify both the Land Registry and the bankrupt. In the event of re-vesting the property will not be treated as after acquired property s283A(4).

Where a petition was presented prior to 1 April 2004 and an order subsequently made transitional rules apply.

The transitional rules state that the three year rule for dealing with the sole or principal properties will also apply. However the three year period will run from 1 April 2004. Therefore the trustee must deal with the interest by 1 April 2007 or it will re-vest in the bankrupt.

R6.237 provides that the three year period may be reduced where the trustee sends an appropriate notice to the bankrupt confirming that:

▸ Trustee considers the continued vesting of the property in the estate to be of no benefit to creditors, or

▸ Trustee considers that the re-vesting will facilitate a more efficient administration of the bankrupt's estate.

In such circumstances the property will re-vest in the bankrupt after one month from the date of the notice.

This provision will ensure that where a trustee is unable to realise his interest in the matrimonial home he will not be precluded from seeking his release under s332(2).

The effect of s283A is that the trustee must take some positive step to deal with the property in the three year period. From the date of issue of any court application time running on such application will be suspended. The legislation sets out the following potential steps:

▸ Realising the interest in the property.
▸ Applying for an order for sale of the property.
▸ Applying for an order for possession.
▸ Obtaining a s313 charging order on the property.
▸ Entering into an agreement with the bankrupt in respect of a liability for the interest.

If the bankrupt has more than one property then s283 would apply to the non-principal properties and any interest would vest in the trustee. This property (or properties) would not be subject to the three year rule.

If the trustee fails to take steps to realise the bankrupt's interest within the three year period he may be subject to proceedings under s303 and s304.

Lewis & Anor v Metropolitan Property Realizations Ltd (2008)

The trustee had sold his interest in a bankrupt's dwelling house to a third party, but the bulk of the consideration was deferred and became payable upon the property being sold in the future. The bankrupt claimed that the trustee had not 'disposed' of his interest within the meaning of s283A as the sale consideration had not been paid in full and accordingly the property should revert back to him.

The court held that as the trustee's interest had been absolutely assigned the transfer had been completed and the property 'realised' notwithstanding that the consideration would only be payable in the future.

Upon appeal however the court held that a sale by a trustee in bankruptcy of the debtor's interest in his dwelling house for a deferred consideration did not constitute 'realisation' of that interest within three years for the purposes of s283A.

Although the trustee had power to sell for a deferred consideration, the realisation was only complete when all the cash had been collected in.

Interactive question 3: Penny Black

You have recently been appointed trustee of Penny Black. She lives with her husband and three children, aged three, six and eight in a four bedroomed house. The property was purchased jointly with her husband when they married 11 years ago.

Requirement

What are your options, as trustee, when dealing with the matrimonial home?

See **Answer** at the end of this chapter.

6.5 Miscellaneous provisions

6.5.1 The right of survivorship and the deceased bankrupt

Under basic land law principles if land is held as joint tenants on the death of one of the joint tenants it will pass to the other by virtue of the right of survivorship. This applies irrespective of any of the provisions contained in the deceased's will or under the laws of intestacy.

If the estate of a deceased debtor is subsequently subject to an Insolvent Administration Order (IAO) the question arises as to whether or not the trustee can recover any value lost to the estate by the operation of the said right (see chapter 14 for more detail).

In the case of *Re Palmer*, it was held that the right of survivorship defeated the claim of a trustee appointed under an IAO. The position was changed by s421A that states that where a petition for an IAO is presented after 2 April 2001 a trustee can recover any value lost to the estate by the operation of the right of survivorship. This is subject to the proviso that the petition must be presented within five years of the debtor's death. There is no transfer of property rights but the survivor can be ordered to pay value to the estate.

The legislation in s421A(2) makes it clear that an order is at the courts discretion. It is suggested that the courts will probably make an order unless there are 'exceptional' circumstances.

Note that if a debtor dies between the presentation of a petition but before the granting of a bankruptcy order the trustee can attack the transfer under the right of survivorship pursuant to s284.

If a debtor is already bankrupt on death the right of survivorship would not apply. The interest of the deceased bankrupt in the property will have already vested in the trustee.

Mountney v Treharne 2002

A property adjustment order (PAO) was made on 6 July 2000 by way of ancillary relief in matrimonial proceedings under s24(1)(a) of the Matrimonial Causes Act 1973, whereby Mrs Mountney's husband was ordered to transfer his sole interest in the former matrimonial home to his former wife. On 14 July 2000 Mr Mountney was made bankrupt on his own petition. At the date of the bankruptcy order no transfer documents had been executed, either by the husband or the district judge. The issue to be decided in the case was whether a post order transfer to the wife of the bankrupt husband's share would be invalid as a void disposition.

The court held that the decision of the matrimonial court created a property right in the wife. The right was to have the husband's share of the property transferred to her in accordance with the terms of the court order. The trustee in bankruptcy took the property subject to this pre-existing right of the wife (see s283(5)). The trustee could not therefore prevent the execution of a transfer of the bankrupt husband's share to the wife.

Hill v Bangham and Haines 2007

In appropriate circumstances the trustee in bankruptcy can however, challenge a transfer of a share of the matrimonial home by the bankrupt to his wife as having been made at an undervalue. The fact that the transfer is made by virtue of a court order does not preclude it having been made at an undervalue.

6.5.2 New Land Registration Rules

If a bankrupt is the sole owner of property the trustee will now protect his interest by way of a Bankruptcy Restriction Notice not an inhibition as previously. A restriction is automatically placed at the Land Registry when a bankruptcy order is made. The notice puts on record that the bankrupt is no longer the legal owner of the property and does not have the ability to sell the property or enter into any other dealings in connection with the property.

If a bankrupt owns property jointly the trustee will protect his interest by way of a Form J Restriction, not a caution as previously. This is a record of the trustee's beneficial interest in the property. It means that the Land Registry must notify the trustee of any dealings in connection with the property.

Definition

Beneficial interest: the bankrupt's interest in the proceeds of sale of the property.

Appendix 1 – Insolvency Guidance Paper

Bankruptcy – family homes

This Guidance Paper was introduced by the Joint Insolvency Committee on 15 October 2005 to assist insolvency practitioners when dealing with a debtor's residential property.

Introduction

It is in the interests of the debtor and the creditors and in the wider public interest, that a family home and any other residential property available for use by the debtor or the debtor's immediate family are dealt with fairly and expeditiously in a bankruptcy. This can happen only if the debtor and others who may have an interest in the properties have sufficient information to understand how the bankruptcy affects them and the options available to them. Failure by a trustee to provide information and explanations can prolong the realisation process, cause unnecessary distress to those involved and also give rise to complaints.

Affected parties

Where the debtor has an interest in a property falling within the estate, the trustee should consider at an early stage whether the property is or has been the home of any person other than the debtor and if that person could be affected by the bankruptcy and the sale of the property.

Those potentially affected include:

- The debtor's spouse, former spouse, unmarried partner or civil or former civil partner.
- Members of the debtor's immediate family.
- A joint legal owner.
- Anyone who has contributed towards the purchase of a property (including making mortgage payments).
- Anyone in occupation of the property other than under a formal tenancy agreement and
- A trustee under a previous bankruptcy.

The trustee should make enquiries of the debtor to establish the properties within the estate and whether any other persons may have an interest in them. It is recommended that a trustee should write to the debtor and any other affected parties as soon as possible after the appointment or of becoming aware of the property or the third party interest. An initial communication may give a broad explanation of the process and timescales to be followed in the proceedings, with further, more specific, information provided as it becomes available. This is in addition to the trustee's statutory obligations.

Information to be provided

A trustee should provide the debtor and any other affected parties with sufficient information at appropriate times to enable them to understand the possible consequences of the bankruptcy, so that they can make an informed decision or seek advice. The information to be provided might include (as appropriate to the circumstances):

- An explanation of the trustee's interest and why that interest may continue after discharge from bankruptcy.
- The circumstances in which the property will revert to the debtor and why it may not revert.
- An explanation of why the trustee needs to realise the property.
- The way in which the property and the trustee's interest would be valued.
- An explanation of how any changes in the value of the property and payments under a mortgage, may be treated.

Personal Insolvency

- How any mortgage, or other security for the repayment of any loan, may be treated.
- Details of the steps that the trustee can take and any timetable, for realising the property.
- A copy of the Insolvency Service leaflet 'What will happen to my home'.

It is also recommended that a trustee:

- Seeks offers from affected parties as appropriate, giving sufficient time for responses and explaining any deadlines.
- Be prepared, in appropriate circumstances, to meet the debtor and other affected parties to discuss any problems that may arise.
- Advises that affected parties should take independent advice.

Timing of communications

After the initial communications outlined above, it is recommended that a trustee writes regularly to the debtor and other affected parties pending realisation of the property. Whilst such communications should be as circumstances dictate, it is recommended that this should normally be every 12 months. The matters to be dealt with might include (as appropriate to the circumstances):

- Whether the trustee's intentions have changed and the effect on the likely timetable for realisation.
- Any changes in the value of the property and the trustee's interest.
- Any changes to the positions of the affected parties and
- Whether the trustee is seeking offers for the estate's interest in the property.

Dealing with offers

A trustee has a duty to obtain a proper price for the benefit of the estate, but the bankruptcy should not be unnecessarily protracted and account should be taken of the effect of future costs. It is recommended that the consequences of any action or delay in respect of a property should be explained to affected parties and where appropriate, to creditors.

If an affected party makes an offer to purchase the trustee's interest in the property the trustee should deal expeditiously with the offer. If the offer is rejected, the trustee should normally provide an explanation of why the offer was regarded as inadequate.

The trustee should advise the debtor and other affected parties to take independent advice in relation to the property for example from a solicitor or the Citizens' Advice Bureau.

Duty of care

The guidance paper does not impose or imply any duty of care by an insolvency practitioner to a debtor, or any person with an interest in a property, over and above what may be imposed by legislation or case law.

Summary and Self-test

Summary

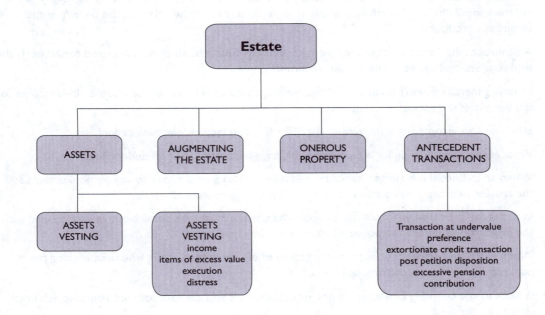

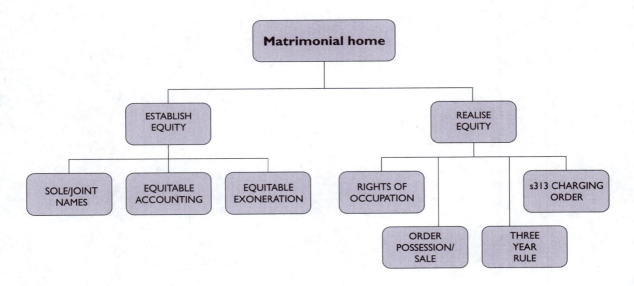

Personal Insolvency

Self-test

Answer the following questions.

1 What is the definition of the bankruptcy estate?

2 What assets are excluded from the bankruptcy estate?

3 A bankrupt owns an antique table which is valued at £15,000 for insurance purposes. He claims that the table should be excluded from his estate because he and his family sit at the table every day to eat their meals. What, if anything, can the trustee do to realise the asset for the benefit of the bankrupt's creditors?

4 A bankrupt inherits a sum of money from an aunt eight months after he is declared bankrupt. Is the bankrupt entitled to retain the monies received?

5 Income generally doesn't form part of the bankrupt's estate. How may the trustee claim income for the benefit of the estate?

6 How does an income payment agreement differ from an income payment order?

7 What is the relevant time for a trustee to challenge a transaction at an undervalue?

8 When an individual is adjudged bankrupt and he has given a preference to any person, under s340 the trustee may apply to court for an order. What is a preference?

9 In order for the three year rule not to apply the trustee must take some positive step to deal with the property. What are the potential steps which he could take?

10 When will it be necessary to apply the principle of equitable accounting when establishing the bankrupt's share in the matrimonial home?

Now, go back to the Learning Objectives in the Introduction. If you are satisfied that you have achieved these, please tick them off.

Answers to Self-test

1. The estate comprises all property belonging to or vested in the bankrupt at the commencement of bankruptcy (s283(1)).

2. The following assets do not form part of the bankrupt's estate:

    Such tools, books, vehicles and other items of equipment as are necessary to the bankrupt for use personally by him in his employment, business or vocation.

    Such clothing, bedding, furniture, household equipment and provisions as are necessary for satisfying the basic domestic needs of the bankrupt and his family.

    Property held by the bankrupt on trust for any other person.

    Income for reasonable domestic needs.

    After acquired property.

    Assets subject to forfeiture clauses (for example, a commercial lease usually provides for forfeiture and re-entry on non-payment of rent or on bankruptcy).

    Peerages and titles of honour.

    Liens on books, papers or records of the bankrupt are unenforceable to the extent they would deny possession to the trustee – s349.

    Rights under an approved pension scheme for petitions presented after 29 May 2000.

    Student Loans.

3. s308 allows the trustee to claw back assets where it appears that the realisable value of the property exceeds the cost of a reasonable replacement.

    He must give the bankrupt written notice, within 42 days of becoming aware of the asset, that he is claiming it for the benefit of the estate.

    The trustee has a duty to provide a reasonable replacement, however he needn't do this until sufficient funds are in hand.

4. Assuming the bankruptcy has not been discharged then the bankrupt has a duty to notify the trustee of any after acquired property within 21 days. The trustee can, by written notice, claim the money for the bankrupt's estate. The trustee must serve notice within 42 days of first becoming aware of the asset.

5. Under s310(1) the trustee can apply to court for an order that part of the bankrupt's income be paid over.

    The procedure is laid down in r6.189:

    - The trustee applies to the court.
    - 28 days' notice of the venue must be given to the bankrupt together with a copy of the application and a short statement of the grounds of the application.
    - The bankrupt can now either consent, in writing, to the application (to the trustee and the court) or attend the hearing and show why the IPO should not be made.
    - At the hearing two types of order may be made:
        - bankrupt to pay the trustee, or
        - person who pays the bankrupt to pay trustee direct.

    The order must leave the bankrupt with sufficient income for meeting the reasonable domestic needs of the bankrupt and his family.

The IPO can last for a maximum of three years from the making of the order (s310(6)).

6 An IPA is a written agreement between the bankrupt and his trustee by which the bankrupt voluntarily agrees to pay specified sums into the estate for a specified period of time. There is no court involvement with an IPA.

7 The relevant time is (s341):

- At a time in the period of five years ending with the day of the presentation of the bankruptcy petition on which the individual is adjudged bankrupt.

- From five to two years pre-commencement will not qualify as a relevant time unless the individual is insolvent at that time or becomes insolvent in consequence of the transaction. (Insolvency will be presumed if the other party to the transaction was an associate (but not an employee)).

- From two years to commencement will be a relevant time and there is no need to prove insolvency.

8 An individual gives a preference to a person if (s340(3)):

That person is one of the individual's creditors or a surety or guarantor for any of his debts or other liabilities and

The individual does anything or suffers anything to be done which has the effect of putting that person into a position which, in the event of the individual's bankruptcy, will be better than the position he would have been in if that thing had not been done.

9 Realise the asset.
Apply for an order for sale of the property.
Apply for an order for possession.
Obtain a s313 charging order on the property.
Enter into an agreement with the bankrupt in respect of a liability for the interest.

10 Where the bankrupt owns the house jointly with his spouse and the couple have separated and only the spouse in occupation is now responsible for mortgage payments and outgoings.

Answers to Interactive Questions

Interactive question 1: James Bolton

Under s307 the trustee may, by notice in writing, claim for the bankrupt's estate any property which has been acquired by, or has devolved upon, the bankrupt since commencement of the bankruptcy. This would include the money won in the competition.

Upon the service on the bankrupt of the notice under s307 the property to which the notice relates vests in the trustee as part of the bankrupt's estate.

The property having been vested on the trustee upon service of the notice, his title to that property then has relation back to the time when the property was acquired by, or devolved upon the bankrupt.

However, where, whether before or after service of a notice under s307 a person acquires property in good faith for value and without notice of the bankruptcy, or a banker enters into a transaction in good faith without such notice, the trustee is not, in respect of that property or transaction, entitled by virtue of s307 to any remedy against that person or banker or any person whose title to any property derives from that person or banker.

Under r6.202 any expenses incurred by the trustee in acquiring title to after acquired property are to be paid out of the estate in the prescribed order of priorities.

Under s309 a trustee may not, except with the leave of the court, serve a notice under s307 after the end of a period of 42 days beginning with the day on which it first came to the knowledge of the trustee that the property in question had been acquired by, or had devolved upon, the bankrupt.

Income payments order

The court may, on the application of the trustee, make an income payments order claiming for the bankrupt's estate so much of the income of the bankrupt during the period for which the order is in force as may be specified in the order (s310).

The court may not make an income payments order the effect of which would be to reduce the income of the bankrupt below that which appears to the court to be necessary to meet the reasonable domestic needs of the bankrupt and his family.

R6.189: Where the trustee applies for an income payments order the court must fix a venue for the hearing of the application.

Notice of the application and of the venue must be sent to the bankrupt at least 28 days before the day fixed for the hearing, together with a copy of the trustee's application and a short statement of the grounds on which it is made.

The notice must inform the bankrupt that:

- Unless at least seven days before the date fixed for the hearing he sends to the court and to the trustee written consent to an order being made in the terms of the application he is required to attend the hearing.
- If he attends he will be given an opportunity to show cause why the order should not be made, or an order should be made otherwise than as applied for by the trustee.

An income payments order must, in respect of any payment of income to which it is to apply either:

- Require the bankrupt to pay over the sum to the trustee, once it is received by the bankrupt.
- Require the person making the payment to deduct it at source and pay it directly to the trustee instead of to the bankrupt.

R6.190: where the court makes an income payments order, a sealed copy of the order must, as soon as reasonably practicable, be sent by the trustee to the bankrupt.

If an order has been made for deduction of the income at source a sealed copy of the order must also be sent by the trustee to the person making the payment.

Personal Insolvency

Initially, contact the debtor and seek to agree terms of an Income Payments Agreement in order to avoid costs of obtaining an Income Payments Order via the court.

Interactive question 2: Fred Band

Mr and Mrs Band
Equitable Accounting Schedule
As at May 10

		Mr Band	Mrs Band
Proceeds of sale	385,000		
Less Barwest Bank PLC	(184,000)		
Equity	201,000		
Apportion equity 50:50		100,500	100,500
Conservatory		(12,500)	12,500
Mortgage Payments;			
Capital Nov 08 to Aug 09		(3,000)	3,000
Sept 09 to May 10		(2,700)	2,700
Occupational rent (Nov 08 to May 10)		4,750	(4,750)
Mortgage Payments;			
Interest Nov 08 to Aug 09		(2,000)	2,000
Sept 09 to May 10		(1,800)	1,800
Share of equity		83,250	117,750
Less Business Loan		(30,000)	
Final equity		£53,250	

WORKINGS

(1) **Equity**

In the absence of other information, assume equity is to be split 50:50. Shares are ascertained at the date of acquisition but valued at the date of sale.

(2) **Conservatory**

Should credit Mrs Band with the lower of

    (i)   The cost of improvements.
    (ii)   The increase in the value of the property resulting from those improvements.

Assume the value of the property has increased by £25,000 as a result of the new conservatory.

(3) **Mortgage payments**

The period to take into account is from Nov 08, when Mr Band left the property, to May 10, the date of sale (19 months).

Assume the capital value of the equity in the property is increased proportionately to the capital payments made by Mrs Band.

    Capital
    Nov 08 to Aug 09   (10 months)   600 × 10 = 6,000
    Sept 09 to May 10   (9 months)   600 × 9 = 5,400

    Interest
    Nov 08 to Aug 09   (10 months)   400 × 10 = 4,000
    Sep 09 to May 10   (9 months)   400 × 9 = 3,600

The interest payments are credited to Mrs Band, to be netted off against occupational rent (can only reduce occupational rent to zero).

(4) Occupational rent
This should be charged from the date Mr Band is excluded from the property. In the absence of other information, assume Fred is no longer welcome from the date of separation.

(5) Business loan
There are two possible treatments:

(i) Treat both parties to the transaction and therefore loan should be deducted equally from both parties, leaving equity of:

	£
Mr Band	68,250
Mrs Band	102,750

(ii) Assume Mrs Band was not party to the loan and as she did not receive any benefit from it, it should be repaid from Mr Band's equity only.

Interactive question 3: Penny Black

1. Must first establish whether there is any equity in the property:
   - obtain up to date valuation and mortgage redemption statement.

2. Determine how much of that equity vests in the trustee:
   - is the property in sole names/ joint names?
   - is there an express trust determining in what shares the property is held?
   - the trustee may be able to attack the declaration as a transaction at an undervalue if it provides for the non-bankrupt spouse to receive an over generous share.
   - in the absence of other information, assume held 50:50.
   - may be able to refute this, need to consider who provided the deposit, who makes ongoing mortgage payments etc.

3. Ensure equity is protected:
   - ensure that ongoing mortgage payments continue to be made to prevent repossession proceedings by the mortgagee.
   - confirm property is covered by insurance.
   - notify building society/ bank of trustee's interest in the property.

4. Trustee has a number of informal options when realising the property:

   (i) Approach non-bankrupt spouse with a view to buying out the bankrupt's share of the property (trustee may be willing to accept a lower value due to not incurring costs of sale/ possession).

   (ii) Could put house up for sale on the open market with the agreement of spouse.

   (iii) Come to an agreement with the debtor whereby the debtor incurs a specified liability to the estate in consideration for which the interest in the property will cease to be part of the estate.

5. If non-bankrupt spouse is unable or unwilling to purchase the equity, the trustee may apply to the court for an order for possession and sale (s14 Trust of Land and Appointment of Trustee's Act 1996).

   The court shall make such order as it thinks just and reasonable having regard to:
   - interests of the bankrupt's creditors.
   - conduct of spouse/ former spouse as contributing to the bankruptcy.

- needs and resources of spouse/ former spouse.
- needs of any children.
- all circumstances of the case (but not the bankrupt's interests).

The non-bankrupt spouse will have a right of occupation under s1 MHA and the bankrupt will have a right of occupation under s337 where she:

- has a beneficial interest in the property, and
- any person under 18 has their home (at the time of presentation of the petition) with the bankrupt.

After a period of one year from the date of appointment of the trustee:

- the court shall assume that the interests of the bankrupt's creditors outweigh all other considerations.
- unless the circumstances of the case are exceptional.
- hardship to wives and children is not exceptional, sudden grave and unforeseen illness would be exceptional.

The trustee must obtain sanction from the creditors' committee (or Secretary of State) before taking action.

6   If, for any reason, the trustee is unable to realise:
- an interest in a dwelling house, occupied by the bankrupt, spouse or former spouse.
- trustee has a power under s313 to apply to court for an imposition of a charge.

The benefit of the charge is comprised in the bankrupt's estate and the property re-vests in the bankrupt. The trustee loses control of how and when the property is sold.

If equity is low, ie. less than £1,000, the court is unlikely to grant a charging order.

The trustee has three years from the date of the bankruptcy order to deal with the equity in the property. After this time the property will re-vest in the bankrupt.

11

Proofs of debt

Contents

Introduction
Examination context
Topic List
1 Proofs of debt
2 Special cases
3 Distributions
4 Order of payment
Summary and Self-test
Answers to Self-test
Answer to Interactive Question

Introduction

Learning objectives

- Understand how a creditor proves his debt, which debts are provable and which debts are not
- Understand the rules regarding interest
- Understand the statutory regulations regarding the payment of dividends

Tick off

Working context

In a working environment it is likely that you will be asked to assist a trustee in bankruptcy in determining the creditor's claims received. It is important therefore to understand the rules relating to what debts are provable and which are not.

Stop and think

Why does a creditor have to prove his debt? Why are rules required regarding the order of payments made by the trustee?

PROOFS OF DEBT 11

Examination context

Creditor's claims and proofs of debt can appear as a topic in any of the three JIEB exam papers so should be learnt thoroughly.

Exam requirements

Past questions to look at include:

2008	Question 3 (a)
2004	Question 5 (ii)
2001	Question 2 (a)
1994	Question 1 (b)
1993	Question 3 (a)

211

Personal Insolvency

1 Proofs of debt

Section overview

A creditor of the bankrupt will establish his right to vote at meetings of creditors and his right to a dividend by submitting a proof of debt form. It is for the trustee to decide whether or not the creditor has established his right to be treated as a bankruptcy creditor within the provisions of the Act and Rules.

Definitions

Prove: a creditor who claims (whether or not in writing) is referred to as 'proving' for his debt (r4.73).

Proof: a document by which a creditor seeks to establish his claim.

1.1 Debts for which a creditor may prove (s382)

Creditors may prove for bankruptcy debts which are defined in s382. This includes all debts and liabilities to which the bankrupt is subject at the commencement and any debt or liability to which he may become subject after the commencement of the bankruptcy (including post discharge) by reason of any obligation incurred before commencement. It is clear, therefore, that liabilities in tort are provable providing the cause of action accrued prior to commencement and it is immaterial whether the debt or liability is present or future, certain or contingent.

S382(2) makes it clear that it is immaterial whether the debt or liability is:

- Present or future.
- Certain or contingent.
- Fixed or liquidated or is capable of being ascertained by fixed rules or as a matter of opinion.

1.2 Debts that are not provable

Pursuant to r12.3, the following debts are not provable. Any:

- Fine imposed for an offence.

- Obligation arising under an order made in family proceedings or under a maintenance assessment made under the Child Support Act 1991. (Note that lump sum and cost orders are provable from 1 April 2005 but still survive the bankruptcy).

- Obligation arising under a confiscation order made under s1 Drug Trafficking Offences Act 1986 (Proceeds of Crime Act) or s71 Criminal Justice Act 1988.

Student debts. (Any student who becomes bankrupt after 1 September 2004 and who has not completed their education is able to receive further student loans and such loans do not form after acquired property and should not be taken into account when assessing whether or not to obtain IPA/IPA.)

If a claim is not provable it follows that although the creditor will not be able to receive a dividend in respect of it, the debt will at least survive the discharge of the bankruptcy.

Certain claims under the Financial Services and Markets Act 2000 and the 1987 Banking Acts are only provable once all other creditors are paid in full.

R12.3 specifically states that it is without prejudice to other rules of law under which particular types of debt are NOT provable.

1.3 Proving for dividend and voting purposes

These must be distinguished for two reasons.

- **Future debts**: These need to be discounted in accordance with r11.13 for dividend but not for voting purposes.

- **Unspecified debts**

    For voting purposes r6.93(3) provides that a creditor shall not vote on such debts unless the chair agrees to put upon the debt an estimated minimum value.

    For dividend purposes s322(3) provides that the trustee shall estimate the value of any debt which by reason of its being subject to a contingency or for any other reason does not bear a certain value.

1.4 Contents of a proof of debt

A creditor wishing to recover his debt in whole or in part must submit his claim in writing to the official receiver or to the trustee (r6.96).

The creditor must be sent a proof of debt form upon request, otherwise the trustee will send out proof of debt forms at his discretion.

The Official Receiver will issue proof of debt forms when a creditors' meeting is convened for the appointment of a trustee.

R6.98 provides for the contents of a proof of debt. The contents are:

- The creditor's name and address and, if a company, its company registration number.
- The total amount of his claim as at the date of the bankruptcy order.
- Whether or not that amount includes outstanding uncapitalised interest.
- Whether or not the claim includes VAT.
- Details of any reservation of title in respect of goods to which the debt refers.
- Particulars of how and when the debt was incurred by the debtor.
- Particulars of any security held, the date when it was given and the value which the creditor puts upon it.
- The name, address and authority of the person signing the proof if other than the creditor himself.

The trustee may, if he thinks it necessary, require a claim of debt to be verified by affidavit.

The trustee shall, so long as proofs lodged with him are in his hands, allow them to be inspected by:

- A creditor who has submitted his proof of debt and it has not been rejected for the purposes of dividend or otherwise.
- The bankrupt.
- Any person acting on behalf of either the above.

The costs of proving a debt are met by the creditor.

1.5 Interest

1.5.1 Pre-commencement interest

Pre-commencement interest is provable as part of the debt. It should be proved for unlike post-commencement interest that will automatically be paid if the trustee is in funds. The rate of bankruptcy interest is governed by r6.113.

- S322(2) states that where a bankruptcy debt bears interest, that interest is provable as part of the debt except in so far as it is payable in respect of any period after the commencement of bankruptcy.

Personal Insolvency

- If the contract itself provides for payment of interest the contractual rate of interest will apply unless it is extortionate.

- On a debt due by virtue of a written instrument and payable at a certain time, for example, a debt due by virtue of a bill of exchange, the rate of interest will be that specified in s17 of The Judgements Act 1838 on the date of the bankruptcy order (currently 8%).

- In all other cases interest will only be payable if the creditor, prior to the date of presentation of the petition, serves written demand for payment of interest stating that interest would be payable from the date of service of the demand to the date of the bankruptcy order. The rate of interest charged is again that in the Judgements Act unless the demanded rate of interest is lower in which case that will apply.

Note. Interest rates can be challenged under s343 as a possible extortionate credit transaction.

1.5.2 Post commencement interest

S322(2) states that interest in respect of any period after the commencement of the bankruptcy is not provable.

S328(4) provides that if all preferential or unsecured creditors (except for deferred debts) are paid in full then any remaining funds are to be used for the payment of interest on those debts.

The interest is paid in respect of the period that the debts have been outstanding since the commencement of bankruptcy.

The interest payable under s328(4) ranks equally even if the debts themselves do not rank equally.

The rate of interest payable is the greater of:

- The rate specified in s17 of the Judgements Act 1838 on the date of commencement.
- The rate applicable to that debt apart from the bankruptcy.

1.5.3 Late payment of commercial debts

The Late Payment of Commercial Debts (Interest) Act 1988 (LPCD) gives businesses a statutory right to claim interest on the late payment of commercial debts by making an entitlement to interest an implied contractual term.

The LPCD applies to contracts for the supply of goods and services where both parties are acting in the course of business. It does not apply to consumer credit agreements, mortgages and charges.

The Act was brought fully into effect on 7 August 2002.

Interest under the LPCD runs from the day following the agreed date of payment, or if no agreed date, from 30 days after the supplier performs their obligation under the contract.

The rate of interest is 8% over the base rate in force on 30 June or 31 December immediately before the day on which the interest starts to run.

Parties cannot contract out of the LPCD unless there is a substantial contractual remedy for late payment of the debt.

Where advising individuals, IPs should draw the LPCD to their attention, interest under LPCD should be provided for in any statement of affairs, both in respect of creditors and debtors.

Where an annulment of a bankruptcy order on the grounds of payment in full is sought, interest due under the late payment legislation (up to the date of the bankruptcy order) must be paid in full, in the same way as interest due under any other contractual or statutory provision.

In bankruptcy, where there is a surplus, interest is paid at the higher of the judgment rate, or the rate applicable apart from the bankruptcy. Therefore, it appears that if debts bear interest under the LPCD, the creditor will be entitled to the payment of interest at 8% over base rate.

IPs will also need to consider whether an individual is entitled to claim interest under the LPCD when collecting book debts.

2 Special cases

Section overview

A number of claims in bankruptcy require special treatment These are summarised below:

2.1 Debts payable in foreign currency

The amount of the debt must be converted into sterling at the official exchange rate (ie Bank of England mid-market rate) on the date of the bankruptcy order (r6.111).

2.2 Discounts

The creditor must deduct all trade and other discounts that would have been available to the bankrupt (r6.110). Early settlement discounts should not be deducted.

2.3 Payments of a periodical nature

This includes rent and other payments and permits the creditor to prove for any amounts due and unpaid up to the date of the bankruptcy order. This would include all amounts payable in advance (r6.112).

If amounts are accruing on a daily basis, the creditor may prove for so much as would have fallen due as at the date of the bankruptcy order.

2.4 Negotiable instruments

Unless the trustee provides otherwise proofs in relation to money owed on a negotiable instrument must be accompanied by the instrument or a certified copy (r6.108).

2.5 Future debts

If a creditor has proved for a debt that is not due at the date of declaration of a dividend, the amount of the admitted proof must be reduced for dividend purposes. This is necessary, as the creditor will have enjoyed early repayment of the debt. Note the change to r11.13 from 1 April 2005.

R11.13 provides a formula to calculate the percentage discount:

The formula to apply is: $\dfrac{x}{1.05^n}$

Where: x = amount of the debt

n = the period beginning with the relevant date and ending with the date on which the payment of the creditor's debt would otherwise be due expressed in years and months in a decimalised form. Relevant date is the date of the bankruptcy order.

2.6 Double Proof

One debt cannot be the subject of more than one proof in the same estate for example where a debt has been guaranteed, the creditor and the guarantor may not both prove in the bankruptcy.

It is usual to admit the primary creditor.

2.7 Gaming debts

Gaming debts are generally void for public policy. However s6 Gaming Act provides that a cheque drawn to enable a person to take part in gaming on licensed permits is enforceable providing:

Personal Insolvency

- It is not post-dated.
- Exchanged for cash or chips at par.
- Presented to bank for payment within two banking days.

2.8 Non-EU tax claims

These are not enforceable in UK courts (*Government of India v Taylor*). Such claims are not, therefore payable in bankruptcy. Pursuant to the EU Regulation, EU claims (except Denmark) are provable.

2.9 Set-off *allowed*

S323 applies where, before the commencement of the bankruptcy, there has been mutual credits, debts or other mutual dealings between the bankrupt and a creditor.

S323(2) states that an account should be taken of what is due from each party to the other in respect of the mutual dealings and the sums due from one party shall be set-off against the sums due from the other.

S323(3) states that set-off should not occur when one of the parties is aware that a petition for bankruptcy was pending.

Only the balance is provable in the bankruptcy. If the effect of set-off is that the third party owes money to the bankrupt then this amount must be paid to the trustee.

2.10 Landlords

Landlords may have a number of claims arising from the lease.

Claims for arrears of rent and/or service charge may be admitted in full.

A claim for rent payable in advance which straddles the date of the bankruptcy order should be admitted in full.

Claims for dilapidations and future rent are unspecified and must be estimated. The landlord has a duty to mitigate his loss.

In *Re Park Air Services plc* it was held that the landlord's compensation is measured by reference to the difference between the rents and other payments which the landlord would have received in the future but for any disclaimer and the rents and other sums which the disclaimer would enable the landlord to receive by re-letting.

Allowance should also be made for early receipt using the yield on gilt-edged securities for an equivalent term from the date of disclaimer. This should be used rather than r11.13 as the landlord's entitlement is a present right to immediate payment rather than a future payment.

2.11 Secured creditors

The secured creditor can prove in three situations (r6.109):

- Creditor realises security and proves for balance.
- Creditor proves for whole debt by voluntarily surrendering his security for the general benefit of creditors.
- Creditor estimates value of security in his proof and proves for the unsecured balance:
    - If the security is subsequently realised the original valuation is substituted for that shown in the proof (r6.119).
    - If trustee disagrees with value put on security can require the security to be realised (r6.118):
        - Terms will be set by the court in default of agreement.
        - If property auctioned – trustee and creditor can both bid.
    - If creditor fails to disclose his security in the proof – must surrender that security.

Exception – If court provides relief on grounds of 'inadvertence or honest mistake'.

Creditor can by written notice force trustee to decide in a period of six months whether he will or will not redeem.

- Creditor can revalue the security given in the proof with:
  - The court's permission if he petitioned or voted with unsecured balance.
  - Either the courts or the trustee's permission in any other case.
- Trustee may redeem the security at value given in proof (costs of transfer will be born by estate). Procedure:
  - Must give 28 days' notice to creditor.
  - Creditor now has 21 days in which to revalue the security.
  - If creditor revalues, trustee can now only redeem at that new price.

2.12 Debts to spouse

S329 applies to bankruptcy debts owed in respect of credit provided by a person who (whether or not the bankrupt's spouse or civil partner at the time the credit was provided) was the bankrupt's spouse or civil partner at the commencement of the bankruptcy.

Such debts rank in priority after all other debts and interest have been paid.

Interactive question: Proofs

You are presented with a bundle of proofs of debt, the details of which are as follows:

(1) A claim by HM Revenue and Customs for unpaid VAT of £1,200 per month for the 14 months next before the date of the bankruptcy order.

(2) A claim by the Secretary of State for £2,450 paid out of the Redundancy Fund to Sam Platt an employee of the bankrupt in respect of eight weeks arrears of wages and six weeks arrears of holiday pay (at £175 per week) which were due to Mr Platt at the commencement of bankruptcy.

(3) A claim by the bankrupt's brother for £8,000 which was lent to the bankrupt eight years ago.

(4) A claim by the bankrupt's wife for £5,000 lent by her two years ago during their engagement.

(5) A claim by Satby Bank plc for an overdraft which had increased by £3,000 after the date of the bankruptcy order. The sum of £3,000 represents a cheque which was written and presented before the date of the bankruptcy order, but which was only cleared and credited to the payee's account after the bank had been informed of the commencement of bankruptcy.

Requirement

State, with reasons, how you would deal with each proof.

See **Answer** at the end of this chapter.

3 Distributions

Section overview

Whenever the trustee has sufficient funds in hand for the purpose he shall, subject to the retention of such sums as may be necessary for the expenses of the bankruptcy, declare and distribute dividends among the creditors in respect of the bankruptcy debts for which they have proved (s324).

3.1 Notice of intention to declare dividend

The trustee must give notice of his intention to declare a dividend (or notice that no dividend is due to be declared) to all creditors whose addresses are known to him and who have not proved their debts (r11.2).

Unless he has previously by public advertisement invited creditors to prove their debts, give notice of the intended dividend by public advertisement. As soon as reasonably practicable the notice shall be Gazetted and may be advertised in such other manner as the trustee thinks fit.

The notice must state a last date for proving, which must be not less than 21 days from that of the notice.

The dividend must be declared within four months from the last date for proving.

The trustee must, within seven days from the last date of proving, deal with every creditor's proof by admitting it or rejecting it in whole or in part, or by making such provision as he thinks fit in respect of it. He is not obliged to deal with proofs lodged after the date for proving, he may do so if he thinks fit (r11.3).

Where a creditor's proof has been rejected, the trustee must send his reasons for rejecting the proof, in writing to the creditor, who then has 21 days to appeal to court for the decision to be reversed or varied r6.105.

If, in the period of four months referred to in r11.2(3):

(i) the trustee has rejected a proof in whole or in part and an application is made to the court for his decision to be reversed or varied, or

(ii) an application is made to the court for the trustee's decision as a proof to be reversed or varied, or for a proof to be expunged, or for a reduction of the amount claimed, the trustee can postpone or cancel the dividend.

3.2 Calculation of dividend

In the calculation and distribution of a dividend the trustee shall make provision:

- For any bankruptcy debts which appear to him to be due to persons who, by reason of the distance of their place of residence, may not have had sufficient time to tender and establish their proofs.
- For any bankruptcy debts which are the subject of claims which have not yet been determined, and
- For disputed proofs and claims.

The trustee may distribute property in specie (s326):

- This is where it cannot be readily or advantageously sold.
- Specific sanction of the creditors' committee is required (if not obtained, the committee can ratify but only if no undue delay and trustee acted in a case of urgency).
- Innocent third parties are not concerned as to whether sanction has been obtained.

3.3 Declaration of dividend

Where the trustee has declared a dividend, he must give notice of the dividend and of how it is proposed to distribute it to all creditors who have proved their debts (r11.6).

The notice must include the following details:

- Amounts realised from the sale of assets, indicating amounts raised by the sale of particular assets.
- Payments made by the trustee in the administration of the estate.
- Provision made for unsettled claims and funds retained for that particular purpose.
- The total amount to be distributed and the rate of dividend.
- Whether, and if so when, any further dividend is expected to be declared.

The dividend may be distributed simultaneously with the notice declaring it.

Payment of dividend may be made by post, or arrangements may be made with any creditor for it to be paid to him in another way, or held for his collection.

3.4 Notice of no further dividend

If the trustee gives notice to creditors that he is unable to declare any dividend or further dividend, the notice must contain a statement to the effect either that (r11.7):

- No funds have been realised.
- The funds realised have already been distributed or used or allocated for defraying the expenses of the administration.

3.5 Final distribution

When the trustee has realised all the bankrupt's estate, or so much of it as can, in the trustee's opinion, be realised without needlessly protracting the trusteeship, he shall give notice in the prescribed manner either:

(a) of his intention to declare a final dividend, or
(b) that no dividend, or no further dividends, will be declared.

The notice shall require claims against the bankrupt's estate to be established by the final date specified in the notice, and shall contain the following information:

- A date (the last date for proving) up to which proofs may be lodged. The date shall be the same for all creditors and not less than 21 days from that of the notice.
- Statement that the trustee intends to declare a final dividend within the period of four months from the last date for proving.

After the final date specified in the notice, the trustee shall:

- defray any outstanding expenses of the bankruptcy out of the bankrupt's estate, and
- if he intends to distribute a dividend, declare and distribute that dividend without regard to the claim of any person in respect of a debt not already proved in the bankruptcy.

3.6 Rights of creditors

A creditor who has not proved for his debt before the declaration of any dividend is not entitled to disturb, by reason that he has not participated in it, the distribution of that dividend or any other dividend declared before his debt was proved (s325).

However, once a creditor does prove he will become entitled to payment of the missed dividends. These will be paid from funds available to pay further dividends before those further dividends are paid. Having proved, the creditor will now also be entitled to such further dividends.

No action lies against the trustee for a dividend but if the trustee refuses to pay a dividend, the court may, if it thinks fit, order him to pay it. It is open to the court to order payment out of the trustee's own money. Interest can also be awarded on any withheld dividend together with an order for costs against the trustee.

3.7 Unclaimed dividends

Dividend cheques unclaimed by creditors should have their bottom right hand corner cut off and should be returned to the Central Accounting Unit in accordance with Reg 15(7) Insolvency Regulations 1986. No attempts should be made to pay them back into the ISA.

4 Order of payment

Section overview

The Act and the Rules contain regulations detailing the order of payment of funds coming into the hands of the trustee.

The order for payment of debts is as follows:

- Costs of the bankruptcy (see 4.1 for more details).
- Any debts specifically preferred (by virtue of s328(6)).
- Preferential debts (s328(1), s386 and Schedule 6).
- Ordinary debts (s328(3)).
- Interest on debts above outstanding for the period after the bankruptcy order.
- Debts in respect of credit supplied by a person who is the spouse or civil partner of the bankrupt at the date of the bankruptcy order. On such debts interest of the type referred to above will rank in this category (s329).
- Debts specially postponed (s328(6)).

If any surplus remains after payment of the above debts it must be paid to the bankrupt (s330(5)).

4.1 Costs of the bankruptcy

The order of priority of these is set out in R6.224.

- Expenses properly chargeable or incurred by the OR or the trustee in preserving, realising or getting in any of the assets of the bankrupt, including those incurred in acquiring title to after-acquired property.
- Any other expenses incurred or disbursements made by the OR or under his authority, including those incurred or made in carrying on the business of the debtor or bankrupt.
- Any other fees payable under any order made under s415, including those payable to the OR, and any remuneration payable to him under general regulations.
    - The fee payable under any order made under s415 for the performance by the OR of his general duties as OR.
    - Any repayable deposit lodged by the petitioner under any such order as security for the fees mentioned. (Except where the deposit is applied to the payment of the remuneration of an insolvency practitioner appointed under s273 (debtor's petition).
- The cost of any security provided by an interim receiver, trustee or special manager in accordance with the Act or Rules.
- The remuneration of the interim receiver.
- Any deposit lodged on an application for the appointment of an interim receiver.
- The costs of the petitioner and of any person appearing on the petition whose costs are allowed by the court.
- The remuneration of the special manager.
- Any amount payable to a person employed or authorised to assist in the preparation of a statement of affairs or accounts.
- Any allowance made, by order of the court, towards costs on an application for release from the obligation to submit a statement of affairs, or for an extension of time for submitting such a statement.

- The costs of employing a shorthand writer in any case other than one appointed by an order of the court at the instance of the OR in connection with an examination.
- Any necessary disbursements by the trustee in the course of his administration (including any expenses incurred by members of the creditors' committee or their representatives and allowed by the trustee under r6.164).
- The remuneration or emoluments of any person (including the bankrupt) who has been employed by the trustee to perform any services for the estate, as required by or under the Act or the Rules.
- The remuneration of the trustee, up to any amount not exceeding that which is payable to the OR under Schedule 6.
- The amount of any capital gains tax on the realisation of any asset of the bankrupt (without regard to whether the realisation is effected by a trustee, a secured creditor or a receiver and manager appointed to deal with a security.
- The balance of any remuneration due to the trustee.
- Any other expense properly chargeable by the trustee in carrying out his functions in bankruptcy.

Summary and Self-test

Summary

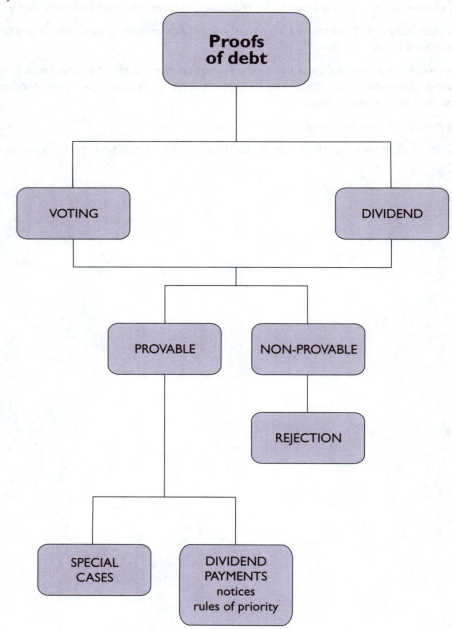

Self-test

Answer the following questions.

1 Which debts are not provable?

2 Who is permitted to inspect proofs of debt held by the trustee?

3 A trustee gives notice of his intention to declare a dividend. Within what period of time should the trustee declare the dividend?

4 Within how many days from the last date of proving must the trustee deal with every creditor's proof?

5 What details must be included in the notice of dividend?

6 As trustee you have just paid a first dividend. A creditor notices that he has not proved for all of the debt due to him and now wishes to do so. Advise the creditor what, if anything, can be done to pursue the dividend on the balance of his claim and the effect any possible payment would have on any further dividend?

Now, go back to the Learning Objectives in the Introduction. If you are satisfied that you have achieved these, please tick them off.

Answers to Self-test

1. Any fine imposed for an offence.

    Any obligation arising under an order made in family proceedings or under a maintenance assessment made under the CSA 1991. (Lump sum and cost orders are provable but survive bankruptcy.)

    Any obligation arising under a confiscation order made under s1 Drug Trafficking Offences Act 1986 (Proceeds of Crime Act) or s71 Criminal Justices Act 1988.

2. A creditor who has submitted his proof of debt and it has not been rejected.

    The bankrupt.

    Any person acting on behalf of either of the above.

3. Within the period of four months from the last date for proving specified in the notice.

4. Within seven days.

5. The notice must include the following details:

    (a) Amounts realised from the sale of assets.
    (b) Payments made by the trustee.
    (c) Provision made for unsettled claims and funds retained for that particular purpose.
    (d) The total amount to be distributed and the rate of dividend.
    (e) Whether, and if so when, any further dividend is expected to be declared.

6. The creditor can prove for the balance of his debt, however he cannot disturb the dividend already paid before he proved his debt. He will be entitled to receive payment of the first dividend on his debt before any further dividends are paid by the trustee.

Answer to Interactive Question

Interactive question 1: Proofs

(1) VAT is no longer a preferential claim. Admit £16,800 as an unsecured claim.

(2) Under Schedule 6 any amount which is owed by the debtor to a person who is or has been an employee of the debtor and is payable by way of remuneration in respect of the whole or any part in the period of four months next before the date of the bankruptcy order ranks as a preferential claim provided it does not exceed the amount prescribed by order of the Secretary of State (£800).

In addition, any amount owed by way of accrued holiday remuneration in respect of any period of employment before the date of the bankruptcy order to a person who was employed by the debtor has been terminated whether before, on or after that date, ranks as a preferential claim.

Accordingly, in this case, £1,850 (£800 wages plus £1,050 holiday pay) ranks as a preferential claim and £600 ranks as an unsecured claim.

(3) It has been held in cases such as *Re General Rolling Stock Company 1872* that if a debt, although at one time valid and enforceable, has become statute barred through lapse of time, the creditor will be unable to lodge a proof in the insolvency and the trustee will be under duty not to pay out any dividend in respect of that claim.

The limitation period for contract debts is six years and therefore the claim by the bankrupt's brother is statute barred, the loan having been made some eight years previously.

(4) Under s329 any bankruptcy debt owed in respect of credit provided by a person who (whether or not the bankrupt's spouse at the time the credit was provided) was the bankrupt's spouse at the commencement of the bankruptcy, ranks in priority after the preferential and ordinary unsecured debts and also ranks after any interest payable on such debts pursuant to s328(4).

Under s329 the debt to the spouse is payable with interest in respect of the period during which it has been outstanding since the commencement of the bankruptcy and that interest has the same priority as the debt on which it is payable.

(5) Under s284 a disposition of property made by the bankrupt in the period beginning with the day of the presentation of the bankruptcy petition and ending with the vesting of the bankrupt's estate in a trustee is void except to the extent that it is or was made with the consent of the Court or is or was subsequently ratified by the court.

Where after the commencement of the bankruptcy the bankrupt has incurred a debt to a banker or other person by reason of the making of a payment which is void under s284, that debt is deemed to have been incurred before the commencement of bankruptcy unless:

(a) That banker or person had notice of the bankruptcy before the debt was incurred,

(b) It is not reasonably practicable for the amount of the payment to be recovered from the person to whom it was made.

In the present case, the disposition is deemed to take place, not when the cheque is written and presented but instead on the date it is cleared and credited to the payee's account.

Since the bank was aware of the making of the bankruptcy order when the cheque was cleared, the disposition cannot therefore be treated as one made before the commencement of the bankruptcy and accordingly the claim is not provable against the bankrupt's estate.

12

Closure of bankruptcy

Contents

Introduction
Examination context
Topic List
1 Discharge
2 Bankruptcy Restrictions Order
3 Annulment of bankruptcy
4 Vacation of office
5 Closure checklist

Summary and Self-test
Answers to Self-test

Personal Insolvency

Introduction

Learning objectives

- Understand the different rules re discharge
- The circumstances when a court will annul a bankruptcy order
- The effects of a Bankruptcy Restrictions Order
- Understand the different ways a trustee can vacate office
- Identify practical and regulatory matters to be dealt with by the trustee on closure of bankruptcy

Tick off
☐
☐
☐
☐
☐

Working context

It is likely that in a work environment you will be asked to review cases for closure. It is important to understand what matters are required to be dealt with prior to closure by the trustee before he can obtain his release. You may also be asked to explain to a bankrupt how they are discharged from bankruptcy and what discharge actually means in practical terms.

Stop and think

How does a trustee close a bankruptcy case? What is discharge and annulment? What do they mean for the debtor? What is a Bankruptcy Restrictions Order? How does such an order affect the bankrupt? How does it differ from a Bankruptcy Restrictions Undertaking?

CLOSURE OF BANKRUPTCY 12

Examination context

The topics covered in this chapter are regularly examined in the JIEB exam.

Exam requirements

Past questions to look at include:

2008	Question 1 (b)
2008	Question 3 (c)
2002	Question 1 (i)
2001	Question 2 (b)
1997	Question 5
1994	Question 1 (b)
1992	Paper II, Question 6 (c)

Personal Insolvency

1 Discharge

Section overview

Bankruptcy commences on the date that a bankruptcy order is made and continues until the bankrupt is discharged. On discharge, the liabilities that the bankrupt has been subject to will be lifted and he will be released from most civil bankruptcy debts. The discharge does not mark the end of the administration of his estate. The trustee will not be released until he has finished administering the estate and consequently the duty of the bankrupt to assist the trustee continues after discharge. Assets that have vested in the trustee will not re-vest in the bankrupt following discharge.

1.1 Effect of discharge

The bankrupt will be released from all bankruptcy debts and interest thereon.

Bankruptcy debts are defined in s382 as any debt or liability to which:

- The bankrupt is subject at the commencement of the bankruptcy.
- He became subject after the commencement of the bankruptcy by reason of any obligation incurred before commencement.

There are some debts that the bankrupt will not be released from. Consequently the creditors concerned will be free to sue the bankrupt and will not require leave.

The debts the bankrupt will not be released from are:

- Secured debts.
- Debts arising from fraud or fraudulent breach of trust.
- Fines and recognisances (exception: revenue penalties where bankrupt can be released with treasury consent).
- Lump sum orders and costs awarded in family proceedings.
- Damages for personal injury awarded in tort or contract.
- Student loans.

Disabilities will no longer apply.

- S11 CDDA (Disqualification of undischarged bankrupt no longer applies).
- Disqualification under other sections are unaffected.
- Duty to notify persons offering credit of £500 or more comes to an end.

The estate will not re-vest in the bankrupt. Assets not yet realised and distributed remain vested in the trustee. The powers and duties of the trustee in relation to the estate are unaffected by discharge. The Act and Rules continue to apply.

Discharge does not mark the end of the administration of the estate. The trustee will not be released until he has finished administering the estate.

Duty of the bankrupt to assist the trustee continues.

Discharge has no effect on the rights of creditors to prove in the bankruptcy.

If the bankrupt is subject to either a Bankruptcy Restrictions Order or Undertaking some of the disabilities/ obligations that arise on bankruptcy will continue beyond discharge (see Section 2 later).

230

CLOSURE OF BANKRUPTCY

1.2 When is a bankrupt discharged?

Section 256 EA 2002 amends s279. The maximum period of bankruptcy is now one year from commencement. Discharge will operate automatically. There are however exceptions to this basic position.

Pursuant to s279(2) the time period for automatic discharge will be less than one year if during the first year following commencement the OR files a notice at Court stating that an investigation into the conduct and affairs of the bankrupt is either unnecessary or has been concluded (s289(2)).

Prior to the filing of this notice creditors and any trustee will be given notice of the intention to file and will have 28 days in which to provide information showing why the bankrupt should not be discharged (r6.214A). If no such objection is made the OR can file the notice at court.

The bankrupt will be discharged from the bankruptcy from the date of the filing of the notice. If objection is made the OR shall not file the notice under s279(2) until he has given notice of the rejection of the objection to the complainant and the time period for any appeal under r7.50(2) has expired (or if appeal proceedings are commenced the appeal has been determined) r6.214A(5).

Despite the provisions introduced by EA 2002 there is still scope within the legislation to suspend the period of automatic discharge (s279(3)).

Either the trustee or the OR can make an application to the court for time to cease to run on the basis that the bankrupt is not complying with his obligations. The application must be made to court within the 12-month period of bankruptcy and the suspension will run for a specified period or until the bankrupt has complied with a specified condition.

Applications should only be made when all other possibilities to obtain the bankrupt's co-operation have been exhausted, for example if the debtor fails to make voluntary payments an IPO should be obtained.

The Court must be satisfied that the bankrupt has failed, or is failing, to comply with one or more of his obligations under IA 1986. The procedure to be followed on such application is set out in r6.215/6.

The court will notify the OR/trustee of the hearing and send him a copy of any order made. The trustee must send a copy of any evidence submitted in support of an application to the OR and the bankrupt at least 21 days before the date fixed for the hearing. The bankrupt may, not later than seven days before the date of the hearing, file in court a notice specifying any statements in the OR's/trustee's evidence in support which he intends to deny or dispute. A copy must be sent to the OR/trustee.

The bankrupt must be notified of any order made.

It should be remembered that suspension of discharge is separate from any application for a bankruptcy restrictions order (BRO) or bankruptcy restrictions undertaking (BRU). Following discharge the bankrupt is released from bankruptcy debts and the disabilities and obligations imposed by IA 1986 (albeit that some restrictions might still apply if a BRO/BRU is in force). Where a suspension is in force the bankrupt will enjoy no such release. Further the fact that a suspension is in force will not affect the courts ability to annul the bankruptcy s279(7).

Criminal bankrupts will still have to apply to court for their discharge (s279(6)). A criminal bankrupt is defined in s264(1)(d). Application is made under s280 and cannot be commenced until five years from the start of the bankruptcy. The procedure for such application is contained in r6.217.

1.3 Second or subsequent bankruptcies

There is no longer a separate rule for discharge in the case of second or subsequent bankruptcies. Where after 1 April 2004 a person is made bankrupt for a second (or subsequent) time they will automatically be discharged after one year in the usual way. However, where the bankruptcy is within six years of discharge of an earlier bankruptcy this is a consideration for a Bankruptcy Restrictions Order (see below).

Where the second or subsequent bankruptcy commenced prior to 1 April 2004 the bankrupt will be discharged on 1 April 2009 unless the court discharges them earlier. No application to court can be made for five years from the date of the bankruptcy order.

Personal Insolvency

1.4 Certificate of discharge

Under r6.220 the former bankrupt may apply, on payment of a fee, for a certificate of discharge. This applies to both automatic discharge and discharge by court order. Application can also be made to the Secretary of State to advertise notice of the discharge although the Secretary of State need not proceed until he is put in funds in respect of the advertising costs. As soon as reasonably practicable, such notice shall be Gazetted and may be advertised in such other manner as the bankruptcy order to which it relates was advertised (r6.220(2)).

2 Bankruptcy Restrictions Order

Section overview

Bankruptcy Restrictions Orders (BRO) were introduced by the Enterprise Act 2002 for bankrupts whose conduct has been irresponsible, reckless or otherwise culpable. It is a civil procedure which provides an alternative to prosecution for bankrupts whose conduct warrants further action. The effect of a BRO is to extend the period during which the disabilities resulting from bankruptcy apply. The provisions are set out in s281A and Schedule 4A.

2.1 Mechanics of a BRO

Only the Secretary of State or OR's can apply to the court for a BRO (ie Not the trustee). Application must be made within one year of the date upon which the bankruptcy commenced unless a suspension has been granted or the court has given permission.

Only the court can make a BRO, however as with disqualification of directors the Insolvency Service can accept a Bankruptcy Restrictions Undertaking (BRU) to avoid the costs of applying to court for an order.

A BRU is where the bankrupt agrees, in writing, to restrictions being imposed upon him.

A BRU between the bankrupt and the Secretary of State takes effect when signed by both parties, with a copy being sent to the bankrupt and the court.

A BRU may be annulled on application by the bankrupt, who gives 28 days' notice of the hearing to the Secretary of State with a copy of the application and an affidavit of any evidence to support it. If the court annuls the BRU, two sealed copies of the order are sent to the Secretary of State, one of which is forwarded to the bankrupt (r6.249-r6.251).

Like a disqualification undertaking, a BRU is likely to lead to a shorter period of restriction. It will have the same legal effect as a BRO and the same time frames should be considered.

When considering whether or not to accept a BRU the Secretary of State will have regard to the requirements of Schedule 4A.

It will come into force on the date it is accepted by Secretary of State and ends on the date specified in the BRU.

Pursuant to Schedule 4A Para 9(3) the bankrupt can apply to court to either annul or shorten its duration.

Any reference to a BRO in IA 1986 should be construed as extending to a BRU and hence the effect is the same.

2.2 Effect of a BRO

A BRO is intended to impose restrictions on the bankrupt after they have been discharged from their bankruptcy and will last for a period of between two and 15 years. The view is that they are similar to disqualification orders for directors and as such the criteria for the length of a BRO has been split as follows:

2–5 years	Negligent
6–10 years	Negligent/self-serving conduct
11–15 years	Fraud/criminal activity

During this period the bankrupt will continue to be subject to the normal bankruptcy offences and also some of the restrictions placed on undischarged bankrupts. The bankrupt will be disqualified from:

- Acting as a receiver and manager.
- Acting as an IP.
- Acting as a director or being concerned with the promotion, formation or management of a company.

Breach of these provisions constitutes a criminal offence.

The bankrupt is discharged from the bankruptcy debts in the usual way. These provisions apply notwithstanding the fact that the bankrupt may have received his discharge.

2.3 Grounds for a BRO (Schedule 4A)

Pursuant to Schedule 4A Para 2(2) the matters that should be taken into consideration when deciding whether an application for a BRO should be made include:

- Failing to keep records that account for the loss of property by the bankrupt or a business carried on by them. The loss must be in the two years prior to the petition and ending on the date of the application.
- Failure to produce records on demand of the OR/trustee.
- Entering into a transaction at an undervalue.
- Giving a preference.
- Making excessive pension contributions.
- Failure to supply goods/services which were wholly or partly paid for which gave rise to a provable claim in the bankruptcy.
- Trading at a time before commencement of the bankruptcy when the bankrupt knew or ought to have known that they were unable to pay their debts
- Incurring a debt before commencement with no reasonable expectation of being able to repay it.
- Failure to account to the OR/trustee/court for the loss of property.
- Gambling or rash and hazardous speculation or unreasonable extravagance between the petition and the commencement of bankruptcy which materially contributed to the extent of the bankruptcy.
- Neglect of business affairs.
- Fraud or fraudulent breach of trust.
- Failing to co-operate with the OR/trustee.
- Undischarged bankrupt in previous six years.

2.4 Interim BRO

Given the shortened period of automatic discharge the new regime introduces the idea of the interim BRO. The interim BRO can be applied for at any time after an application for a BRO. Obviously this will before the date of the substantive hearing of the BRO.

The order will be made if there are prima facie grounds to suggest the substantive application would be successful or it is in the public interest to make the interim order.

The interim BRO can only be made on the application of the Secretary of State, or the OR acting on the direction of the Secretary of State.

Personal Insolvency

For an interim BRO to be made an application for a BRO must have already been issued at court but not yet heard.

An interim BRO has the same effect as a substantive BRO. It comes into force when it is made but will cease to have effect:

- On determination of application for a full BRO.
- On acceptance of a BRU offered by bankrupt.
- Where the court discharges an interim BRO following application of either the bankrupt or Secretary of State/OR.

Where an interim BRO is superseded by a full BRO its commencement date is backdated to the date that the interim BRO commenced.

2.5 Bankruptcy Restrictions Register

The Secretary of State maintains a register of any BRO, interim BRO or BRU, which is in effect.

This register (as with the Individual Insolvency Register) will be open for public inspection on any business day between 9am and 5pm.

Such information will be removed:

- immediately if the bankruptcy order is annulled or rescinded.
- after three months from the date of discharge (r6A.4, r6A.5).

Information on a BRO or BRU will be deleted immediately on it expiring or ceasing to have effect.

3 Annulment of bankruptcy

Section overview

Annulment, by contrast to discharge, restores the bankrupt to his pre-bankruptcy status and he remains liable in full for all his bankruptcy debts. Annulment does not release the trustee, who remains liable to account for all his actions in respect of the estate. He will only be released at the court's discretion (see r6.214(4)).

3.1 Power of the court to annul s282(1)

The court may do this where either:

- The order ought not to have been made (s282(1)(a)).
- To the extent required by the rules, the bankruptcy debts and the expenses of the bankruptcy have all, since the making of the order, been either paid or secured for, to the satisfaction of the court s282(1)(b). *Re Robertson (A Bankrupt) 1989* – annulment refused where failure to prove all debts.
- An IVA is approved in regard to an undischarged bankrupt (s261).

The court has power to annul whether or not the bankrupt has been discharged (s282(3)). (Confirmed in *Re Johnson 2006*).

Bankruptcy debts are defined by s382 and include interest provable under s322(2). Interest provable under s322 does not include post bankruptcy order interest.

A scenario which came up in a recent JIEB exam is where a trustee has been appointed to realise an unrealised interest in the bankrupt's home. The options for the bankrupt are either to buy out the trustee's interest in the home or to apply for annulment – which, if successful, will have the effect of re-vesting the property in the now ex-bankrupt. Annulment may turn out to be a lower cost option if the bankrupt can maintain the contention that no post bankruptcy order interest is payable. In addition, where the funds are provided by a third party and do not pass through the hands of the trustee there will be no Secretary of State fees as the funds will not have been paid into the Insolvency Service Account. This scenario has been relevant recently because the Enterprise Act transitional provisions provided that for pre 1 April 2004 bankruptcies where unrealised interests in homes formed part of the estate, those interests had to be realised by 1 April 2007 or would re-vest in the bankrupt.

Harper v Bulcher

Despite the wording of s282(1)(b) the court has a discretion and can require the payment of post order interest as a condition for the granting of annulment. This will be particularly relevant where there has been a long delay between the bankruptcy and the application for annulment. The court will also look at the conduct of the bankrupt and whether realisation of the property within the estate would be sufficient to pay both debts and interest.

Wicklow v Duckworth (2005) and Gill v Quinn (2004)

One way for the bankrupt to ensure that it will not be necessary to pay statutory interest on an application for annulment is to obtain the consent of the bankruptcy creditors. The bankruptcy orders in these two cases had been made in 1992 so that there were practical problems in tracing creditors and obtaining their consent. The cases show that where it has proved impossible to obtain the consent of significant creditors the court is unlikely to allow non-payment of statutory interest.

Where a bankruptcy is annulled following approval of a voluntary arrangement, any sums required to settle the OR's debit balance will not attract Secretary of State administration fees.

3.2 Effect of annulment

The court can order that the property of the bankrupt vested in trustee now vest in such person as it shall appoint. In default of such appointment the property will re-vest in the bankrupt (subject to any terms imposed by court).

The annulled bankruptcy is disregarded for the purpose of working out whether the next bankruptcy is a 'second or subsequent' bankruptcy.

The annulment will have no effect on the pre-annulment acts of OR, trustee or court.

Annulment results in the discharge of any BRO/BRU where the bankruptcy is annulled under s232(1)(a) or (2).

3.3 Application for annulment (r6.206)

The application is made supported by an affidavit or witness statement which must specify under which paragraph of s282 the application is made. Where an application is made under s261 (approved VA) the same procedural rules apply as if the application was made on the ground that the order should never have been made, s282(1)(a).

Once the court issues the application and sets a date for the hearing notice must be given to the OR and trustee. If the bankruptcy order is challenged on the ground that it ought not to have been made or because a voluntary arrangement has been approved the creditor who petitioned for bankruptcy must also be notified.

On an application based on repayment of all debts the trustee (or if none the OR) must file a report in court which covers:

▸ The circumstances leading to the bankruptcy.

▸ A summary of the extent of the bankrupt's assets and liabilities at date of the order and application for annulment.

▸ Details of creditors known to have claims who have not yet proved.

▸ The extent to which and the manner in which debts and expenses have been paid or secured (and whether the security is satisfactory).

Personal Insolvency

The applicant has a 'right to reply' and can file affidavits in answer to the report, sending copies to the OR/trustee.

The trustee (if there is one) is also obliged to send the report to the OR. The OR can file an additional report in court sending a copy to the applicant. If the OR does so he must attend the hearing.

R6.209 states that where the report filed in court by the OR/trustee indicates there are known, non-proving creditors, the court can direct the OR/trustee to notify such creditors of the application giving them an opportunity to prove for their debt within 21 days.

The court can also make a direction as to advertising to bring the application to the attention of non-proving creditors.

Before the hearing (and irrespective of the ground of the application) application can be made to the court for an interim order staying proceedings. Two types of application can be made.

- An application to stay bankruptcy proceedings. Here the applicant must send copies of the application to the OR and any trustee. They must have sufficient notice to enable their attendance.
- An application to stay any other proceedings. Here the application may be made without attendance so that notice does not need to be given to the OR/trustee.

At the hearing itself the court will require proof of payment of debts in full and that some provision has been made in the case of disputed debts or untraced creditors. This security will need to take the form of insurance or a payment into court. Where security has been given the court may direct advertising and if it does the security will be released after 12 months if no claim is made.

The trustee will be required to attend the hearing.

If the court makes the order – copies are sent to the applicant, the OR and the trustee and the court. The OR notifies creditors forthwith of the annulment (and expenses are a charge on the property of the former bankrupt).

Within 28 days of the order being made the former bankrupt may require the Secretary of State to give notice of the annulment, as soon as reasonably practicable, in the Gazette and in such other manner as the bankruptcy order to which it relates was advertised.

In an order under s261 or s282 the court shall include provision, permitting vacation of the registration of the bankruptcy petition as a pending action and of the bankruptcy order in the register of writs and orders affecting land.

3.4 Bankruptcy register

R6A.1 – r6A.5 provide for the Secretary of State to maintain a register of bankruptcy orders, to contain specified information entered into it by the OR. Provision is made for the deletion of information contained in the register in the following circumstances on:

- Receipt by the Secretary of State of notice of an annulment under section 282 (1)(a) (that the bankruptcy order ought not to have been made).
- The expiry of three months after the date of the bankrupt's discharge, and
- The annulment under s261(1)(a) (approval of a voluntary arrangement) or s282(1)(b) (payment in full) or a rescission under s375.

CLOSURE OF BANKRUPTCY | 12

4 Vacation of office

Section overview

A trustee can vacate office in a number of ways;
- Resignation.
- By operation of the law.
- On annulment of the bankruptcy order.
- Removal by court or creditor.

Each of these will be looked at in turn.

4.1 Resignation

A trustee can resign in the circumstances set out in r6.126. Resignation is effected by notice to the court s298(7). The grounds in r6.126 are the same as for voluntary and compulsory winding-up and are:

- Ill health.
- Intends ceasing to be an IP (notice must be served in accordance with the rules).
- That there are joint trustees in bankruptcy and it is no longer expedient to have more than one trustee.
- A conflict of interest/change in personal circumstances precludes or makes continuation impractical.

Although s298(7) says that a trustee resigns by giving notice to the court, it is clear from the rules that in the first instance the trustee must call a meeting of creditors to receive his resignation.

The notice of the meeting draws attention to the rules regarding release (r6.127(1)) and is accompanied by:

- An account of the trustee's administration of the estate (r6.126(2)).
- A summary of his receipts and payments.
- A statement that his accounts have been reconciled with those held by the Secretary of State.

Notice of the meeting must be sent to the OR at the same time as the creditors are notified.

There are a number of possible outcomes at the meeting:

Firstly the meeting may be inquorate. The effect is that the meeting is deemed held and the resignation and release are deemed to have been authorised by the creditors (r6.126(5)).

Secondly the creditors resolve NOT to accept resignation. Here:

- The trustee applies to the court for leave to resign (r6.128(1)).
- If leave is granted the court will determine the date of release (r6.128(2)).
- The Court sends two copies of the order to the trustee who transmits one to the OR.
- Finally the trustee files in court his formal notice of resignation and sends a copy to the OR.

Thirdly the creditors agree to accept the resignation but refuse to grant release:

- The trustee gives notice of resignation to the court 'as soon as reasonably practicable' and copies in the OR. The notice is accompanied by a copy of the account of the trustee's administration which was originally sent to all the creditors. The chair of the meeting sends a certificate of acceptance of resignation and a copy of the resolution to the OR.
- The OR files a copy of the s298(7) notice. Resignation is effective from the date of filing (r6.127(7)).
- The trustee applies to the Secretary of State for his release on the prescribed Form 6.49 (r6.135(3)).
- When the Secretary of State gives the release, a certificate is sent to the OR who files it in court whilst a copy is sent to the trustee.
- Release is effective from the date of the certificate.

Personal Insolvency

Finally, the creditors accept resignation and grant release:

- The procedure on resignation is the same as where resignation is accepted but release refused.
- Both resignation and release will be effective from the date endorsed on the copy s298(7) notice which the OR files in court.

If a new trustee is appointed they must state in the notice of appointment that the previous incumbent has resigned and been released (r6.134).

The resigning trustee delivers up assets, books, records etc to the new trustee.

4.2 By operation of law

There are three circumstances when this will happen:

- Death.
- An ceasing to be an IP.
- On annulment. Remember that annulment does not in itself release (the trustee) and he must comply with the usual requirements to obtain his release.

Vacation of office happens automatically rather than resigning or being removed.

4.3 On annulment of the bankruptcy order

A trustee vacates office on annulment of the bankruptcy order (s298(9)). This is an effect of annulment, the trustee is neither resigning nor being removed.

However, annulment does not of itself release the trustee and in particular as with resignation and removal the rules require that the trustee 'accounts for all his transactions in connection with the former bankrupt's estate' (r6.214(1)) by:

- Submitting a copy of his final accounts to the Secretary of State, as soon as practicable after the court's order annulling the bankruptcy.
- Filing a copy of that account in court.

The final account must include a:

- Summary of the trustee's receipts and payments.
- Statement of reconciliation with the Secretary of State's account.

The court determines the time of release taking into account compliance with the above rules and whether any security under r6.211(3) has been or will be released (re disputed or untraceable creditors).

4.4 On removal by the creditors or the court

Removal by the creditors:

The trustee can be removed by a creditors' meeting where the trustee was:

- Appointed by a meeting of creditors.
- The supervisor in relation to the bankrupt's IVA.

If the trustee was appointed by the Secretary of State, or by the court or where the trustee is the OR, a trustee can only be removed if the:

- Court directs.
- Trustee consents.
- Meeting resolving to remove has been called on a 25% requisition (by value) from the creditors.

Procedure for removal by creditors:

- The creditors and OR must be given notice of the meeting. The notice must state that the purpose of the meeting is to remove the trustee and must draw the creditor's attention to the statutory rule s299(3) on the trustee's release.
- The trustee or his nominee may act as chair (others can so act). If a resolution to remove has been proposed the chair can only adjourn the meeting with a simple majority of the votes cast.

Possible outcomes of the meeting:

1. The creditors vote against removal. Clearly the trustee remains in office.

2. The creditors vote for removal and refuse to give release:
   - r6.129(4) the chair sends, within three days, a copy of the resolutions to remove and to refuse to release to the OR as well as a certificate that the meeting has removed the trustee.
   - the OR checks that the Secretary of State has certified that the removed trustee has reconciled his accounts with the Secretary of State. (If not, the procedure cannot progress further).
   - r6.131 the OR now files the Certificate of Removal in court and removal is effective from the date of filing. Copies of the certificate, endorsed with date of filing, are sent to the now removed trustee and to any new incumbent.
   - the trustee must apply to the Secretary of State for his release. The procedure is the same as where a meeting has accepted resignation but refuses release.

3. The creditors vote for removal and to grant release:
   - the procedure is as above but there is no need to apply to the Secretary of State for release and release is therefore effective from the time of filing of the Certificate of Removal in Court.

4.5 Removal by the Court

The Court has powers pursuant to s298(1) to remove the trustee from office.

Application can be made either to remove the trustee or for an order directing the trustee to summon a meeting of creditors for that purpose.

Application is made on the prescribed Form 6.48.

The Court now has a choice, it can:

- dismiss the application (but must not do so unless it has given the applicant the opportunity to attend the court for an ex parte hearing on seven days' notice) or
- fix a venue to hear the application. At least 14 day's pre-hearing the applicant sends to the trustee and OR:
  - notice stating venue.
  - copy application.
  - any evidence which the applicant intends to adduce in support.

r6.132 (4) provides that, subject to any contrary order, costs do not fall on the estate. The usual party to pay costs would be the applicant where the application turns out to be unmeritorious or the trustee where the trustee's conduct appears to the court to warrant costs being awarded against him.

Where the Court removes the trustee it sends copies of the order to the trustee and OR. The Court can also make consequential provision including the appointment of a new trustee.

Under r6.135 (3)(b) the trustee must apply to the Secretary of State for his release. When the Secretary of State gives the release he certifies it accordingly and sends the certificate to the OR. The OR files the certificate in Court. The Secretary of State sends a copy of the certificate to the former trustee. The trustee's release is effective from the date of the certificate.

Personal Insolvency

4.6 Application to Secretary of State for release

Where the creditors have resolved against the trustee's release he must apply to the Secretary of State on Form 6.49 including:

- a copy of the minutes of the final meeting where the resolution against his release has passed.
- a copy of the voting schedule for that meeting.
- the names and addresses and amount of claim for each objecting creditor.

If the Insolvency Practitioner Unit (IPU) is satisfied that the bankruptcy proceedings and disposal of property have been dealt with satisfactorily, release will be granted.

4.7 Claims against the trustee

Pursuant to s304, an application may be made by the OR, the Secretary of State, a creditor or the bankrupt to seek a remedy against a trustee that has caused loss to the estate. The court must be satisfied that:

- The trustee has misapplied, or retained, or become accountable for, any money or other property comprised in the estate, or
- An estate has suffered any loss in consequence of misfeasance or breach of fiduciary duty by the trustee in the carrying out of his function

In such circumstances the court may order the trustee to make such recompense as it thinks fit.

Leave will be required if the applicant is the bankrupt and the trustee has obtained his release.

4.8 The effect of the trustee's release

From the time of the trustee's release, he is discharged from all liability in respect of any act or omission whilst he was trustee (save for the court's power under s304).

5 Closure checklist

Section overview

There are a number of practical and statutory matters which must be dealt with by the trustee prior to and upon closure of the bankruptcy estate to ensure that all aspects of the administration have been dealt with and that his conduct cannot be the subject of criticism.

5.1 Closure checklist

Below is a checklist of matters to be dealt with by the trustee. This list is not exhaustive. If you can think of any other matters please add them to the end of the list.

- Review statement of affairs to ensure that all available assets have been realised including matrimonial home, income etc.
- Reconcile receipts and payments account with the ISA, obtain a certificate of balance from the ISA.
- Ensure all creditors' claims have been dealt with.
- Ensure received all proofs initially sent to OR.
- Ensure all agents and solicitor's fees have been paid.
- If dividend to be paid ensure dealt with properly:
  - Given notice of intention to declare a dividend.
  - Declare dividend within four months of last date for proving.
  - Request cheques from ISA.

CLOSURE OF BANKRUPTCY

- Give notice of dividend to all creditors who have proved their debts.
▶ Give notice of no further dividend.
▶ Call final meeting of creditors – 28 days' notice to creditors.
▶ Prepare trustee's final report to present to final meeting.
▶ Report to court re outcome of final meeting.
▶ Close bordereaux.
▶ Ensure remuneration is agreed and drawn.
▶ Close ISA account.
▶ Complete IP Records.

5.2 Final meeting

Where the trustee is other than the OR he shall give at least 28 days' notice of the final meeting of creditors to be held under s331. The notice shall be sent to all creditors who have proved their debt and the bankrupt.

The notice of the first meeting can be sent out along with notice of the final dividend but the meeting cannot be held until the final dividend has been paid.

The final meeting should be called in accordance with s331.

The purpose of the meeting is to provide the creditors with the trustee's report of his administration of the bankrupt's estate and to ask the creditors whether or not the trustee shall have his release.

If there is no quorum present at the final meeting, the trustee must report to court that a final meeting was summonsed in accordance with the rules, but that there was no quorum present. The final meeting is then deemed to have been held and the creditors deemed not to have resolved against the trustee having his release.

If should be remembered that the final meeting cannot take place unless the matrimonial home has been dealt with. Either the trustee will have realised his interest or obtained a s313 charge or the property will have re-vested in the bankrupt.

As soon as practicable after the final meeting, the trustee must file a copy of his final account in court and submit a copy to the Secretary of State. The account must contain a summary of the receipts and payments in the administration, it must also state that the trustee has reconciled his account with that held by the Secretary of State.

Once the trustee has dealt with the account he will be in a position to seek his release.

Personal Insolvency

Summary and Self-test

Summary

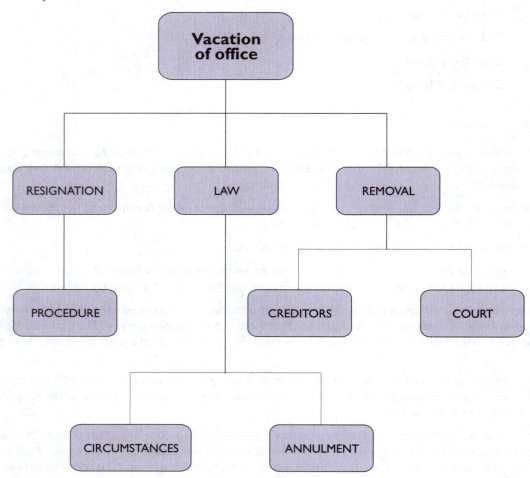

Self-test

Answer the following questions.

1. What is the effect of discharge on the trustee?
2. What is the effect of annulment on the trustee?
3. In what circumstances will the time period for automatic discharge be for less than one year?
4. How long may a bankruptcy restrictions order last for?
5. What is the effect on a bankrupt of a bankruptcy restrictions order being made?
6. In what circumstances does the court have the power to annul a bankruptcy order under s282?
7. How can a trustee vacate office?
8. On what grounds may a trustee resign?
9. What is the purpose of the final meeting of creditors?
10. How many days' notice must be given to creditors of a final meeting?

Now, go back to the Learning Objectives in the Introduction. If you are satisfied that you have achieved these, please tick them off.

CLOSURE OF BANKRUPTCY

Answers to Self-test

1. Discharge does not bring the bankruptcy to a close. The trustee is not released until he has finished administering the estate. Assets remain vested in the trustee and his duties continue.

2. Annulment releases the trustee, however he remains liable to account for all his actions in respect of the estate and will only be released at the court's discretion (r6.214).

3. When, during the first year following commencement, the OR files a notice at court stating that an investigation into the conduct and affairs of the bankrupt is either unnecessary or has been concluded (s289(2)). The bankrupt will be discharged from the date of filing of the notice.

4. Two to 15 years depending on the behaviour of the bankrupt.

5. A BRO imposes restrictions on the bankrupt after they have been discharged from their bankruptcy and will last for a period of between two and 15 years. During this period the bankrupt will continue to be subject to the normal bankruptcy offences and also some of the restrictions placed on undischarged bankrupts. The bankrupt will be disqualified from acting as:

    - A receiver and manager.
    - An IP.
    - A director or being concerned with the promotion, formation or management of a company.

    Breach of these provisions constitutes a criminal offence.

    The bankrupt is discharged from the bankruptcy debts in the usual way. These provisions apply notwithstanding the fact that the bankrupt may have received this discharge.

6. (a) When the order ought not to have been made (s282(1)(a)).

    (b) Where, to the extent required by the rules, the bankruptcy debts and the expenses of the bankruptcy have all, since the making of the order, been either paid or secured for, to the satisfaction of the court (s282(1)(b)).

    (c) Where an IVA is approved in regard to an undischarged bankrupt (s261(2)).

7. Resignation.
    By operation of the law.
    On annulment of the bankruptcy order.
    Removal by the court or creditors.

8. Ill health.

    Intends ceasing to be an IP.

    That there are joint trustees in bankruptcy and it is no longer expedient to have more than one trustee.

    A conflict of interest/change in personal circumstance precludes or makes continuation impractical.

9. To provide creditors with the trustee's report of his administration of the bankrupt's estate and to ask creditors whether or not the trustee shall have his release.

10. 28 days' notice to all creditors who have proved their debts.

13

Partnership law

Contents

Introduction
Examination context
Topic List
1 Partnership law
2 Options for creditors of insolvent partnerships
3 Options for insolvent partners
4 Partnership voluntary arrangements
5 Priority rules
Summary and Self-test
Answers to Self-test
Answer to Interactive Question

Introduction

Learning objectives

- Identify the legislation governing insolvent partnerships
- Understand the options available to insolvent partners and creditors of insolvent partnerships
- Understand the procedure to follow to obtain agreement to a partnership voluntary arrangement

Working context

Many individuals work in partnership with others and it is likely therefore in a work environment that you will be asked to assist with an insolvent partnership or an insolvent individual who is in partnership with another. It is important therefore to have an understanding of the main issues regarding insolvent partnerships and the provisions of the Insolvent Partnership Order 1994.

Stop and think

Why, when dealing with a partnership, is it necessary to look at the individual partner's assets and liabilities as well as the partnership assets and liabilities? How does the bankruptcy of one partner affect the partnership as a whole?

PARTNERSHIP LAW

Examination context

Partnerships are not regularly tested in the JIEB exam however it is important to have an overview of the options available to partners and creditors.

Exam requirements

Past questions to look at include:

2008	Question 4
2001	Question 3
1998	Question 3

1 Partnership law

Section overview

Unlike a company a partnership is not a separate legal entity from the members who make it up. If a simple partnership becomes insolvent it will have far reaching implications for the partners involved as they all share joint and several liability for the debts of the creditors. This may result in the personal insolvency of individual members. Also, the personal insolvency of an individual member may have consequences for the partnership as a whole. The partners may be companies or individuals (these notes will assume they are individuals).

Definition

Partnership (a firm): the relationship between persons carrying on business in common with a view to profit (s1 Partnership Act 1890).

1.1 Nature of a partnership

Unlike a company a partnership is not a separate legal entity from the members who make it up. Consequently as a partnership has no legal personality:

- It cannot enter into a contract with a partner.
- 'Partnership property' belongs collectively to all the partners not to the firm.
- The name of the firm is merely a convenient collective noun for the aggregate of the partners.

As a partnership is a relationship rather than a legal person any change in membership (eg by retirement or expulsion or inviting a person to join the firm) strictly speaking dissolves the old partnership and gives rise to a new one between the remaining partners. This is sometimes called a 'technical dissolution'.

Despite the above, it is often convenient to treat a firm as if it were a separate legal person. Examples of when it is treated as such include:

- VAT registration.
- Partnership accounts and bank accounts in the name of the partnership.
- Where the partnership is insolvent where as we will see, it can be wound up as if it were an (unregistered) company.

For taxation purposes however HM Revenue and Customs assesses each partner on his or her share of the profits as if that partner were a sole trader.

1.2 The relationship between the partners

In a company the relationship between the company and its directors and shareholders is governed primarily by the Articles of Association. In a partnership the relationship between the partners is governed by the partnership contract (often in practice executed as a deed).

If there is no deed or the deed is silent the terms of the Partnership Act 1890 (PA 1890) will apply. Key provisions of the 1890 Act are set out below.

1.3 Powers of management

All partners have a right to participate in management.

Ordinary matters are decided by majority.

Unanimity is required however, for:

- The introduction of a new partner, or
- A change in the nature of the partnership business. This would probably include the partners initiating an insolvency procedure.

Expulsion of a partner is only possible if the partnership contract allows it.

1.4 Power to bind the firm to a contract (agency)

S5 PA 1890 provides that partners are agents of the firm and the other partners.

On ordinary agency principles a partner will therefore bind the firm/the other partners to a contract providing he acts within his:

- Express authority, or
- Usual (implied) authority (ie doing any act 'for carrying on in the usual way business of the kind carried on by the firm'). There are two exceptions:
    - Where the third party knows that the partner they are dealing with is acting outside their actual authority, or
    - The third party does not believe or know that the person they are dealing with is a partner.
- Ostensible or apparent authority. This applies where a person may not have express or implied authority to enter a contract – but they are held out by the principal as if they did. The third party is entitled to rely on such a representation and the firm/partners will again be bound.

1.5 Duties of partners

The relationship between partners is fiduciary (of the 'utmost good faith').

This has the following implications:

- Partners have a duty to make full disclosure to other partners. S28 PA 1890 requires partners to render full accounts and information on all matters affecting the partnership.
- They must account to the firm for any benefits received personally (s29 PA 1890).

If they compete with the firm (ie make a secret profit) must hand over any profits to the firm (s30 PA 1890).

1.6 Liability

The liability of partners for the firms debts is unlimited (although limited liability partnerships are possible under the Limited Liability Partnership Act 2000 (LLP 2000).

By s9 PA 1890 every partner is liable jointly with the other partners for all debts of the firm incurred while a partner.

A partner who settles a debt due from the firm personally is entitled to a contribution from the other partners.

The basic principle of the Partnership Act in the absence of contrary agreement is equality. All partners:

- Share equally in capital and profits.
- Contribute equally to losses.

Liability in tort (eg for negligence) is 'joint and several'. The distinction between joint (one obligation of all the partners) and joint and several (each partner separately liable) is of much less practical significance since the Civil Liability (Contribution) Act 1978.

1.7 Dissolution

The Partnership Act 1890 lists circumstances where a partnership is dissolved.

The rules on dissolution are particularly important where a partnership is solvent. Here the 1890 Act and not the IPO 1994 will tend to apply.

1.8 When will a partnership be dissolved?

There are three sets of circumstances by:

- By notice.
- By operation of law.
- By court decree.

1.9 Dissolution by notice

This is where any Partner gives written notice to all other partners (s26(1) PA 1890). Date of dissolution will be the date specified in the notice – or if none the date of communication.

This right to dissolve the firm at will is often modified in the partnership deed.

1.10 Dissolution by operation of law

(S33(1) PA 1890) bankruptcy of any partner (see later).

(S33(1) PA 1890) death of any partner.

(S32(a) PA 1890) expiration of fixed term partnership or termination of single undertaking/adventure (s32(b) PA 1890).

(S34 PA 1890) occurrence of an event which renders business unlawful (eg loss of necessary licence).

(S33(2) PA 1890) at a partner's option where a partner charges his or her share of the partnership property with personal debts.

1.11 Dissolution by decree of the court on application by any partner

This would be particularly relevant where the partnership agreement does not permit dissolution by notice and the partnership is solvent.

The grounds are:

- Insanity or other permanent incapacity to perform obligations under the partnership agreement (s35 PA 1890) on the part of any partner.
- A partner's conduct is prejudicial to the firm's business.
- A partner is wilfully or persistently in breach of the agreement, or conduct is such that it is not reasonably practicable for the firm to continue.
- Business can only be carried on at a loss.
- It is just and equitable to dissolve the firm.

1.12 The effect of dissolution on the partnership relationship

Any partner may publicly notify dissolution (s37 PA 1890).

The rights, duties and agency of the partners only continues so far as necessary to:

- Wind up the affairs of a partnership, or
- To complete transactions (s38 PA 1890).

1.13 Distribution of assets

The general position (s39 PA 1890) is that property of the partnership is applied in:

- Payment of debts and liabilities of the firm.
- With any surplus going to the partners, deducting any sums owed to them by the firm.

Losses according to s44(a) PA 1890 are to be paid:

- Out of profits of the firm, then
- Out of capital of the firm, then
- By the partners individually in the proportions of their respective profit shares.

Assets are distributed in the following order when settling accounts between partners (s44(b)):

- To pay debts and liabilities of the firm.
- To re-pay advances made by partners to the firm (ie partners are deferred).
- To pay partners back their capital advances.
- Any surplus distributed as per profit share.

Remember that these rules will apply only where the insolvency legislation is not invoked. The partners may well be able to distribute assets as above by agreement between themselves. If the matter cannot be settled amicably the court has powers to wind up the partnership and appoint a receiver if necessary.

1.14 The law on insolvent partnerships

Pre IA 1986 all insolvent partnerships were dealt with under bankruptcy law. The IA 1986 did not make specific provision for insolvent partnerships but it gave the Lord Chancellor the power to make rules (s420). The result was the Insolvent Partnership Order 1986 which introduced the concept that an insolvent partnership could be wound up as an unregistered company pursuant to s221 IA. The Insolvent partnerships Order 1986 was revoked on 1 December 1994 by the Insolvent Partnerships Order 1994. This is not a stand alone piece of legislation, it must be read in conjunction with the IA 1986. The legislation has been further amended by the Insolvent Partnerships (Amendment) No 2 Order 2002.

2 Options for creditors of insolvent partnerships

Section overview

There are a number of options available to creditors of insolvent partnerships. These are dealt with below.

2.1 Sue and obtain judgment on the debt

The creditor has a choice either to sue the firm or individual partner(s):

Sue the firm. (Remember that, although for convenience the creditor will sue the firm in the firm's name, this is really an action against all the partners collectively.)

It is the partners at the date the cause of action accrued (eg date the debt was incurred) who are defendants to the action.

This will include partners who since this date have retired, died or been expelled.

Personal Insolvency

Under the terms of a professionally drafted partnership agreement ex-partners of this type will normally have an indemnity against the firm.

Once judgment has been obtained against the firm execution can be levied:

- Against partnership property, or
- Against the personal property of one or more partners (but formal proof of partner status will be required eg the person has acknowledged service of the papers as a partner).

Sue an individual partner or partners. (This might be appropriate where an individual partner has substantial assets whilst the firm itself appears to be insolvent.)

If the partner sued pays up he will have a right to claim a contribution from the other partners.

The disadvantage of obtaining judgment against an individual partner is that execution can only be levied against that partner's personal estate. However, s23(2) of the 1890 Act gives judgment creditors the right to apply to court for a charging order over that partner's share of the partnership property.

2.2 Bankrupt one or more partners in the usual way without seeking to wind up the firm

This is specifically provided for by Insolvent Partnership Order 1994.

The apparent advantages of this route are:

- Relatively simple procedure (effectively we are ignoring the IPO).
- The chance of 'queue-jumping' the creditors of the firm.

However, where it comes to the attention of the court that the bankrupt is a member of an insolvent firm the court may apply the terms of the IPO 1994 to the future conduct of the bankruptcy of that partner.

This might result in the creditors of the firm generally ranking *pari passu* with all other creditors of the bankrupt (including the petitioning creditor). This would negate the apparent advantage of this route.

Possible outcomes where a creditor seeks to bankrupt individual partners, the partner:

- Pays the outstanding debt to stave off bankruptcy. This partner will now have a right of contribution against the other partners.
- Applies for an interim order (IVA).
- Is made bankrupt.

Effect of bankruptcy of a partner:

- The partnership is automatically dissolved in the absence of contrary intention in the deed.
- The bankrupt's estate, including his or her share in the partnership, vests in the trustee on appointment.
- The deed often provides for expulsion of the bankrupt partner, continuation of the firm between the remaining partners and some mechanism for valuing and buying out the bankrupt's share. If this buy-out is for full value it is valid.
- If there is no such buy-out of the partner's share the trustee may have to bring proceedings against the firm to realise the bankrupt's interest in the partnership business. Ultimately this may involve winding-up the firm.

2.3 Wind-up the firm as an unregistered company without seeking to bankrupt individual partners under Article 7 of IPO 1994

Advantages

May be appropriate where the major source of assets appears to be the firm rather than the estates of individual partners.

Can always bankrupt individual partners later if necessary (and again court has power to order that creditors of the firm rank equally with personal creditors of the now bankrupt partners).

Lower costs than winding-up the firm and bankrupting partners.

Disadvantages

If 'wait and see' before bankrupting the individual members of the firm there is a risk that in the intervening period, the value of their estates will have diminished.

Legal risk that court will not exercise discretion to order pari passu distribution to firm and individual creditors.

Procedure

The firm is wound up as an unregistered company. Effectively the procedure mirrors that of a compulsory winding-up initiated by a creditor's petition. Note that there are three grounds for a petition of this type:

▶ Inability to pay debts. This is proved by the statutory demand method or by giving the firm notice of a proceeding for debt brought against it to which the firm does not respond in 21 days.

▶ Partnership dissolved, has ceased to carry on business or is carrying on business only for the purpose of winding up its affairs.

▶ Just and equitable.

Trustees of partners who have been bankrupted can also petition for winding-up. It should be straightforward to make out one of the above grounds as:

▶ Bankrupting of the partner for inability to pay a debt of the firm is proof of insolvency of the firm.
▶ Bankruptcy often has the effect of dissolving the partnership.

2.4 Wind-up the firm as an unregistered company and bring concurrent petitions against one or more partners (Article 8 IPO 1994)

Although this is a more complex and costly route, it probably maximises a creditor's chances of getting at least some of his money back.

The rules for winding-up the firm are exactly the same as for winding-up without concurrent petitions except that the *only* ground permissible is inability to pay debts.

To bankrupt the individual partners the creditor will need to prove inability to pay a joint debt (ie one or more of the firm's debts). Proof is by:

▶ Serving a statutory demand on the individual for a joint debt(s) worth £750 or more.
▶ Also serving a written demand on the firm.
▶ The debt remaining unpaid 21 days after the serving of the last of the two demands.
▶ No application to set aside etc. being made.

2.5 Petition the court for a Partnership Administration Order

As in corporate insolvency, creditors have the power to do this but may find difficulty in compiling sufficient information about the business to draft an independent report. It is unlikely that creditors would consider this an attractive option.

3 Options for insolvent partners

Section overview

There are many options for insolvent partners which are detailed below.

3.1 To propose an IVA or IVAs

A partner can always seek to put a proposal for an IVA to his or her own creditors. This might be where:

- A creditor of the firm is seeking to 'pick-off' this partner's assets by petitioning for bankruptcy, or
- The other partners cannot or will not agree to trying to set up a PVA.

All the partners intend proposing IVAs, which will be drafted in similar terms (interlocking IVAs).

The major advantage of the partners proposing interlocking IVAs is that the interim order should prevent:

- Legal processes against individual and partnership property.
- Winding-up orders being made against the firm or bankruptcy orders against the partners.

One IP will be instructed to act as nominee in relation to interlocking IVAs. The IP should:

- Ensure that the partners understand that they are each responsible for a separate retainer to the IP.
- That if there is any risk of conflict that the partner concerned is advised in writing to seek independent advice.

Interlocking IVAs will be more commercially attractive to the firm's creditors if the proposals provide for:

- Partnership creditors to be paid out of the firm's assets.
- Any deficit to rank equally with individual creditors of the partners against the separate estates.
- Any claims of partners to be deferred.

Interlocking IVAs are not appropriate where there are large number of partners, material conflicts of interests or the position regarding the firm's debts is a complex one.

3.2 To propose a Partnership Voluntary Arrangement (PVA)

The partners of the firm must propose a PVA. Most partnership deeds will not provide expressly for what majority is required to decide to propose a PVA. As seen earlier changes in the nature of the partnership business require unanimous approval, so that the decision to propose a PVA would seem to require unanimity.

PVAs can also be proposed by:

- Any administrator of a Partnership Administration Order, or
- Any liquidator of the firm.

It is important to remember that PVAs are modelled on CVAs. Consequently following the amendments to the Act and the Insolvent Partnerships (Amendment) Order 2002 it is now possible to apply for an interim order. However note that although approval of the PVA will protect the partners' individual estates from partnership creditors there will be no protection for the partners from their individual creditors. Such creditors will not be notified of the PVA meeting because they are not creditors of the firm. They cannot therefore be bound by the terms of the PVA proposal. In practice, it may be necessary to consider setting up IVAs for partners at risk from individual creditors. The PVA procedure is very similar to that in CVA.

(See Section 4 for more details.)

3.3 To petition to wind-up the firm as an unregistered company under Article 9 IPO 1994 (s220 to s229 IA)

Any partner can petition although if there are less than eight partners in the firm court leave is required (and will only be given where the petitioning partner has unsuccessfully served a statutory demand or levied execution).

Where the firm has eight or more partners the permissible grounds are as for creditor's petitions (ie inability to pay debts /just and equitable/or dissolution/cessation of business).

PARTNERSHIP LAW 13

3.4 To petition to wind up the firm as an unregistered company and present concurrent petitions against ALL partners (under Article 10 IPO 1994)

This procedure is subject to strict conditions:

- The only available ground is the firm's inability to pay debts.
- The petitions must be for orders against all partners including the petitioning partners.
- Each partner must be willing to have an order made against him or her.
- All petitions must be presented to the same court on the same day. The petition against the firm is advertised.
- Each petition must refer to all the other petitions.
- The hearing of the petition against the firm comes first and against the partners immediately after.

3.5 Joint bankruptcy petition presented by individual partners without winding-up the partnership as an unregistered company

One petition is presented by all the partners (known as a Form 16 petition under Article 11 IPO 1994). The only ground is inability to pay debts. This is the partnership equivalent of the debtor's petition. It can only be presented where all the partners are individuals. If one or more of the partners is a corporate member, the position must be presented under Article 10 IPA 1994.

The court will order that:

- Each partner is bankrupted.
- The trustee winds-up the partnership business (without liquidation as an unregistered company) and administers the partnership property.

One trustee of both the estates of the individual bankrupt partners and of the firm will be appointed by a combined meeting of all creditors (whether of individual partners or the firm) failing which Secretary of State appointments can be made in the usual way, or the OR will become the joint trustee.

3.6 Petition for a Partnership Administration Order

Any partner (or creditor) can petition the court. In practice administration orders were usually sought to obtain the protection of the moratorium before seeking a PVA. Now that the interim order is available in a PVA, PAO are of little importance.

4 Partnership voluntary arrangements

Section overview

The Insolvent Partnerships Order 1994 (IPO 1994) introduced (amongst other things) a partnership voluntary arrangement (PVA). The legislation for partnership voluntary arrangements is contained in the IPO 1994 as amended by the Insolvent Partnership (Amendment) Order 2002 and IA 1986. Partnership voluntary arrangements are modelled on company voluntary arrangements and the following sections of the IA 1986 apply:

- S233
- Part VIII (but not s250 IA)
- Parts XII and XIII
- S411 IA, s413, s414, s419 Part XV
- Parts XVI – XIX

4.1 Advantages of PVAs

Provides breathing space to enable the reorganisation and restructuring of the partnership.

One proposal – one creditors' meeting.

Limited disclosure – deals with partnership assets and liabilities only, not personal ones.

Partner's claims may be deferred.

Simple and cheap – costs are less than other insolvency options such as winding up as an unregistered company.

No court involvement necessary (but can apply for interim order).

Interim order provides protection from pressing creditors.

Partners remain in control of day-to-day partnership affairs.

Should provide a better return for creditors than other insolvency options.

4.2 Disadvantages of PVAs

No automatic interim order.

Unanimity is required.

Doesn't deal with personal liabilities, IVA may be required to protect individual's assets.

Joint and several liability.

Need to be careful when considering voting rights of partners, conflicts may arise.

May well be unfair prejudice in relation to junior/salaried/retired or newly admitted partners.

Proposal must also deal with effect of subsequent liquidation of the partnership or bankruptcy of individual partners.

Time period involved usually three-five years.

4.3 Who may propose a PVA?

A PVA may be proposed by:

- The partners (but not if partnership is in administration, or being wound up as an unregistered company, or if an order has been made under Article 11 IPO 1994).
- The administrator (if partnership is subject to a Partnership Administration Order).
- The liquidator (if partnership being wound up as unregistered company).
- Trustee of the partnership (where an order has been made by virtue of Article 11 IPO 1994).

4.4 Role of nominee/supervisor

Nominee acts in relation to the VA either as trustee or otherwise for the purpose of supervising its implementation.

The nominee must be a person who is qualified to act as an IP.

Upon acceptance of the arrangement by the creditors the IP will become supervisor of the arrangement.

4.5 PVA checklist for IP instructed by partners

Many of these items would be important in any case where an IP is instructed by partners of an insolvent firm and not only where they wish to propose a PVA.

Who are the partners?

The IP should obtain a full list of the names and addresses of all the partners in the firm. Identifying partners is important because:

- The decision to propose a PVA must probably be taken unanimously.
- All partners must be notified of the meeting to approve the PVA.
- If any partner is bankrupted this will dissolve the partnership in the absence of contrary intention.

Sources of information include the partners, firm's notepaper, list of partners at principal place of business, the partnership agreement etc.

The IP needs to consider the status of salaried, junior and associate partners. Prior to 1 January 2003 partners who had no right to vote within the partnership were nevertheless entitled to vote on any proposal. Although the vote would not be counted towards the majority required to approve a PVA it did mean that such partners were entitled to challenge the meeting's decision. Since 1 January 2003 a partner with no right to vote at the meeting is unable to challenge a PVA. (Note: if a person participates in profits and management he will generally be a partner in the true sense).

Valid resolution of partners is required authorising:

- Proposing a PVA.
- The agreement of the firm to pay the nominee's fees in relation to the PVA.

Information concerning the firm:

- Description of the partnership business including:
    - Last accounts and trading history.
    - Background to the insolvency.
    - Major assets and liabilities of the partnership.
    - Details of all creditors and their status.
- Intentions regarding the conduct of the partnership business. If this is to continue the partners should be advised of the need to obtain business plans, cash flow forecasts, budgets and arrangements for the provision of trading information to the supervisor
- Information regarding the partners:
    - Solvency of each individual.
    - To what extent the personal assets of each partner will be brought into the PVA.
    - Whether partners are prepared to defer their claims against the firm to all other creditors.

The proposal for a PVA must demonstrate that a PVA offers creditors a better commercial outcome than any other available option.

The proposal must comply with r1.3 (as modified) and SIP 3.

4.6 Moratorium

Members of the partnership are able to apply for a moratorium under Sch 1A(1) IPO 1994 if certain criteria are met. To be eligible the partnership must satisfy two of the following conditions:

- Turnover not more than £6.5 million.
- Assets of not more than £3.26 million.
- No more than 50 employees.

The partners cannot apply for a moratorium if:

- Partnership is in administration.
- Partnership is being wound up as an unregistered company.
- There is appointed an agricultural receiver.
- A voluntary arrangement has effect in relation to the insolvent partnership.
- A provisional liquidator has been appointed.

Personal Insolvency

- An order has been made by virtue of Article 11 of IPO 1994.
- A moratorium has been in force for the insolvent partnership at any time during the period of 12 months ending with the date of filing and no VA came into effect.

The effect of the moratorium is that:

- No petition may be presented for the winding-up of the partnership as an unregistered company.
- No meeting of the members of the partnership may be called or requisitioned except with the consent of the nominee or leave of the court.
- No order may be made for the winding-up of the insolvent partnership as an unregistered company.
- No administration application may be made in respect of the partnership.
- No administrator of the partnership may be appointed under para 14 or 22 of Schedule B1.
- No agricultural receiver of the partnership may be appointed except with the leave of the court and subject to such terms as the court may impose.
- No landlord or other person to whom rent is payable may exercise any rights of forfeiture by peaceable re-entry in relation to premises forming part of the partnership property or let to one or more officers of the partnership in their capacity as such except with leave of the court.
- No other steps may be taken to enforce any security over the partnership property or to repossess goods in the possession, under any HP agreement, of one or more officers of the partnership, except with leave of the court.
- No other proceedings and no execution or other legal process may be commenced or continued and no distress may be levied, against the insolvent partnership or the partnership property except with leave of the court.
- No petition may be presented and no order may be made, by virtue of Article 11 IPO 1994.
- No application or order may be made under s35 Partnership Act 1890.

4.7 Procedure – members' proposal, no application for moratorium

The procedure to be followed by members is as follows:

- The members give notice of the proposal to the nominee to include:
    - Document setting out terms of the proposed VA.
    - Statement of the partnership affairs (particulars of partnership creditors, debts and other liabilities, details of partnership property and such other information as may be prescribed).
- Within 28 days after receiving notice, the nominee must submit a report to court (s2(2) Sch 1 IPO 1994) stating:
    - Whether, in his opinion, the proposed voluntary arrangement has a reasonable prospect of being approved and implemented.
    - Whether, in his opinion, meetings of the members of the partnership and of the partnership's creditors should be summoned to consider the proposal.
    - If in his opinion such meetings should be summoned, the date on which, and time and place at which, he proposes such meetings should be held.
    - Whether there are in existence any insolvency proceedings in respect of the insolvent partnership or any of its members.
    - Whether any insolvency proceedings in respect of the partnership or any of its members are in existence.
- Convening meetings of members and creditors:

    Nominee must summon creditors' meeting for the time, date and place stated in his report to court.

All creditors of the partnership of whose claim and address the nominee is aware must be given notice.

- Creditors' meeting:

    The purpose of the meeting is to decide whether or not to approve the PVA (with or without modifications).

    Any modifications cannot affect the rights of secured or preferential creditors without their consent.

    A modification may be agreed which nominates another person to act as nominee/supervisor.

- After meeting:

    The chair must report the result to the court and give notice of the result of the meeting to all creditors who were sent notice of the meeting.

    If the decision taking by the creditors' meeting differs from that taken by the meeting of the members of the partnership, a member may, within 28 days of the meeting, apply to the court.

    The court may order the decision of the meeting of the members of the partnership to have effect instead of the decision of the creditors' meeting, or make such other order as it sees fit.

- Appeals:

    Under s6(1) Sch 1 IPO 1994 an appeal may be made by:

    - A person entitled to vote at either of the meetings.
    - A person who would have been entitled to vote at the creditors' meeting if he had had notice of it.
    - The nominee.

    Any appeal must be made within 28 days of the reports being made to court.

    An appeal may be made on the grounds of:

    - That the interests of a creditor, member or contributory of the partnership are unfairly prejudiced.
    - That there was some material irregularity at or in relation to either of the meetings.

- Effect of approval:

    The approved VA takes effect as if made by the members of the partnership at the creditors' meeting and binds every person who was entitled to vote at the meeting (whether or not he was present or represented at it) or would have been so entitled if he had had notice of it.

4.8 Powers of supervisor

The supervisor has few statutory powers, his powers will be derived from the proposal which must be detailed enough to include any powers he may need.

The following statutory powers are available:

- May apply to court for directions (s7(4) Sch 1 IPO 1994).
- May apply to court for the winding-up of the partnership as an unregistered company or for an administration order to be made in relation to the partnership.
- May dispose of charged property as though it were not subject to the charge (s20 Sch 1 IPO 1994).
- Power to obtain supplies from utilities (s233).
- Power to take action in respect of transactions defrauding creditors (s423).

4.9 Duties of supervisor

If it appears to the nominee/supervisor that any past or present officer of the insolvent partnership has been guilty of any offence in connection with the moratorium or voluntary arrangement, for which the officer is criminally liable, the nominee/supervisor must (s7A(2) Sch 1 IPO 1994):

Personal Insolvency

- Report the matter to the Secretary of State.
- Provide the Secretary of State with such information and give him access to and facilities for inspecting and taking copies of, documents.

The supervisor is not required to report on the conduct of the partners under CDDA.

Records should be kept of all meetings of members and creditors.

4.10 Resignation and release

There are no statutory provisions dealing with the resignation and release of a supervisor of a PVA. The terms of the arrangement would have to be checked to ascertain the mechanism by which the supervisor may resign or be released from office. In the absence of a specific clause the supervisor would need to obtain a court order to deal with his release.

4.11 Procedure when made by liquidator or administrator

The procedure is the same as for the members however, the statement of affairs will be that already obtained in the existing proceedings and a report to court and nominee's comments are not required.

5 Priority rules

Section overview

Technically a firm cannot own property. Partnership property is simply the collective property of the partners. Each partner's estate includes their share of the firm's assets.

However, for practical reasons the IPO does distinguish between:

- The joint estate – the partnership property of an insolvent partnership.
- The separate estate – the personal property of an insolvent member.
- Joint debts – the debts of an insolvent partnership.
- Separate debts – the debts for which a member of a partnership is liable other than the joint debts.

The basic principle is that (as far as possible) joint expenses and debts are payable out of the joint estate and separate expenses and debts out of the separate estate.

5.1 Priority of debts and expenses

Step 1
Paying the expenses of winding-up the partnership and bankrupting the members

As far as possible, pay the joint expenses of winding-up out of the joint estate.

If there is a deficit apportion this unpaid balance between the separate estates of the bankrupt partners equally.

These joint expenses will rank behind the separate estate expenses but ahead of the separate estate creditors.

If any of these separate estates is unable to meet the burden of its share of the joint expenses deficit you take the unpaid balance and re-apportion it amongst the remaining partners.

Not surprisingly, the rules are the same for separate expenses. Try and pay them out of the separate estate. If there is a deficit this is now payable out of the joint estate ranking behind joint expenses but ahead of joint creditors.

PARTNERSHIP LAW 13

Worked example: A13 Joiners

Darren, Carly and Wayne are partners in the firm of 'A13 Joiners'. The firm is being wound-up and the partners are bankrupt. After payment of winding-up expenses out of the joint estate there is a deficit of £600.

A13 Joiners

	£'000
Assets	500
Less winding-up expenses	(1,100)
	(600)

	Darren £'000	Carly £'000	Wayne £'000
Assets	850	1,000	400
Less bankruptcy expenses	(300)	(300)	(300)
Less deficit re winding-up expenses	(200)	(200)	(200)
	350	500	(100)

The deficit of £100 on Wayne's estate in respect of the balance of joint expenses will now be apportioned between Darren and Carly's estate leaving £300 and £450 respectively to meet the claims of creditors.

Note. that the responsible IP can with sanction of the committee or the court pay joint and separate expenses *pari passu*.

Step 2
Paying debts of the partnership

This assumes that there is a surplus after payment of expenses.

The usual order of priority applies:

- Preferential creditors.
- Ordinary unsecured creditors.
- Interest on preferential and unsecured creditors.
- Postponed debts.
- Interest on postponed debts.

If there is a surplus after payment of all debts including interest this will be distributed amongst the partners in accordance with the partnership agreement. This will increase the amount available to distribute to the separate estate creditors.

If there is a deficit the IP acting as liquidator of the firm proves for that deficit in each of the bankrupt partners' estates.

That deficit will rank equally with the separate creditors of each bankrupt partner. Notice that the whole deficit is proved for in each of the separate estates. This is NOT a breach of the rule against double proof. The liquidator is proving for the deficit in a number of estates. Double proof prevents more than one creditor from proving for the same debt in the same estate.

Worked example: Harlow New Town 'Blondes' Fitness Club'

Kylie, Shelley and Dean are partners in the Harlow New Town 'Blondes' Fitness Club – a partnership. The firm is being wound-up and the partners are bankrupt.

'Blondes' Fitness Club

	£'000
Assets	20,000
Total liabilities	(120,000)
Deficit	(100,000)

Personal Insolvency

The liquidator will now prove for the £100,000 in each of the individual partner's separate estates

	Kylie £'000	Shelly £'000	Dean £'000
Assets	50,000	100,000	50,000
Liabilities			
Separate	120,000	180,000	300,000
Joint (deficit)	100,000	100,000	100,000
Total liabilities	(220,000)	(280,000)	(400,000)
Deficit	(170,000)	(180,000)	(350,000)

The outcome

Kylie pays	22.73p in the pound
Shelley pays	35.71p in the pound
Dean pays	12.50p in the pound

Note that separate and joint debts rank *pari passu*.

This much improves the position of the partnership creditors (compared to IPO 1986). Here they will receive:

	£
Partnership assets	20,000
Dividend from Kylie	22,730
Dividend from Shelley	35,710
Dividend from Dean	12,500
	90,940

ie a dividend of 75.78% (total of dividend of £90,940 divided by the total liabilities of £120,000).

Interactive question: Archers Limited

Sarah, Brian and Harry were partners in a clothing business which traded under the name of Archers Limited. Insolvency orders were made on the same day against the partners and against the partnership on 11 March 2008. Jim was appointed trustee of the partners and liquidator of the partnership. All realisations have now been made and Jim wishes to distribute the estate.

Before doing so however, he shows you the following proofs of debt:

(1) A claim by Blue Jeans Ltd for £10,000 in respect of pairs of jeans sold and delivered.

(2) A claim by Surfsup Ltd for £92,000 in respect of the price of a boat sold to Harry. (Note: this sum has been jointly and severally guaranteed by Sarah and Brian).

(3) A claim by HM Revenue and Customs for £15,000 unpaid VAT on clothes sold in the 10 months before the making of the insolvency orders (representing £1,500 VAT per month).

(4) A claim by Satby Bank plc for £18,000 on a promissory note signed by Sarah, which is not due and payable for a further six months.

(5) A claim by Sarah's husband for £15,000 which he lent to her to clear her personal overdraft.

Requirement

Advise Jim how he should adjudicate on each of these proofs and also advise him in which estate they will rank for dividend.

See **Answer** at the end of this chapter.

Summary and Self-test

Summary

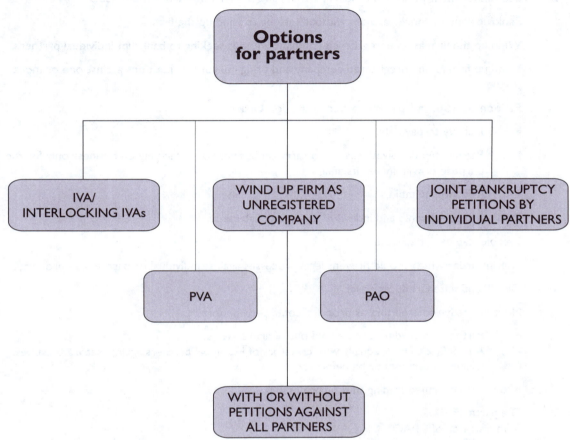

Self-test

Answer the following questions.

1. What document governs the relationship between partners?
2. List the options available to a creditor of an insolvent partnership.
3. On what grounds may a partnership be wound up as an unregistered company?
4. What are the main advantages of partners presenting interlocking rather than individual IVAs?
5. Who may propose a PVA?

Now, go back to the Learning Objectives in the Introduction. If you are satisfied that you have achieved these, please tick them off.

Answers to Self-test

1. The partnership contract (or if none, the terms of the Partnership Act 1890 will apply).

2. Sue (either the firm or an individual partner) and obtain judgement on the debt.

   Bankrupt one or more partners without seeking to wind up the firm.

   Wind up the firm as an unregistered company without seeking to bankrupt individual partners.

   Wind up firm as an unregistered company and bring concurrent petitions against one or more partners.

   Petition court for a Partnership Administration Order.

3. ▸ Inability to pay debts.
   ▸ Partnership dissolved, ceased to carry on business or is carrying on business only for the purpose of winding-up its affairs.
   ▸ Just and equitable.

4. Deals with partnership and individual assets and liabilities.

   Flexible, can exclude assets.

   Interim order which should prevent legal processes against individual or partnership property.

   One IP appointed, reduces costs.

   More attractive to creditors as proposal could provide for:

   ▸ Partnership creditors to be paid out of firm's assets.
   ▸ Any deficit to rank equally with creditors of individual partners against separate estates.
   ▸ Claims of partners to be deferred.

   Allows for continued trading of the partnership.

5. The partners.
   Administrator of a PAO.
   Any liquidator of the firm.

Answer to Interactive Question

Interactive question: Archers Limited

(1) **Blue Jeans Ltd**

This would appear to be an ordinary unsecured business debt and is accordingly provable as against the estate of Archers Ltd.

(2) **Surfsup Ltd**

There is no evidence that the guarantee is secured by way of charge or mortgage and accordingly it ranks as an ordinary unsecured claim.

The primary debtor is Harry, but since there was a joint and several guarantee from Sarah and Brian, the debt is provable in the separate estates of all three partners, subject only to the proviso that the creditor is not to receive more than 100% of the amount due.

(3) **Revenue and Customs**

VAT no longer ranks as a preferential debt. Since the VAT appears to have arisen out of the carrying on of the business, it is provable as an unsecured claim against the estate of Archers Ltd.

(4) **Satby Bank plc**

This is a debt payable at a future time and r11.13 provides that the debt may be proved for subject to an adjustment where the payment of the dividend is made prior to the due date for payment of the debt.

The debt should be reduced using the following formula:

$$\frac{x}{1.05^n}$$

Where x = amount of the debt due

n = decimalised amount of time from the date of the bankruptcy order to the date the debt is due.

This debt would rank in Sarah's estate (as signatory) unless it is shown that the debt incurred was in the ordinary course of the partnership's business in which case it would rank in the estate of Archers Ltd.

(5) **Sarah's husband**

Under s329 debts owed by the bankrupt to a person who (whether or not the bankrupt's spouse at the time the credit was provided) was the bankrupt's spouse at the commencement of bankruptcy, are admissible to rank for dividend after preferential and ordinary and unsecured debts and after interest has been paid on such debts under s328 out of any surplus funds. Interest will be payable on the husband's claim equally with the amount of the principal sum due.

The claim will rank in the separate estate of Sarah.

Personal Insolvency

14

Administration of the estate of insolvent deceased individuals

Contents

Introduction
Examination context
Topic List
1 Administration of the estate of insolvent deceased individuals
2 Death of existing bankrupt
3 Death of debtor after presentation of bankruptcy petition
4 Effect of death on voluntary arrangements
Self-test
Answers to Self-test

Personal Insolvency

Introduction

Learning objectives

- Understand how to deal with the estate of an insolvent deceased individual
- Understand how the death of a debtor affects an existing bankruptcy or IVA

Tick off
☐
☐

Working context

You may be asked to deal with the estate of an insolvent deceased individual it is important therefore to have an understanding of how such an estate should be dealt with.

Stop and think

Why are the debts of an individual not cancelled upon their death? How does the death of a debtor affect a voluntary arrangement?

ADMINISTRATION OF THE ESTATE OF INSOLVENT DECEASED INDIVIDUALS

Examination context

How to deal with the estates of deceased individuals is not regularly tested in the JIEB exam however this subject did form the basis of an exam question in 2007.

Exam requirements

Past questions to look at include:

2007 Question 1
2003 Question 3

Personal Insolvency

1 Administration of the estate of insolvent deceased individuals

Section overview

It is a common misconception that when a person dies his debts are automatically discharged. Debts are not discharged upon death unless specific provision has been made for them to be discharged eg by an insurance policy. All debts that are not provided for must be met from the assets of the deceased debtor. Where the assets are insufficient to meet all the debts, the estate is insolvent.

This area is governed by the Administration of Insolvent Estates of Deceased Persons Order 1986 – referred to here as 'DPO 1986' for ease of reference.

The purpose of DPO 1986 is to modify the IA 1986 in respect of insolvent estates. In the event of any conflict between the two the DPO 1986 prevails.

The DPO 1986 applies whether an existing bankrupt dies or where following the death of a person it is revealed that his estate is insolvent. Either way the estate must be administered for the benefit of the estate creditors and not the beneficiaries of any will or intestacy.

1.1 Insolvent estate

Where a person dies before the presentation of a bankruptcy petition and it is found that the estate is insolvent the provisions of any will made relating to beneficiaries do not apply. The estate should be administered under the provisions of the DPO 1986 and s421 IA. In all cases funeral and administration expenses are paid before any other debts. The balance of the assets must then be distributed in accordance with the law of bankruptcy as amended by the DPO 1986.

IA references	DPO 1986 modifications
The bankrupt, the debtor	The deceased debtor or his personal representatives
The bankrupt's estate	The deceased debtor's estate
The commencement of bankruptcy	The date of the insolvency administration
A bankruptcy order	An insolvency administration order
An individual being adjudged bankrupt	An insolvency order being made
A debtor's petition	A petition by the personal representatives of a deceased debtor for an insolvency administration

1.2 Insolvency administration order (IAO)

Although it is possible to deal with an insolvent estate without an IAO it is usual for a petition to be lodged in all but the simplest of cases.

Definition

Insolvency administration order: an order for the administration in bankruptcy of the insolvent estate of a deceased debtor.

Insolvency administration petition: a petition for an IAO.

ADMINISTRATION OF THE ESTATE OF INSOLVENT DECEASED INDIVIDUALS

The following persons may apply for an IPO:

- Personal representatives (PR): on the grounds that the deceased is insolvent. This will be shown by a statement of affairs. If the court is satisfied as to the deceased's insolvency it must make the order.

- Creditors or supervisor of an IVA in relation to the deceased: on the ground that the estate is insolvent:

    - the debtor must have owed the petitioning creditor a debt/ debts of at least £750.
    - the debt must be for an unliquidated amount.
    - the debt must be unsecured.

The court may make the order if it is satisfied that the debt is due and owing or there is no reasonable prospects of it being paid when it falls due AND there is a 'reasonable probability' that the estate will be insolvent. The petition must be served on the PR.

1.3 Interim receiver

If necessary for the protection of the deceased's property the court can appoint the OR as interim receiver prior to the appointment of the trustee.

The OR's duties may be restricted by the order appointing him. The OR, as interim receiver, will have all the powers and duties of a receiver and manager. The PR has a duty to co-operate with the interim receiver and to provide details of the assets which should be taken into immediate possession pending the hearing of the petition.

1.4 Effect of the administration order

The OR is appointed receiver and manager of the deceased's estate. Control of the estate passes from the PR to the OR.

On receipt of the IAO the OR should contact the deceased debtor's PR as soon as possible. The PR is either:

- The person named as executor in the deceased debtor's will with the responsibility of administering the estate of the deceased, or

- Where the deceased debtor dies without making a will (intestate), a person who is known as the administrator, who is granted letters of administration by a court of probate.

Where there is no PR or administrator, the OR should contact the closest surviving relative of the deceased debtor.

The PR (or other such person as the court may direct) is required to submit to the OR, within 56 days of the IAO being made, a statement of affairs. The statement of affairs should contain both the position at the date of death and at the making of the IAO and should be completed on Form SADI.

The PR owes a number of duties to the OR:

- Notify the OR of any assets which may be claimed for the estate by the trustee.
- Provide an inventory of the estate to the OR.
- Attend on the OR as reasonably required.
- Provide information regarding the assets, liabilities and affairs of the deceased debtor.

Failure to comply may be a contempt of court. The OR may apply to the court for the PR to be privately examined if he does not comply with his obligations.

The PR may not dispose of estate assets once they have received notice of the petition without leave of the court (s284 IA as modified by DPO 1986 Sch 1). A bona fide purchaser for value, without notice, is however protected.

If there are sufficient assets a trustee may subsequently be appointed in much the same way as if the bankrupt was not deceased. The OR should call a meeting of creditors, however the notices and forms sent out should be amended to make it clear that the meeting relates to the IAO and not to a bankruptcy order. The proof of debt forms should show the date of death as being the date to which claims should be made.

1.5 Items excluded from the estate

S283(2) IA is modified by DPO 1986 Article 3 so that the only personal and household effects that are excluded from the estate are those belonging to the family of the deceased. The trustee can claim items of excess value and after acquired property (from death) as per bankruptcy.

1.6 Matrimonial home

When dealing with the matrimonial home similar considerations apply as in normal bankruptcy. Prior to IA 2000 it was not possible for the trustee to attack any share of the matrimonial home that had passed to a surviving joint tenant(s) by the right of survivorship (the deceased debtor's interest in property owned under a joint tenancy passes automatically to the other joint owners by right of survivorship and never becomes part of the insolvent estate). However, s421A IA enables a trustee to apply to court for an order that a surviving joint tenant pay an amount equivalent to the deceased's share of the property to the trustee for the benefit of the estate.

The court is not compelled to make the order and must have regard to all the circumstances of the case including the interests of the creditors and surviving tenant(s) (co-owners). The court may therefore make such order as it thinks fit.

1.7 Investigation of the deceased's affairs/conduct

The OR is not under any duty to investigate the conduct or affairs of the deceased debtor but may if he thinks fit report to the court on the activities of the deceased debtor (s289 IA as amended by DPO 1986 Article 3).

1.8 Antecedent transactions

The trustee can investigate antecedent transactions. The only way in which the rules on antecedents different in respect of a deceased bankrupt is that the relevant time (as per s341 IA) is now assessed up to the date of death of the deceased debtor rather than the date of the presentation of the petition (Article 3 DPO 1986).

1.9 Potential criminal offence under DPO 1986

Pursuant to Article 3 DPO 1986 a third party is guilty of an offence if, in the twelve months before the date of the death of the deceased he acquired or received property from the deceased knowing or believing that the deceased debtor owed money in respect of the property and did not intend, or was unlikely to be able, to repay it (s359(2)).

It is a defence to such a charge that the acquisition or receipt of property was in the ordinary course of business.

The price paid for the property will be taken into account.

1.10 Control of trustee

As in bankruptcy the creditors may form a committee for the control of the trustee. In addition, s303 (as modified) applies, hence the trustee is subject to the general control of the court.

1.11 Creditors' claims

The same rules apply as in bankruptcy.

ADMINISTRATION OF THE ESTATE OF INSOLVENT DECEASED INDIVIDUALS

1.12 Order of priority

As per bankruptcy – the relevant date for preferential creditors and interest is the date of death.

The trustee must however have regard to any claim by the PR for reasonable funeral, testamentary and administrative expenses in dealing with the estate. If the trustee is in funds these claims will be paid out in priority to the remaining debts.

Any surplus is returned to the PR.

1.13 Rules re distribution of the estate

As per bankruptcy.

2 Death of existing bankrupt

Section overview

The administration of the estate continues as if the bankrupt were alive (s5(1) DPO 1986). The reasonable funeral and testamentary expenses of the PR have priority to preferential debts.

3 Death of debtor after presentation of bankruptcy petition

Section overview

Although the court can order otherwise the proceedings continue as if the debtor were still alive (s5(3) DPO 1986).

If an order is made by the court it is a bankruptcy order and is administered accordingly with some necessary modifications. The deceased debtor's PR (or other appropriate person) is required to complete the statement of affairs.

Where a deceased debtor owned property under a joint tenancy and died after a bankruptcy petition was presented but before a bankruptcy order was made, the deceased debtor's interest in the property passes to the surviving tenant and does not form part of the estate. S421A IA does not apply in this case and the value lost to the estate cannot be recovered.

The reasonable funeral and testamentary expenses relating to the deceased debtor have priority over preferential debts but notice of these expenses must be communicated to the trustee.

4 Effect of death on voluntary arrangements

Section overview

As the debtor will be insolvent at the time of death DPO 1986 will apply with the estate being administered for the benefit of the deceased creditors.

If a debtor dies pre-approval by the creditors' meeting, the proposed arrangement is brought to an end. The nominee must notify the court of the death and any interim order will be cancelled (as will any creditor's meeting already scheduled).

Personal Insolvency

If a debtor dies post approval of a VA:

▸ **Post creditors' meeting, pre report to court**

Although VAs normally take effect as at the date of the creditors' meeting (and not the date of the chair's report to court) the DPO 1986 brings the VA to an end. The reason for this is that s260 IA to s262 IA no longer apply on the debtor's death (DPO 1986 Part III para 4).

▸ **Post report to court**

Whether or not the VA continues depends upon the terms of the arrangement and whether or not death will result in failure. The proposal should also deal with the effect of such failure (see *NT Gallgher*).

Self-test

Answer the following questions.

1   Under the Administration of Insolvent Estates of Deceased Persons Order 1986, who may present a petition for an Insolvency Administration Order?

2   Under what grounds may an Insolvency Administration Order be applied for by a personal representative?

3   What is the effect of an Insolvency Administration Order being made?

4   What duty does the OR have to investigate the conduct or affairs of the deceased debtor?

5   How is the bankruptcy of a debtor affected if they die prior to discharge?

Now, go back to the Learning Objectives in the Introduction. If you are satisfied that you have achieved these, please tick them off.

Personal Insolvency

Answers to Self-test

1. The personal representatives of the deceased.
   His creditors.
   Supervisor/creditor of an IVA.

2. Only on grounds of inability to pay debts.

3. OR is appointed receiver and manager of the deceased's estate.

   An interim receiver may be appointed if necessary.

   Personal representatives must submit a statement of affairs to the OR.

   Personal representatives must deliver up all books, papers and records in relation to the insolvent estate that are within their control.

   All dispositions of property following the death of the debtor are void unless permitted by the court.

4. OR has no duty to investigate but he may, if he thinks fit, report to the court on the activities of the deceased debtor.

5. The administration of the estate continues as if the bankrupt were alive. Reasonable funeral expenses incurred by the personal representatives may be paid in priority to the preferential creditors.

15

Numbers questions

Contents

Introduction
Examination context
Topic List
1 Statement of Affairs
2 Estimated outcome statement
3 Receipts and payments accounts
Answer to Interactive Question

Personal Insolvency

Introduction

Learning objectives

- Prepare and present a statement of affairs
- Prepare and present an Estimated Outcome Statement from information available
- Record and account for receipts and payments made by an office holder in a way that fulfils the statutory requirements of the submission of annual returns

Tick off
☐
☐
☐

Working context

Office holders are frequently required to present financial information to debtors and creditors in a format which is easily understood. This includes statements of affairs, estimated outcome statements and receipts and payment accounts. It is likely that from a junior level you will be asked to assist in preparing these statements for inclusion in reports to creditors and other interested parties.

Stop and think

What does a statement of affairs show? How does it differ to an estimated outcome statement? To whom should the office holder submit accounts of his receipts and payments and why?

Examination context

The JIEB is a very practical exam, with a numbers question appearing in most exam papers. You are most likely to be asked to prepare a statement of affairs or an estimated outcome statement.

Exam requirements

Past questions to look at include:

2008	Question 1 (c)
2007	Question 2
2007	Question 4
2006	Question 3
2006	Question 4 (b)
2004	Question 4 (ii)
2004	Question 5 (i)
2003	Question 3 (i)
2002	Question 1 (ii)
2002	Question 5 (i)
2001	Question 5 (a) (c)
1999	Question 5 (b)
1998	Question 5 (a) (b)
1995	Question 3 (i) (ii)
1993	Question 3 (b)
1989	Question 3 Paper II

Personal Insolvency

1 Statement of Affairs

Section overview

It is a statutory requirement under the IA 1986 to produce a Statement of Affairs in a prescribed format.

Definition

Statement of affairs: A picture of the individual's financial position as at the date of:

- **Bankruptcy** – as at the date of the bankruptcy order (creditor's petition), as at the date of the petition (debtor's petition).

- **Individual voluntary arrangement** – the statement of affairs must be made up to a date not earlier than two weeks before the date of the notice to the intended nominee under r5.5(4).

1.1 Content of statement of affairs

R6.59 and r6.68 define the content of the statement of affairs in bankruptcy as being all of the particulars required by Forms 6.33 and 6.28 respectively.

The statement must include the following details:

- List of secured creditors, name, address of creditor, amount owed, nature and value of assets subject to security.

- List of unsecured creditors, name, address of creditor, amount claimed by creditor, amount bankrupt 'thinks' he owes.

- Inventory of assets including cash at bank or building society, household furniture and belongings, life policies, debtors, stocks in trade, motor vehicles and other property, and in each case, the value of the asset.

R5.5(3) details the contents of the statement of affairs in a voluntary arrangement.

- A list of his assets with estimated values.
- Details of secured creditor claims.
- Names and addresses of preferential creditors with the amounts of their respective claims.
- Names and addresses of unsecured creditors with the amounts of their respective claims.
- Particulars of any debts owed by or to the debtor.
- Such other information as the nominee may require.

Exam hints

- Always show your workings. Easy marks are always available for showing full workings and assumptions.

- Leave plenty of space. This makes it easier to read and mark. Marks are always available for presentation.

2 Estimated outcome statement

Section overview

The statement quantifies the outcome of a particular course of action for one or more interested parties. It can be used to:

▶ Make a comparison of alternative offers for the sale of a business or assets.

▶ Calculate the return to creditors of pursuing a voluntary arrangement rather than opting for bankruptcy.

▶ Enable a trustee or supervisor to decide whether to continue trading by comparing outcomes of ceasing to trade with continuing.

2.1 Layout

There is no standard layout for an Estimated Outcome Statement, this will be determined by the information available and the purpose for which it is prepared.

When estimating returns to creditors it is useful to follow the format of the Statement of Affairs as a guide, with comparative Statement of Affairs figures shown wherever possible.

When comparing offers/comparable outcomes, always try to show the relevant figures side by side. This makes comparisons easier.

Full workings and assumptions made should always be shown clearly. Marks are often awarded to supporting workings.

In order to prepare Estimated Outcome Statements the following knowledge is required:

▶ The order of distribution of funds in insolvency cases.
▶ How to calculate the various categories of preferential creditors.
▶ Preparation of a simple trading account for the period.

Interactive question: Jane Brown

Jane Brown has contacted you for some advice. She has, for many years, operated a hat shop in Chester. Eighteen months ago her husband suffered a serious illness and required constant care, as a result Jane's business affairs have been neglected.

She provides you with the following information:

1. The shop operates from freehold premises which have recently been valued at £135,000. They are subject to a fixed charge in favour of Natby Bank PLC in the sum of £115,000. No payments in respect of this loan have been made for a number of months and Jane tells you that the bank are considering repossessing the property unless the monthly arrears totalling £3,600 are paid immediately.

2. Stock is held with a retail value of £16,000. If the shop were to close the stock would realise 20% of its retail value.

3. Fixtures and fittings in the shop are estimated to realise £12,000 on a going concern basis and £3,500 on a forced sale basis.

4. Jane lives with her husband in the jointly owned matrimonial home. It is worth about £160,000. They have a standard repayment mortgage with North Building Society which currently stands at £80,000.

5. Jane's other assets comprise £1,500 Premium Bonds, £750 British Telecom shares and a Volkswagen Golf which is worth around £12,000 but there is an outstanding credit balance of £7,900.

6. Jane owes £4,500 on a personal overdraft and approximately £36,000 on various credit cards. Business creditors are also owed a total of £68,000.

Personal Insolvency

7   Jane's husband is now well and she is determined to get the business back to its former levels. Based on previous years trading she expects to make the following profits, 75% of which would be available to pay her creditors.

Year 1	£4,000
Year 2	£10,000
Year 3	£18,000
Year 4	£22,000

8   Jane would like to enter into an IVA to avoid the stigma of bankruptcy. She is seeking to exclude the matrimonial home from the arrangement in return for a payment of £30,000 from her husband. This sum would not be available were she to be made bankrupt.

9   You estimate that supervisor's fees would be £2,500 per year during the arrangement and nominee's fees would total £3,500. If she were made bankrupt trustee's fees would be calculated using the Schedule 6 scale. The OR's administration fee is £1,715.

Requirement

Prepare an estimated outcome statement from the information available comparing bankruptcy with an IVA, on the basis that trade would cease if Jane were to be made bankrupt.

See **Answer** at the end of this chapter.

3 Receipts and payments accounts

Section overview

A receipts and payments account is prepared by office holders to:

▶   Provide information to creditors and other interested parties.
▶   To fulfil statutory requirements under IA 1986 re submission of annual returns.

3.1 Format

Reports to members, creditors, committees and other interested parties should include in the body of the report, or by way of an annex, details of the office holder's receipts and payments.

The receipts and payments account is a summary of all receipts and payments made by the office holder during the relevant period.

The procedure for preparing a receipts and payments account is the same for whatever purpose the account is being prepared.

The layout will be determined to some extent by the requirements on individual cases. SIP 7 provides guidance to office holders when preparing receipts and payments accounts.

3.2 Additional considerations

The following points regarding presentation should be regarded as best practice:

As far as possible, receipts and payments summaries in bankruptcies and IVAs should show receipts and payments classified under the headings used in the statement of affairs so as to facilitate comparison.

Estimated to realise figures on the statement of affairs should be shown so that comparisons with the actual realisations made to date may be made.

Results of trading (if any) should be distinguished from realisations of assets existing at the date of appointment and costs of realisation.

Any payments to pre-insolvency creditors should be stated separately or by category indicating:

- Amounts paid under duress.
- Reservation of title or in respect of liens.
- Payments to preferential creditors.
- Any other pre-insolvency items.

Asset realisations should be shown gross. Costs of realisation should be shown separately as payments.

If assets are sold direct by a mortgagee so that the proceeds do not come into the account, this fact should be stated in a note and a 'nil' realisation included in the account.

Where assets are sold by the office holder which are subject to prior charges, the gross realisation should be shown as a receipt and related costs and the amounts accounted for to the chargeholder shown as payments.

Where a debenture holder insists on a separate bank account being opened for fixed charge realisations, these transactions should be incorporated into the account without the need to specify that a separate bank account has been operated.

As an alternative to showing amounts inclusive of VAT it is acceptable to show receipts and payments net of VAT with the total net VAT being shown separately. This method is also acceptable for producing periodic summaries for creditors in any insolvency proceeding.

The practitioner's fees should be stated separately including any additional management fees or fees for other services which should be separately described. The practitioner's fees may be stated net of out of pocket disbursements (which should be shown separately and appropriately described).

The cost of professional services and advise from third party advisors etc to the practitioner should be shown separately (or by category). The information given in this respect should include not only advisors, but also other hired assistants and such sub-contract labour or self-employment staff as are involved in assisting the practitioner in his function (as opposed to being employed in the ordinary course of the debtor's business). Any fees to the practitioner's own firm and any firm or person with whom he has a profit or work referral arrangement should be distinguished and shown separately.

Other amounts received and banked which are not part of the estate and are subsequently paid to the true owner should be shown as a receipt with the payment being shown as a deduction from receipts. Assets collected by the office holder on behalf of a mortgagee should be dealt with similarly and any additional fee charged therefore should be disclosed.

3.3 Summary of statutory of returns.

Statutory requirements for the filing of returns are laid down in the IA 1986 and rules, a summary of which is provided below.

	Submit to	Timescale re submission	On closure
Individual voluntary arrangement r5.31(2)+(3)	Court The debtor Bound creditors	Within two months after the end of 12 months from the date of appointment; and every subsequent 12 month period	Within 28 days of completion of the arrangement
Trustee in bankruptcy	Upon request of Secretary of State		Within one month of ceasing to act

Answer to Interactive Question

Interactive question: Jane Brown

Jane Brown
Estimated Outcome Statement
As at X.X.00

		Bankruptcy £	IVA £
Realisations:			
Shop premises	1.	135,000	
Less Natby Bank PLC		(115,000)	
Equity		20,000	
Stock	2.	3,200	
Fixtures and fittings	3.	3,500	
Matrimonial home	4.	40,000	
Premium bonds		1,500	1,500
BT shares		750	750
Motor car	5.	Nil	Nil
Contributions from profits	6.		40,500
Contribution from husband			30,000
Total realisations		68,950	72,750
Costs:			
Supervisor's fees	7.		10,000
Nominee's fees			3,500
Duress payment Natby Bank PLC			3,600
Secretary of State administration fees	8.	11,381	
Trustee's fees	9.	10,298	
OR's administration fees		1,715	
		(23,394)	(17,100)
Available for creditors of £112,100/£108,500		45,556	55,650
		40.64p in £	51.29p in £

WORKINGS

(1) Shop:

Sold by trustee in bankruptcy.

Retained to enable trade to continue in VA. Arrears on loan (£3,600) will be paid as a duress creditor to prevent repossession proceedings. Shop will be outside VA therefore Natby Bank Plc will not be bound by IVA and prevented from taking action by interim order.

(2) Stock:

Bankruptcy – realise 20% of value on forced sale basis.

IVA – retained to facilitate ongoing trading. Enquire as to possible sale of surplus stock?

(3) Fixtures and fittings:

Bankruptcy – realised

IVA – retained to facilitate ongoing trading.

(4) Matrimonial home:

Value	£160,000
Less Mortgage	(£80,000)
	£80,000

Assume held 50:50

Jane's share £40,000.

Excluded in VA.

(5) Golf:

Value	£12,000
Less Credit	(£7,900)
	£4,100

Bankruptcy – could be claimed as an exempt asset as required for business. If not required trustee would seek to sell.

Assume retained by Jane in both scenarios.

(6) Profits from trading:

Year 1	£4,000
Year 2	£10,000
Year 3	£18,000
Year 4	£22,000
	£54,000 @ 75% = £40,500

(7) Supervisor's fees:

Assume duration of four years.

4 × £2,500 = £10,000

(8) Secretary of State administration fees:

17% on realisations over £2,000.

£68,950 - £2,000 @ 17% = £11,381

(9) Trustee's fees:

Calculated on Schedule 6 Scale.

Realisations:

5,000 × 20%	1,000
5,000 × 15%	750
58,950 × 10%	5,895
68,950	£7,645

Distributions:

5,000 × 10%	500
5,000 × 7.5%	375
35,556 × 5%	1,778
45,556	£2,653

Total remuneration £7,645 + £2,653 = £10,298.

(10) Creditors:

	IVA	Bankruptcy
Personal overdraft	4,500	4,500
Credit cards	36,000	36,000
Business creditors	68,000	68,000
Landlord arrears	3,600	
	£112,100	£108,500

Personal Insolvency

Index

INDEX

A
Advisor, 42
After acquired property, 134, 182
Annulment, 234
Antecedent transactions, 272
Appeals, 82
Approval, 81

B
Bankruptcy, 32, 110
   offences, 137
   order, 130
   restriction order, 232
Bordereau, 141

C
Cash flow test, 28
Category 1 disbursements, 168
Category 2 disbursements, 169
Closure checklist, 240
Code of Ethics, 4
Commencement, 110, 178
Completion, 101
Composition, 42
Compromise, 34
Concertina order, 73
Confidentiality, 4
Consolidation of debts, 29
Convenor, 143
Creditors' committee, 146
Creditor's petition, 110

D
Death of debtor after presentation of bankruptcy petition, 273
Death of existing bankrupt, 273
Debt management plan, 29
Debtor's petition, 116
Debts payable in foreign currency, 215
Deceased individuals, 270
Deceased's affairs/conduct, 272
Declaration of dividend, 219
Deed of arrangement, 32
Disabilities of the bankrupt, 130
Discharge, 230
Disclaim, 183
Discounts, 215
Dissolution, 250
Distress, 136
Double Proof, 215
Duties – supervisor, 94
Duties of the trustee, 156

E
Effect of death on voluntary arrangements, 274
Equitable accounting, 191
Equitable exoneration, 193
Estate, 178
Estimated outcome statement, 281
Excluded from the estate, 272
Execution, 135
Extortionate credit transactions s343, 188

F
Failure, 99
Fast track VAs, 80
Final meeting, 241
Final meetings of creditors, 145
Fundamental principles, 4
Future debts, 215

G
Gaming debts, 216
Greystoke v Hamilton-Smith, 45

H
Hearing, 115
High value dealer, 10

I
Income, 180
Income payments agreement, 180
Income payments order, 180
Individual voluntary arrangement, 31
Insolvent estate, 270
Insolvent partnerships, 251
Integration, 8
Integrity, 4
Interim order, 72
Interim receiver, 120, 271
Interlocking IVAs, 254
IP Record, 142
Items of excess value, 179
IVA protocol, 56

L
Landlords, 216
Late payment of commercial debts, 214
Layering, 8
Low value homes, 196

INDEX

Matrimonial home, 189, 272
Money Laundering, 8
    Reporting Officer, 9
Moratorium, 258

Negotiable instruments, 215
Nominee, 42
Nominee's report, 74, 79
Notice of intention to declare dividend, 218
Notice of no further dividend, 219

Objectivity, 4
Obligations of the bankrupt, 131
Occasional transaction, 10
Official Receiver, 139
Onerous property, 183
Order for possession and sale, 194

Partnership, 248
Partnership (a firm), 248
    Administration Order, 254
    Voluntary Arrangement, 254
Payments of a periodical nature, 215
Pensions, 182
Personal insolvency, 28
Petition, 111
Placement, 8
Post commencement interest, 214
Post petition dispositions, 135
Powers – supervisor, 94
Powers in Schedule 5 1A, 161
Pre-commencement interest, 213
Preferences s340, 187
Private examination, 158
Professional behaviour, 4
Professional competence and due care, 4
Proof, 212
Proofs of debt, 212
Property, 178
Proposal, 46
Prove, 212
Public examination, 133, 157

Reasonable, 180
Receipts and payments accounts, 282

Redirection of mail, 158
Release, 240
Re-mortgaging, 28
Removal, 238
    supervisor, 95
Remuneration, 164
    supervisor, 96
Report to Secretary of State, 81
Resignation, 237
Rights of occupation, 194

S313 charging order, 195
Safeguards, 4
Schedule 6 scale, 165
Secretary of State fees, 166
Secured creditors, 216
Self interest threats, 6
Self review threats, 6
Set-off, 216
Significant relationship, 6
SIP 3, 47, 75
 SIP 9, 96
Special manager, 121
Statement of Affairs, 74, 117, 132, 280
Statements of Insolvency Practice, 16
Statutory demand, 34, 111
Sue and obtain judgement, 34
Supervisor, 42, 94
Supervisor's petition, 118

Tax claims, 216
Technical Releases, 16
Three year rule, 196
Transaction at an undervalue s339, 186
Transaction defrauding creditors s423, 188

Unregistered company, 253
Unsatisfied judgement execution, 111
Unspecified debts, 213

Vacation of office, 237
Variation, 98
Vesting, 178
Voluntary arrangements, 42